ISBN 978-1-333-62689-1
PIBN 10527973

1 MONTH OF
FREE
READING

at

www.ForgottenBooks.com

By purchasing this book you are eligible for one month membership to ForgottenBooks.com, giving you unlimited access to our entire collection of over 1,000,000 titles via our web site and mobile apps.

To claim your free month visit:

www.forgottenbooks.com/free527973

English
Français
Deutsche
Italiano
Español
Português

www.forgottenbooks.com

Mythology Photography **Fiction** Fishing Christianity **Art** Cooking Essays Buddhism Freemasonry Medicine **Biology** Music **Ancient Egypt** Evolution Carpentry Physics Dance Geology **Mathematics** Fitness Shakespeare **Folklore** Yoga Marketing **Confidence** Immortality Biographies Poetry **Psychology** Witchcraft Electronics Chemistry History **Law** Accounting **Philosophy** Anthropology Alchemy Drama Quantum Mechanics Atheism Sexual Health **Ancient History** **Entrepreneurship** Languages Sport Paleontology Needlework Islam **Metaphysics** Investment Archaeology Parenting Statistics Criminology **Motivational**

NIGHT SCENES

IN THE

BIBLE.

BY

Rev. DANIEL MARCH, D.D

AUTHOR OF "WALKS AND HOMES OF JESUS."

———◆———

ZEIGLER, McCURDY & CO.:
PHILADELPHIA, PA.; CINCINNATI, OHIO;
CHICAGO, ILL.; ST. LOUIS, MO.
SPRINGFIELD, MASS.
1869.

WESTCOTT & THOMSON,
Stereotypers, Philada.

PREFACE.

THE Bible is the oldest and the newest of books. It surveys the whole field of time, and it looks farthest into the infinite depths of eternity. It lends the most vivid and absorbing interest to the scenes and events of the past, and it keeps us in the most active sympathy with the time in which we live. It gives us the most reliable record of what has been, and it affords us our only means of knowing what is yet to be. It is so conservative as to make it a solemn duty to study and revere the past, and it is so progressive as to be in advance of the most enlightened age. It is strict enough to denounce the very shadow and semblance of sin, and it is liberal enough to save the chiefest of sinners. It is full of God, and must therefore be read with a pure heart or its true glory will not be seen. It is full of man, and must therefore always be interesting and instructive to all who would know themselves.

The Bible is the plainest of books, and yet it has depths of wisdom which no created mind can sound. It is set up as a beacon to show all wanderers the safe way, and yet its light shines forth from thick clouds of mystery and from abysses of infinite darkness. It describes all conditions of life, and it gives utterance to all desires and emotions of the soul. It has a song of triumph for the victor and a wail of defeat for the vanquished. It sparkles with the fervor and gladness of youth, it celebrates the strength and glory of manhood, it bewails the sorrows and infirmities of age. It exults in the mighty deeds of kings and conquerors, it sympathizes with the poor and lowly, it lifts up the fallen, it delivers the oppressed, and it breathes the blessing of peace upon the quiet homes of domestic life. It describes with startling clearness the seductions of temptation, the conflicts of doubt and the miseries of skepticism. It searches the secret chambers of the heart, and brings to light its purest love and its darkest hate, its highest joy and its deepest grief. It compasses the utmost range of thought and feeling and desire, and it sounds the utmost depth of motive and character and passion.

The composition of the Bible was extended through a long course of years; it was carried on under a great variety of circumstances; it bears the impress of every diversity of individual character. And yet the spirit of inspiration speaks with equal fullness through all the times and circumstances and characters. Thus in the Bible, God and man, earth and heaven, time and eternity speak with one voice and teach the same truth. Thus the Bible is made to be the one book for all ages and all nations, for all classes of men and all states of society, for all capacities of intellect and all necessities of the soul. It sets forth the most spiritual and heavenly truths in the lights and shadows of earthly scenes and human characters. To understand and treasure up the truths we need to know something of the places and the people that stand forth so prominently on the sacred page. It will help us much to apply the lessons of inspiration to the present time and to personal duty if we go back in imagination and sit with Lot at the gate of Sodom, and see angels approach like common travelers in the calm light of the evening, or if we walk with the two disciples into the country and see Jesus joining our company on the way to Emmaus. It will help us make all Scripture profitable for instruction in righteousness if we go a day's journey into the desert with Elijah, and see him cast himself down in despair and wishing to die, or if we listen to the praises sung by Paul and Silas at midnight in the prison at Philippi.

It is with such views of the infinite variety and special adaptation of the Scriptures that the following sketches have been written. The author has endeavored to explore a single vein in this exhaustless and many-chambered mine, and to bring forth some few golden grains for others to use and enjoy. He has tried in a few particulars to read the past in the light of to-day, and to show that the Bible is a fit emanation from the one Infinite Mind, to whom all things are ever present and with whom all have to do. From the NIGHT SCENES in sacred history he has sought to bring forth some rays of light to cheer the dark hours of life, and to guide pilgrims on their way to that land where there shall be no night.

ILLUSTRATIONS.

PAGE

THE NIGHT OF AGONY.. FRONTISPIECE.

JACOB'S NIGHT AT BETHEL... 65

THE NIGHT PASSAGE OF THE SEA.. 127

SAUL'S NIGHT AT ENDOR.. 147

NIGHT WATCH IN MOUNT SEIR.. 247

JESUS' NIGHT ON THE MOUNTAIN... 325

THE NIGHT OF TEMPTATION... 377

THE NIGHT OF FRUITLESS TOIL... 433

ANGEL VISITS IN THE NIGHT.. 451

MIDNIGHT IN THE PRISON AT PHILIPPI.. 469

PAUL'S NIGHT IN THE DEEP... 491

NO NIGHT IN HEAVEN... 529

CONTENTS.

I.

THE LAST NIGHT OF SODOM.

PAGE

Man and angels—Appearance and reality—Things not what they seem—Life, air, electric force—Railway disaster—Death-angel in the night—Strong man struck down—Invisible powers around us—Evening scene—Vicinity of the city—Chief men in the gate—Gay throng—Sunset—Oriental life—Riches of the city—Luxury of the people—Idleness—Security—Angels approach—Common garb—Taken for travelers—Hospitality—Welcomed by Lot—Derided by the people—Clamorous mob—The warning—Old man laughed at—All seems safe—A word of alarm—The departure—Angels hasten—Morning scene—The overthrow—Utter desolation—Cause of the judgment—Work and want—Two words—The choice—Who the mocker—"Wait" a bad word—Hasten—Look not behind.. 23

II.

ABRAHAM'S NIGHT VISION AT BEERSHEBA.

Voice in the night—Abraham an old man—A hard message—Greatest trial last—Age needs repose—The home at Beersheba—Grove, altar, wells—A great household—Herds, riches, only son—A pilgrim's life—Thunderbolt from clear sky—Fourfold severity—A father's grief—Loss of a bad son—Loss of an only and beloved son—Seeming contradiction—Wealth nothing—A bitter cry—Is it a demon's voice—Tent scene—Isaac sleeping—Eastern dawn—The stars of the morning—Sand-cloud from the desert—Human sacrifices on the hill-tops—The grove of terebinth—No voice or face of angel there—Abraham resolves to go—Mysterious journey—Secret departure—No mother's farewell—The road—Grassy plains—Flowers—Caravans—Solitude—The heavy secret—The father's conflict—Night on the journey—The stars again and the promise—Too short a night—The hills—Oaks of Mamre—Hebron—Bethlehem—Second night—Shall he go back?—Third day—The Shechinah—Moriah—Faith triumphs—The altar built—Isaac's wonderful submission—The last look—Hold—Enough—Nothing too precious to give to God—Nothing too precious for God to give to us—Prompt obedience easiest and best... 43

III.

JACOB'S NIGHT AT BETHEL.

PAGE

A long journey—Hasty departure—No protection—The worst traveling com-panion—Jacob timid, home-child—His mother's favorite—Shepherd life—The wild man—Isaac's favorite—The two brothers contrasted—A boisterous visitant—The parental longing for the absent—Common blessings unappre-ciated—A child at seventy—The supplanter—The hungry hunter—A reck-less bargain—Cost of trifling gratifications—The profane person—Poor pay—The stolen blessing—The garment of falsehood—Strange mixture of fraud and faith—The flight—A brother's wrath—Washington in the wilder-ness—A fearful fugitive—Shepherds, caravans, robbers—A solitary place—Bethel at night—Lodging with jackals—A hard pillow and a heavy heart—God's time to help—A sure covenant—The pathway of angels—The gate of heaven—A better life begun—The memorial stone—No such thing as chance—All for good—God's voice in common things—Way to heaven always open—Heaven always near—Night storm in mid-ocean—Sailor-boy's dream of home—The ship the house of God—The miner's Sabbath-eve in Nevada—Work, work, rest—Bethel everywhere.......................... 63

IV.

JACOB'S NIGHT OF WRESTLING WITH THE ANGEL.

Eras in Jacob's life—The Jabbok described—Wild, swift mountain stream—Neighboring country—Wild flowers—Oak forests—Twenty years before—Now rich, brave, strong—God's host at Mahanaim—A wondrous life—Heaven and earth nearer now—God's host still our guardians—God's providence in every wind—Faith and science agree—Esau's band—Jacob prepares to meet them—Adjusts his account with God first—The greatest affliction the greatest mercy—Man must needs pray—All have time and words—Presents to Esau—Alone in the darkness—Alone with infinite power, truth, love—Source of strength, safety, peace—A fearful night—An unknown antagonist—A real encounter—Long and desperate struggle—Victory by self-surrender—The angel entreating—The mightiest man on earth—"Give me Scotland or I die—Life a conflict—With whom to con-tend—Disguised angels—Deep mysteries—God comes in the thick cloud—A great school—Peace through conflict—Power with God—Worth of God's blessing—Three steps of progress—House of God, host of God, face of God. 83

V.

THE LAST NIGHT OF ISRAEL IN EGYPT.

The birth-night of a nation—Sudden emancipation—Rome and the Hebrews—Other ancient nations extinct—Hebrews still live—The first book of history—The teachers of the world—The first great era in history—Night in Egypt—River scenes—Princes and bondmen asleep—Night in the palace—Moses heard for the last time—The shepherd's staff and the sceptre—The plagues ended—Pharaoh sleeps—The priests sleep—Slaves shall not go—Hebrews awake—High expectation—All indoors—Ready to go—Awful suspense— Midnight—The cry? No. The rustle of palms—The lowing of Apis—The great cry at last—The death-angel's stroke—Death everywhere—The groans of ages—A free people on the march—God in history—The great emanci- pator—All in bondage—Immortal freedom—The highest rank—The great inheritance—Slaves cling to their chains—The caged eagle—The eagle in his mountain home—A sadder sight—The heir of the unive —An un- speakable destiny—Salvation very nigh—A day to be much observed—The grandest march—Will you go?—Shipwrecked mariner—Beautiful island— The prison-paradise—The escape—Ready for the voyage...................... 103

VI.

THE NIGHT PASSAGE OF THE SEA.

A great landmark in the nation's life—Effect on other nations—A distinctive national idea—The scene of the passage—The sandy plain—The valley between mountains—Entangled in the land—Encamping for the night— Distress and dejection—First joy over—A sad night—The Egyptians appear behind—An armed host—Sure of their prey—Wait till morning—" We told you so"—Sublime faith—" Fear not"—Hard to hold their peace—A house on fire—Terrible panic—Wailing of the Hebrews—How they came there— The Shechinah guide—Faces the sea—Passes over the Hebrews—Darkness to the Egyptians—A broad highway—The advance—The Egyptians aroused —They pursue— A hard march—The cloud shooting forth lightnings—The confused host—The meeting of the waters—Ourselves girt with infinite power—Miracle and laws of nature—The truest philosophy—A prayerless man—All things of God—Duty to God first—The Christian watchword, " go forward"—Decision makes the man—Do your duty at any cost—Seas divide before the advance of faith—" Go forward" revolutionizes nations, the world—Light to one is darkness to another—The sea all must cross— The safe guide.. 125

VII.

SAUL'S NIGHT AT ENDOR.

Tragic element in Saul's career—Celebrated in poetry and music—Strange con- tradictions—Loved and hated—Contrasts of character—A hero and a cow- ard—A prophet and a demon—Good and evil angel—The crisis at Gilboa— Famous field—Joshua and Napoleon—Gideon and his Spartan band—A great army—An unhappy king—Revolt of tribes—Forsaken—A hero trem- bling—A dark path—The worst fate—Sunset on the battle-plain—Light sought from darkness—The king in disguise—The night journey to Endor —The witch's cave—The hag surprised—Her false pretences—Magical arts —A degraded king—The host without a commander—Unsafe counsel— " Whom shall I bring up?"—An unexpected apparition—Who can call spirits from the deep?—A real man—The words of doom—Perhaps spoken

PAGE

in mercy—A giant prostrate—Return to Gilboa--The shock of battle—
Israel routed—The end of Saul—The last memorial—Seek counsel from the
right source—The shining path—The first law of a kingdom—The work for
all—What is failure?—The worst madness—Is wickedness ever profitable?—
A good purpose—A plain path—How found—The open door—" Nearer,
my God, to thee.".. 145

VIII.

DAVID'S NIGHT AT THE JORDAN.

The third Psalm—When written—A sad night—Sudden surprise—The inner
calm—Absalom planning revolt—Arts to win the people—His splendid
bearing—An accomplished conspirator—His chariots and foot-runners—
The father blinded—Absalom crowned at Hebron—General revolt—No time
to lose—The darkest day in David's life—Order to leave Jerusalem—De-
parture from the palace—Descent into the Kidron—Pause at the last guard-
house—Fidelity of the Philistines—The loyal chief—A loud lamentation—
The hills and valleys weep—The ark sent back—Great men in their fall—
A great soul—The ascent of Olivet—A funeral procession—Pause to wor-
ship on the height—Last look at Zion—A fearful road—Utter desolation—
Shimei cursing—The dog left to bark at the king—Silence the best answer
—Arrival at the Jordan—Bivouac on the sand—Alarm at midnight—Pas-
sage of the Jordan—A morning song—Trust in trouble—From the throne
to the wilderness—What a young man could endure—Hard lot for an old
king—Hard for a high-tempered man—King Lear's imprecations—Con-
trasted with David's psalm—A hymn of trust for all time—A costly lesson
—A man more than a king—What the soul would say—Faith more precious
than science—" My Father's house"—The best knowledge—" Brother, come
home"—The sequel of the rebellion—David at Mahanaim—Stands in the
gate—Troops file before him—Thinks only of saving Absalom—" Gently,
gently with the boy Absalom"—His last word to Joab—The battle—Watch-
man on the tower—The bringer of tidings—"Shalom"—Is Absalom safe?
The cry of parental anguish—The man greater than the monarch—Parental
love ever the same—Its power and persistency—Others forget—Parents
cannot—The Great Father's love—The Father before the sovereign—Voices
of God's paternal love—The universal prayer—The most acceptable dispo-
sition—The Fatherhood of God the great revelation................................ 163

IX.

ELIJAH'S NIGHT IN THE DESERT.

Night in the desert—Solitude—Silence—Starlight—A lonely fugitive—Sick of
life—The mystery of existence—Job cursing his day—The greatest of the
prophets—A fearless and tireless man—His history—Elijah before Ahab—
A fearful oath—A messenger of wrath—Mystery about Elijah—No gene-
alogy—His return expected—Tishbite—Gilead—A wild region—The haunt
of robbers—A life of peril—Jacob wrestling—Jephthah—David's refuge—

Elijah's early life—A hardy mountaineer—A Hercules or a Samson—A
great day's work—A long race—A child of the desert—Ever before Jehovah
—A marked man—The discipline of solitude—The man for the hour—God's
men of the time—Every man on his post—Israel's providential history—
The worship of nature—The gods of Sidon—The God of nature—A grand
contest—Elijah's court dress—" The hairy man"—The king defied—Elijah's
escape—The key of nature lost—Let Baal show his power—Who can give
rain?—Great trial of Elijah's faith—A land of streams and fountains—A
fearful risk—Duty questioned—No scientific ground of faith—The word of
the Lord to every man—Be wise to-day—Always in the presence of Jehovah
—A sanctuary everywhere—Honorable work—Go not out from the presence
of the Lord—Source of all evil—Lo! God is here—Perpetual trisagion—
Tidings to Jezebel and the people—The drought begins—Shepherds,
ploughmen, vintagers mourn—Sky, sun, stars in mourning—Baal's altars
burn in vain—The earth, the grass, the harvests, the forests burnt—Cattle,
men die—Drought dries up all pity—Reason for the judgment—Something
worse than famine—Elijah appears again—His summons to Ahab—The
king awed by the prophet—The gathering to Carmel—Great encampment
on the mount—The eventful morning—The scene of the gathering—Elijah's
challenge—People silent—The trial proposed—Priests of Baal begin—Their
frantic cries and demoniac dance—Elijah mocks the idolaters—He takes
his turn—Awful expectation—The fire descends—Seen afar off—The priests
of Baal slain—Prayer on the mountain—The little cloud—The tempest—A
fearful race—A cold bed—The man to meet Jezebel—The queen's oath—
The hero-prophet alarmed—A wild and hurried flight—To Beersheba, to
the desert—Desolation of the wilderness—Reaction in great minds—Peter,
Paul, Bunyan's Pilgrim—The young disciple—The business Christian—
The reformer—The successful minister: old, deserted, despondent—" It is
enough; it is better to die than live"—Hard to be laid aside—Hard to fail
after success—The world can do without us—Work for all—The greatest
success was accounted failure—God's angel on the wing—Never say, " It is
enough"—Not the chief end of man to succeed.. 187

X.

JONAH'S NIGHT AT NINEVEH.

When Jonah lived—The book written by him—His one prophecy—Long journey
to deliver it—Hardships and peril of the way—Danger when there—A
great and bloody city—No angel guard—Short respite—Utter overthrow—
"I cannot go"—A recreant prophet—Flight to Joppa—His mother's
" dove"—No hiding from God—A hard lesson to be learned—Word of the
Lord comes to many—It seems a hard message—They flee—The path of
perdition—Passage engaged—On board and asleep—Word of the Lord in
the wind—Dreadful sleep—Vengeance swifter than ships—Pagan prayers—
Awake, O sleeper!—Sharp suspicions—Helping transgressors does not pay
—Philosophy overboard—When wicked men like to hear prayer—Jonah no
coward—Early impressions—He is ready—Seamen afraid of him—Over-
board at last—A great calm—Beneath the bottoms of the mountains—The

PAGE

call of duty still loud—How kept alive in the sea-monster—Second com-
mission—Obedience now easy—He starts and travels on—His arrival—The
city described—His one cry of woe—The stricken multitude—A conquered
city—Jonah disappointed with success—Gives no consolation—He spurns
the Ninevites—His night of waiting for the destruction—Angry with him-
self and everything else—The strange plant—It is withered—Jonah's last
word—His probable repentance—No escaping from God—Servants of God
always safe—Duty shunned is duty still—Law of duty supreme.............. 223

XI.

THE NIGHT-WATCH IN MOUNT SEIR.

Night comes with the morning—Lights and shadows among mountains—Camp
of pilgrims—Watching for the morning—Effect of night among mountains
—Dawn—Morning among the hills—Changes wrought by light—Mists form-
ing—Darken the whole scene—Still the day is approaching—They press
on—Such the lot of man—An earthly paradise—Night and storm—A study
of human society—Hopes blasted—Yet the day will come—Peace through
conflict—Struggles of nations to be free—First success—Then again en-
slaved—Storms succeed the sunshine—Still the full day approaching—The
tide in the affairs of men—Man's work perishes—God's temple stands—
Light out of darkness—The pavilion of God's presence—Look to the cloud
for light—The hour before sunrise among mountains—After sunrise darker
—Happy to walk under clouds—The moment of greatest discouragement—
God's way dark from excess of light—Vale of Chamouny at evening—Sun-
rise on Mont Blanc—The veiled mountain most impressive—Do not be
afraid of mystery—Heroes and conquerors—The best days not in the past
—Christianity is progress—Appearances may be adverse—Yet the day is
approaching—The hour before dawn the darkest of the night—Perfect
through suffering—Hope and wait... 245

XII.

THE NIGHT OF WEEPING.

Life a conflict of forces—Law of decay and reproduction—Harmony in contra-
diction—Appearance and reality at variance—Evening clouds—Thunder-
bolt—Morning mists promise a fair noon—The coldest day—The tornado—
The earthquake—The diamond—The eye—Infinite variety in uniformity—
Samson's riddle—The volcano—The rainbow—Paradox and mystery not
alone in spiritual life—The whole creation in travail—Struggle and conflict
in both—Faith grows by conflict—Life a battle and a march—Pain the
price of pleasure—Beauty from the tomb—Why all this?—Why sorrow and
trial and tears?—So ordained of God—Not ours to choose—Still it is so in
all other things—Everything costs—Self-denial not arbitrarily imposed—
The Supreme Giver can give rest only to penitent souls—Tears not a sign
of weakness—Christian building begins at the foundation—Much in the
world to make one weep—"Streams in the south"—Husbandmen watching
for their return—The gladdening rain—The bird of Paradise—Never flies

before the wind—Prosperity disarrays the soul's garments of beauty—The beginning of strength—Worldling in a prayer meeting—He scoffs and is weak—He weeps and is strong—A boy's fault—He denies it and is enslaved—He confesses and deplores and is free and noble—Blessed are they that mourn 265

XIII.

THE NIGHT FEAST OF BELSHAZZAR.

The last of the Babylonian kings—The race of the Chaldeans—Their profligate young men—Luxurious habits—Testimony of history—No wonder that Babylon fell—What kind of young men will ruin any city—Sure way to destroy a nation—Rome, Constantinople, Venice—Delicate, self-indulgent young men dangerous—Belshazzar an absolute monarch—Flattered, capricious, cruel—The banquet-hall—Fine arts flourish in a licentious age—Rome—France—Naples—Debasement under the shadow of St. Peter's—The greatness of Babylon—Belshazzar's palace—Streets, walls, temples—Nebuchadnezzar the mighty builder—Rawlinson's statement—Belshazzar inherited too much—His head turned—Babylon besieged—Enemy withdraw—City given up to riotous mirth—Feasting, illuminations, processions—Belshazzar enters the banquet-hall—The scene at the board—Profanation of sacred things—The vessels of Jehovah brought forth—The writing on the wall—The interpretation—Belshazzar slain—How the city was taken—Death will enter palaces—Last opportunities lost—The gay not always happy—How to find joy in everything—What will lift the weight from all hearts—Danger of wine-drinking—Heathen testimony—The universal witness—God here, God everywhere—Conscience a mighty power—What Belshazzar's life is worth to the world—Weighed and found wanting—The greatest thought 283

XIV.

A NIGHT WITH JESUS AT JERUSALEM.

Napoleon and Alexander at Tilsit—A memorable interview—Arranging the destiny of nations—A more important conference—With less display—Mighty words spoken—Time and place—The great feast—Jerusalem crowded—Number of sacrifices—The temple the chief attraction—The choral service—The most impressive anniversary—Passover still kept—Purging the temple—Power of Jesus' presence—A day in teaching and healing—Place of rest—A venerable listener—Testimony of the Talmud concerning Nicodemus—Private interview impossible by day—Resolves to seek Jesus by night—Leaves his house secretly—Goes out at the eastern gate—Hesitates while seeking the house—Men still hesitate when seeking Jesus—They inquire openly about other things—Inquiry is reasonable—Nicodemus to be commended—The scene of the interview—Contrast between the two persons—The calmness of Jesus—The amazement of Nicodemus—The foundation truth—When the millennium will come—Life from above needed—A great question—What the Bible says about it—Hard

PAGE

names for hard characters—Testimony of history—Joy of the new life—
What is true greatness?—A glorious destiny—The highest work of angels
—Heavenly messengers in humble abodes—The heir of the universe—A
great estate seeking an owner.. 303

XV.

JESUS' NIGHT ON THE MOUNTAIN.

Sublime pre-eminence of mountains—Impressive in every aspect and form—
Records of creative power—Hebrew language impersonates mountains—
Sacred scenes and associations of mountains—The Holy One in Mount
Paran—The chief things of the ancient mountains—Promise firmer than
mountains—Help from the hills—Herald of glad tidings on the moun-
tains—The mountains God's sanctuary—The mountains of Eden—Ara-
rat—Moriah—Sinai—Giving of the law—Elijah in Horeb--Mount Hor
—Death of Moses—These associations confirmed by Jesus—The mount of
temptation—Of the Beatitudes--Of the Transfiguration—Of the Crucifixion—
Of the Ascension—His nights of prayer among mountains—Preceded by a
long day of toil—No rest by day—At night he withdraws alone to the
mountains—He wakes and prays while others sleep—His common practice—
An impressive scene—He must be alone—Modes of living then—Monastic-
ism not encouraged—Retirement to prepare for public life—All great and
true reformers prepare for their work thus—Lofty views from the heights
of prayer—Light from the mount—Go up to the mount of God—The lofti-
est outlook—Traveler among mountains deceived by appearances—All
corrected by view from the loftiest peak—So with human policies and
opinions—Must be viewed from the mount of God—Prayer the most ra-
tional and elevating exercise... 323

XVI.

A NIGHT STORM ON THE SEA.

The Sea of Galilee sacred—Reflections of a traveler on seeing it—Everything
speaks of Jesus—The shore, the waves, the shadows, the towns, the neigh-
boring heights—Now changed and desolate—The doom of Capernaum—One
thing the same—A night storm—The "torment" of the winds—Structure of
the banks and highlands—Sudden and strong winds—A fair day of teach-
ing—Feeding of the five thousand—A calm evening—The disciples caught
in a storm—A night of hard rowing—They are watched by Jesus from the
mountain—He comes to them on the water—Their terror—Natural fear of
spectres—Courage and fear of Peter—His rescue—The great deep of the
soul—Its agitations and conflicts—The Bringer of peace—Men afraid of
their best friend—Men afflicted by the words of consolation—How to be
happy—Mistakes of the young and ardent—Jesus walks abroad in the calm
and sunshine as well as in the storm—What a brave man should fear—
Jesus no spectre—The truest man—He would make true men—To be a
Christian is to be a true man—Whatever prevents following Christ is a
falsity—Only a few steps in the false way—A miserable comforter—A

winter's night call upon a dying young man—"Too late"—A summer's afternoon call upon a dying Christian—A hallowed room—His last word "Victory"... 341

XVII.

THE LAST NIGHT OF THE FEAST.

The feast of Tabernacles—Seven days of festivity—The immense multitude— All out of doors—Jerusalem a forest—Offerings and libations—The annual thanksgiving—The last night the climax of excitement—Illuminations— Dancing and singing of devout men—Orchestra of Levites—Chorus of thousands of the people—"The great Hosanna"—Singing and dancing all night—Silver trumpets hail the dawn—Procession to the fountain of Siloam—The song of Degrees—Water from the fountain poured out—The enthusiasm of the multitude—The great rejoicing—The voice of Jesus heard at such a time—A most startling and impressive cry—The effect of the appeal—That voice still crying to the thirsty—Relief for the deepest need —The fullest possible invitation—The world changed, the soul's necessity the same—Destitution of man without a Saviour—The cry of the soul— What all are seeking—Thirst a fit sign of greatest need—Dying soldiers— Shipwrecked mariners—The crucified—Lost in the desert of Sahara—A Deliverer appears—A glad escape from the desert to paradise—The picture a reality—"Come unto me '.. 361

XVIII.

THE NIGHT OF TEMPTATION.

A hard thing for Jesus to say—Hard for Peter to hear—His sincere attachment —His great surprise—Does my Master trust me so little?—The occasion— Night in the upper chamber—The last words of counsel and comfort—The intercessory prayer—All devoted to him—All shall be offended this night— Peter's declaration—It was called for—He was not blamed for making it— Good professions should be both made and kept—How Jesus' word was fulfilled—His agony while they sleep—Peter follows afar off—He is pointed at—He denies his Master—The hour strikes—Peter himself tells the story— "Lead us not into temptation"—An aspiring young man—Leaves a Christian home—Begins life in the city—Does not fully commit himself for God —There he mistakes—He falls—He is ruined by those whom he despises and who despise him for yielding—A dreadful defeat—Fit words for every young man—Power of No—An old man burdened and sorrow-stricken— A half century of suffering because he did not say, No—Nothing can undo the past—A terrible lesson to the tempted—The way to destruction made inviting and beautiful—Genius and art and wealth and invention enlisted to adorn the broad way—"Destruction made easy"—Temptation never the voice of a friend—The mountain lake with two outlets—The child's sport breaking the levee—The first transgressors—Beware of the beginnings of evil—Requires effort to be good—The Simplon road—The Divine Excelsior. 375

XIX.

THE NIGHT OF AGONY.

PAGE

The approach to Jerusalem from the west—The pass of Beth-horon—Joshua's victory—Christian traveler emerging from the pass—Rejoicings at the first sight of Jerusalem—Many nations and languages take up the cry, "Jerusalem, Jerusalem!"—The view blank and lifeless—The Hill of Zion greatly changed—Olivet the same—Close to the city—Its paths, slopes, terraces and trees—Noah's dove—The Shechinah—The oath of the Almighty—The scene of the final judgment—No need of fable—Abraham's sacrifice— David's place of prayer—His sorrowful ascent of Olivet—The three paths —The footsteps of Jesus here—Bethany beyond—The triumph road—The last prediction — The meeting with Nicodemus — The fruitless fig tree— "The blood-drops of Jesus"—The favorite home of the Son of God—The scene of the agony—Jesus comes forth with his disciples—His mysterious sadness—His disciples amazed—He stops at the gate of the garden—Separates himself from his disciples—Falls upon the ground—Fearful words of the evangelists in describing his emotions—The second and third access of the great agony—Strengthened by an angel—He is now calm and ready for the sacrifice—We dare not analyze this mysterious conflict—It was borne for us—He stood in the sinner's place—Dreadful to bear the full burden of sin for an hour—How much more dreadful to bear it for ever.................... 393

XX.

THE FIRST NIGHT AFTER THE RESURRECTION.

The two great facts in the Gospel history—The resurrection confirms all—The two greatest days in the world's history—The darkest night, the brightest morning—The disciples slow to believe—The rising from the dead still hard to believe—The perplexities of the disciples—Two start for Emmaus at evening—Leave the city at the western gate—A stranger joins them as they walk—He draws from them the cause of their grief—Their hearts burn while he speaks—He goes on with them up and down the steep and stony road—The path described—The most desolate leading out of Jerusalem— The sun has set and they reach the village—They beg the stranger to stay —He blesses the evening meal—They see that it is Jesus, and he vanishes out of their sight—They hurry back to Jerusalem in the darkness—They find the band assembled with closed doors—While they are telling what they have seen and heard, Jesus stands in the midst of them—Their terror —Their joy—The first word of Jesus is, Peace—He comes back from the unseen world to say, Peace—This the word that the world wants most to hear—How the early Christians cherished the word—Jesus rose in his full manhood—His resurrection the pattern of our own—We shall know each other in the resurrection—The risen ones clothed with the beauty of immortality—The blessed life a human and homelike reality............................ 411

XXI.

THE NIGHT OF FRUITLESS TOIL.

PAGE

The last chapter in John a second ending—Why written—The scene described most sacred—Two pictures—The first, night on the Sea of Galilee—Deep calm—The lake, the stars, the watch-tower—Shepherd's cry—Pleasure-boat —Roman patrol—Seven men appear on the beach—Fishermen, yet masters of the world—Peter, John, Thomas, Nathaniel and James characterized— They push off and let down the net—Change their ground, toil all night and take nothing—They think and talk of their Master—Revive the associations of the past—Cannot solve the mystery—Many toilers that take no. thing—Ambitious young man—Toils hard—Becomes very rich—Finds that money will not buy what he wants—Poor-rich man dies disappointed— Easy, self-indulgent young man—Means to enjoy life and take it easy— Succeeds no better—What is success? and how attained ?—A young lady in gay life—Wearies and distresses herself in vain to be happy—The noblest aim of woman's life—Morning on the Sea of Galilee—Signs of the coming day—Jesus walking on the shore—He directs the toil of the disciples, and they succeed—They recognize him and are glad—A good lesson learned at last—Jesus calls from the eternal shore—The night wanes—The morning is breaking on the nations—The full day comes on apace.............................. 431

XXII.

ANGEL VISITS IN THE NIGHT.

View from the mountain-top—From the deck of the ship in mid-ocean—View of the starry sky—Its impressions—Reflections in the dungeon, in the crowd—Feeling that man and earth are everything—Men not the only actors in the world—Thinking, observing and mighty beings all around us —They sometimes have stepped forth into the light of day—Circumstances in which angels have been seen and heard—They have taken part in man's work—What they have done—How they have appeared—How much it enlarges the range of our thought to know this—God's great empire— Angels care little for earthly distinctions—They often find their friends in lowly circumstances—The angel that came to Jerusalem visited a prison in preference to a palace—Faith consecrates dungeons—Peter's chain and cell —Bunyan's prison—The Wartburg—When the whole earth will be holy— Peter slept soundly—A good conscience the best opiate—Glorious to be waked from the sleep of death by the touch of an angel—Peter strongly guarded—Thanks for his chains—Voltaire's boast—Thanks to the Star Chamber—Peter's surprise—His silent obedience to the angel—Passes through guards and doors, not knowing how—Doubts whether it is him-self—It is no dream—So will God's angel deliver the disciple of Jesus from the prison of the body—His surprise on waking in heaven to find death behind—Here we sleep and dream—The true life yet to come... 449

MIDNIGHT IN THE PRISON AT PHILIPPI.

Strange sounds in a heathen prison—Who were the singers?—The events of the preceding day described—Paul and Silas by the river's side—Interrupted by the cries of a slave girl—She is delivered from the demon—Her masters enraged—A tumult excited—The apostles dragged into the city—The magistrates interfere—They take it for granted that the strangers are to blame—They are stripped and beaten with rods—Terrible severity of the infliction—The rabble applaud—They are sent to prison—The jailer charged to keep them safely—The terrible dungeon of the inner prison—Their pitiable condition—The reception which Europe gave the first missionaries—How the world treats its benefactors—The excitement of the day over—Midnight in the prison—Voices heard in the dungeon—Not of wailing—A psalm of victory—Surprise of the other prisoners—The earthquake—The prisoners all unfettered—The despair of the jailer—Paul's assuring call from the dungeon—He lifts them out of the horrible pit—His alarm for himself—The most momentous inquiry—Evidence of a sound mind—We have too many fears and anxieties—How to quiet them—Another experience of the dungeon—The Mamertine prison described—When built—Paul said to have been confined there—His dreadful condition—The chill and damp—The darkness and solitude—Deep beneath the ground—A friend permitted to visit him—Dictates a letter to Timothy—What will he say?—His high aspirations, his great talents and experience—The splendors that surround him in the city—Will he lament the loss of these?—What will be his last voice to the world? Complaint? Disappointment? No—A strain of triumph—A coronation hymn—Tender-hearted still—He glories and rejoices—Paul greater than Nero—The footsteps of Paul more venerated than the palace of the Cæsars—His memory brightens—His power increases with the progress of time—How to make ourselves remembered.............. . 467

XXIV.

PAUL'S NIGHT IN THE DEEP.

Tales of shipwreck often told—Always interesting—Paul's the most suggestive —Our interest for the safety of the man—His dignity and composure—The voyage—Sailing in his time—No chart, quadrant, chronometer or compass —The ship large, heavy, unwieldy—One-masted—Stormy month—First day of the storm—Frapping—Boat taken up—Cargo, except the wheat, thrown overboard—The struggle with the tempest—All hope lost—Breakers ahead at midnight—Sounding, anchoring—Waiting for day—Ship run on shore —Broken in pieces by the waves—Passengers and crew thrown into the breakers—All saved—A word that could not be broken—The post of duty the right place when danger comes—The most precious freight the Mediterranean ever bore—Paul's life, influence and reputation safe—All who trust in Jesus escape safe to the heavenly shore—A great gathering—Out of great variety of circumstances—All there—Unlike the gatherings of earth —Family circles—Regiments return from the war—Storms on the sea—

PAGE

Always some missing—Not so with the sacramental host—Whom to follow as a guide—A large and strong ship—A safe Pilot—Infinite riches easy to acquire—A wonder of growth on the mountains—A greater wonder in the heart—Hope for all—A man overboard—Cling to the rope—A great company and a glad song.. 489

XXV.

THE TEACHINGS OF NIGHT.

Day and night coheralds of the Divine glory—They never cease to proclaim— The many voices of both—No excuse for not hearing them—A lesson from the night—The individuality of our being—Thoughts in a wakeful hour at night—Alone with God—Night more impressive than day—Pastor Harms' wakeful hours—Night fearful to the conscience-smitten—Involuntary confessions of a criminal—His great mistake—Made to be social—Strong emotions will declare themselves—Yet the night has deeper lessons—Jesus retired to desolate mountains—Not nearest to God in the crowd—The mistake of the monks—A night alone on mountains—Solitude of the Alpine heights—Awful impressiveness of the situation—Why Jesus transfigured on a mountain—Too much in society—Why God sends darkness—Retirement of the soul needs not solitude—God's presence felt on the street— Night on the battle-field—God and eternity felt to be near—Night in the streets of a foreign city—Highest idea of human greatness—Night the symbol of sorrow—God near in the cloud—We cannot always see our Father—He covers us with his hand—The angel met in the way—When we shall need a companion—The unerring Conductor............................. 509

XXVI.

NO NIGHT IN HEAVEN.

Review—Light sought from darkness—Abraham in his tent—Lot at the gate of Sodom—Jacob at Bethel and Peniel—Israel in Egypt and at the Red Sea— Saul at Endor—David at the Jordan—Elijah in the desert—Jonah at Nineveh—Belshazzar's feast—Jesus with Nicodemus—Jesus walking on the sea —Peter tempted—Jesus in Gethsemane—Jesus at Emmaus and the Sea of Galilee—Peter delivered from prison—Paul at Philippi—Paul shipwrecked —All these things of earth—Light and shadow intermingled—Appointed to lift our hopes higher—Earth has no home for the soul—This is the land of the dying—The true life yet to come—Bible interpreted by our feelings —What heaven is—This world smitten with curse—None in heaven—This earth the dominion of death—No death in heaven—Here all weep—No tears in heaven—Here all suffer—No pain in heaven—Here everything imperfect—In heaven even the just are made perfect—No night in heaven— Here are mystery, ignorance and uncertainty—What can we know?—Longings for light—Good and evil here strangely adjusted—Spiritual things hard to grasp—Few hours of clear vision—Traveler in a defile of mountains —Helped by whom?—This mist shall all pass away—Perfect knowledge shall be given—Inspiration of such a hope—" No night shall be in heaven " 527

The Last Night of Sodom.

And there came two angels to Sodom at even; and Lot sat in the gate of Sodom: and Lot seeing them rose up to meet them; and he bowed himself with his face toward the ground; and he said, Behold now, my lords, turn in, I pray you, into your servant's house, and tarry all night, and wash your feet, and ye shall rise up early, and go on your ways. . . . And when the morning arose, then the angels hastened Lot, saying: Escape for thy life; look not behind thee, neither stay thou in all the plain; escape to the mountain, lest thou be consumed.—GEN. xix. 1, 2, 15, 17.

Night Scenes in the Bible.

I.

THE LAST NIGHT OF SODOM.

"TARRY all night:" "Escape for thy life." The words of man and the words of angels. The man, a master of courtesy and hospitality: the angels, ministers of mercy and of vengeance. The man speaks of house and home and feasting and rest: the angels speak of impending wrath and swift destruction. The man persuades to the enjoyment of a quiet evening in a luxurious clime, and promises the return of a beautiful day: the angels would hasten an escape from the scene of enchantment and delight at the sacrifice of all earthly possessions. The man speaks from mere feeling and a vivid impression of things as they are passing before his eyes: the angels speak of things as they are, and behind the calm and peaceful aspect of the closing day, they see the fiery tempest of the coming morn.

Such is the contrast between feeling and fact, shadow

and substance, appearance and reality. So unlike and so allied to each other are the sensual and the spiritual; the earthly and the heavenly; the aspect of peace and safety, and the near approach of danger and destruction. Such is the difference between the judgment of man, who is all involved in the cares and toils and pleasures of the passing day, and the judgment of beings who stand outside the range of our mistakes and temptations, and who see the affairs of time in the light of eternity.

Things are seldom what they seem to those who judge only by what they see. We are walking every moment upon the very brink of the awful abyss of death and eternity. We are compassed about at all times, and the very sanctuary of our being is penetrated by influences that we cannot comprehend, and by forces of illimitable power. The flame of life burns so feebly upon the secret altar of our hearts that it can be put out by a sudden jar or a single breath. The partition between us and the unseen world is thin as the garments that clothe our flesh, and as easily pierced as the bubbles that float on the wave. A slight change in the elements of the air we breathe would wrap the whole earth in devouring fire or stop the breath of everything that breathes. The draught of water with which we quench our thirst holds imprisoned an electric force great and terrible enough to darken the heavens with tempests and to shake the eternal hills with its thunders.

Things are not what they seem. The appearance of rest and security is often the thin veil which hides approaching calamity and destruction. The smoothly gliding car flies along its level track, and the voices of gayety and gladness are flung out upon the air, as the changing panorama of mountain and hill and valley and forest and stream unfolds before the happy throng of travelers hastening to their homes or seeking new delight in other scenes. A sudden crash is heard, and the flying palace, with all its living throng of passengers, lies in fragments and in flames beside the track, and the voices of gladness are changed to shrieks of terror and cries of agony and death. A healthful and happy family retire to rest with every feeling and indication of peace and security. The morning looks in upon a darkened chamber and upon a company of mourners, weeping around the bedside of one for whom the death-angel came in the night-watches with so swift a summons as to leave no time to say farewell. The strong man rises with the sun and goes forth from his home rejoicing in his strength. He takes up the burden of his daily toil with eager grasp and tireless energy. In an unexpected moment some secret spring of life is broken, and he falls as if smitten by the lightning-stroke, never to rise again. Thus, while the angels of life and of death were seen by living men in ancient time, we are met in our daily paths and visited in our homes by powers as mysterious and mighty, although we see them not with our eyes. Every day's experience compels us to believe in the reality and awful nearness of forces that take no visible body or form. Let us equally believe in the actual appearance of messengers from the unseen world, stepping out from beneath the shadow of eternity to teach men the great lessons of God's truth and love in ancient time.

Let us study this memorable passage in sacred history with deep reverence and godly fear. The first scene which arrests our attention is one of quietness and security. It is evening. A fair city lies upon the border of a plain that looks like a garden in beauty and fertility. A bright lake stretches away northward between dark frowning hills and the steep wall of the eastern shore is reflected in perfect outline beneath the mirror-like surface of the water. Laborers are coming in from the vineyards and fields on the plain, and shepherds are folding their flocks on the distant hills. There are no signs of wrath in the sky, no voices of wailing in the air, no tremor in the "sure and firm-set earth."

And yet the last night is casting its shadows upon the walls and battlements of the doomed city. According to the custom of the land and the time, the chief men are sitting in the gate. Old and young are all abroad in the open air. The idle multitude are coming and going to gather the gossip of the day and enjoy the cool wind that comes up from the lake outside of the walls. The sun has gone down behind the to go, like a purple fringe on the dusky garments of the coming night. So lingers the crimson flush of health upon the pale cheek of the consumptive while the fires of fever are draining the fountains of life within. So the deluded youth, enticed by the siren voice of pleasure, hesitates at the threshold of the house of death, and then sets his feet in the way to hell with a smile.

The evening is so mild and beautiful in the cloudless clime of the East that the idle and pleasure-loving population give themselves up with childish freedom to its bewitching charm, and the streets of the city and its walks outside the gates resound with the voices of the gay and the loud laugh of the "vacant mind." Theirs is the land of the olive and the vine. The flowers blossom through all the year. The air is loaded with perfume. The light clothes the landscape with dreamy fascination. The evening air woos to voluptuous ease. The night persuades to passion and pleasure.

The plains surrounding the city are like the garden of the Lord in fertility. The most indolent culture secures an abundance for the supply of every want. The distant hills are covered with flocks. The merchants of the East bring their treasures from afar. The camels and dromedaries of the desert lay down their burdens at her gates. And the fair city in the vale of Siddim revels in the profusion of everything that nature and art can produce. The chief men display the luxury and the pride of princes. The common people make a holiday of the whole year. The multitude look as if they were strangers equally to want and to work. Like birds in summer, they enjoy the season as it passes, and they take no thought for the morrow. Idleness and riches stimulate the appetite for pleasure, and they go to every excess in indulgence. They have everything that the sensual can desire, and their only study is to find new ways of gratifying the coarsest and basest passion. According to the testimony of One who knew all history, they eat and drink, they buy and sell, they plant and build, and their whole thought and effort and desire is given to a life of the senses, denying God and debasing the soul. And they are so passionate and haughty in their devotion to earthly possessions and sensual pleasures as to count it a mockery for one to say that there may be guilt or danger in such a life.

Such is the throng of the thoughtless and the gay around the gate of the beautiful city in the vale of Siddim, while for them the shadows of evening are deepening into night for the last time. It would only provoke a smile of incredulity or derision if they were told that they were sporting upon their funeral pile, and that the breath of the divine wrath was just ready to kindle the pile into devouring flame.

Alas! how many millions of immortal men live like the thoughtless and pleasure-loving people of Sodom, all devoted to earthly cares, joys and occupations, until the pit of the grave opens in their path and they sink to rise no more. And alas! how often the solemn lesson of sudden death is lost upon the living! for the crowd press on with hurried and heedless tread in the very path out of which men are constantly passing from time into eternity at a single step.

Two strangers are seen approaching the city. The softened radiance of the evening light shows nothing unusual in their appearance. They seem to be only common travelers coming down from the hill-country, and turning in for shelter by night, that they may rise up early in the morning and go on their journey. God's mightiest messengers of mercy and of wrath often come in a very common garb. We must give earnest heed and keep ourselves upon the watch, or the angels of blessing and of deliverance will come and pass by us unawares, and we shall not receive their help.

There was but one man at the gate of Sodom sufficiently attentive to notice the strangers and invite them to his own house. He did not know who they were, nor did he suspect the awful errand upon which they came. But by treating them with such courtesy as was due to the character of strangers, in which they came, he secured for himself such help as angels alone could give in the time of his greatest need. Fidelity in the most common and homely duties of life opens the door of the house for the greatest of heaven's blessings to come in. The discharge of duties that are fully

The idle throng in the streets deride the hospitable old man for taking the two strangers home to his own house. They see nothing in them worthy of such attention. They are much more ready to treat them with rudeness and contempt, or to make them the subjects of the passion which has given their city a name of infamy throughout all generations. They hoot and jeer at the venerable patriarch when he rises up from his seat in the gate to meet the travelers, and bows himself with his face to the ground, and says with Eastern courtesy, " Behold now, my lords, turn in, I pray you, into your servant's house, and tarry all night." The vilest suggestions are passed to and fro among the lewd and leering rabble as the old man leads his guests away. The hour of rest has not come before a crowd gathers in the streets and besets the house where the strangers have gone to repose. They become more clamorous, with infamous outcries and rude assault, as night wears on. They are so blinded and besotted in their sensuality that they would do violence to God's mighty angels, who can wrap their city in flames and iniquity of the inhabitants was full; the last drop was added to the fiery cup of wrath to be poured upon their heads, when they received the warning as an idle tale and treated the messengers with contempt. So dreadful a thing it is to slight God's offered salvation, even though it should be meant only for once. For when the angels of mercy go back to Him that sent them, it may be that they will kindle behind them the fires of wrath.

The men of Sodom did not think they were doing anything unusual when they beset the house of Lot and came near to break the door. They were no more riotous or dissolute on the last night than they had been many nights before. But there is a point beyond which the Divine forbearance cannot go. And they had reached that point when they clamored against Lot, and would have beaten him down in the streets for protecting his angel-guests. When blindness fell upon them, and they wearied themselves to find the door, they had already passed

> " The hidden boundary between
> God's patience and his wrath."

For the sake of the righteous man, Lot, there was just one thing more to be done. The aged father is permitted to go out and urge his sons-in-law to flee from the doomed city. He makes his way to their houses through the blinded rabble in the streets and gives the warning. But he seems to them as one that mocked. They cannot think it possible that he is in his right mind, to be coming to them at that late hour of the night with such an alarming message. They only tell him to go home and quiet his fears by dismissing the suspicious strangers and going to sleep in his own house. They cannot think of troubling themselves about the anxieties of a wakeful and weak-minded old man, when nothing is wanted but a little rest to dismiss his fears. They will sleep on till morning, and to-morrow they will laugh at the kind-hearted old father about his midnight call.

Alas! how little do sons and daughters know the fears and hopes, the anxieties and sorrows, of Christian parents in their behalf! They jest and laugh the hours of life away, while a father's heart is burdened all day long with the desire and prayer that they would be in earnest about the things that concern their everlasting peace. They sleep soundly while a devoted and self-denying mother spends the long hours of the night in watching and weeping for their sake. This old man, Lot, going into the noisy streets under the cover of darkness, to rouse up his sons-in-law and persuade them to escape from the doomed city, was only doing what faithful parents have been doing ever since, to save their children from the sad consequences of living only for earth and time.

When the disappointed father comes back to his own house, the angels of rescue are waiting for him, and the first streaks of dawn are just beginning to appear in the east. As yet there is no apparent change in the earth or the sky. No trumpet of wrath has blown through the midnight. No earthquake has shaken the hills. No sulphurous fires have flamed up from the bed of the peaceful valley. No threatening wave has rolled upon the shore of the quiet lake. No cloud of vengeance darkens the coming day. The morning star shines with its customary brightness over the mountains of Moab. The cool air, mingled with the perfume of flowers, comes up like refreshing incense from the placid sea, and the song of birds welcomes the returning light.

There is nothing to fear save that one word of the angels: "The Lord will destroy this city." The beautiful skies speak peace and safety. The teeming earth promises riches and abundance. The sleeping city dreams of long life and continued pleasure. The coming day looks down from the eastern hills with a smile. But the angels have said, "The Lord will destroy this city," and that is reason enough for alarm and for immediate flight. When he threatens, it is the part of fortitude to fear. When he commands, it is the first dictate of duty and of safety to obey. A thousand voices from the marts of business, from the haunts of pleasure, from the beds of ease, and from the lips of skepticism may promise peace and safety. But all such voices are nothing against one word from the mouth of the Lord. The desires of the deceiving heart, the seductions of temptation, the example of the multitude, may all say peace to those who are living without Christ and without hope. But God's word has said it is death so to live, and that word is enough.

It is hard for the old man to go and leave a part of his own family and all his worldly possessions behind to perish. But go he must, or even he cannot be saved. He lingers with divided heart and hesitating mind while the hour of doom is fast coming on. The angels urge him to hasten, but he lingers still. With merciful violence, they lay hold upon his hands and upon the hands of those of his family that are with him in the house, and hurry them forth out of the city. And then comes the startling and vehement charge: "Escape for thy life! Look not behind thee, neither stay thou in all the plain. Escape to the mountains, lest thou be consumed."

A few moments' delay will cost him his life. If he only turns to take one longing, lingering look of house and home, and of all that his heart holds dearest on earth—if he only waits to see what will become of the city—he will be consumed in the coming storm. The overthrow is delayed only to give the fugitives time to escape. Their steps across the plain are counting out the last moments of the doomed city. Still the weary and distracted old man begs to be permitted to rest at a little town short of the safe mountains. It is so small that he thinks it need not be involved in the ruin of the greater and guiltier city below. The fond and fearful request is granted, but with a solemn reite-

ration of the charge to hasten, for the fiery storm can_
not long be restrained from its outbreaking wrath.
One of the four fugitives pauses to look back, with a
vain curiosity to see what would become of the city,
and so fails to escape.

The sun is already risen upon the earth, and the
bright morning promises a beautiful day. The early
risers in Sodom are making themselves merry with the
frightened old man who had fled with his family to
the mountains. The sons-in law are on the way to his
house, to laugh at him for walking in his sleep the
night before. The idle and voluptuous are devising
new pleasures for the day; and the profligate are
sleeping through the fresh hours of the morning to
compensate for the late revels of the night.

And just now the hour of doom strikes. And the
Lord rains fire and brimstone out of heaven upon the
city and upon the beautiful plain, that seemed like
Paradise the day before; and the smoke of the burning
goes up as the smoke of a great furnace; and the glare
of the mighty conflagration is seen far off by shepherds
on the hills of Hebron and the mountains of Moab.
And in one moment the fair vale, which had been as
the garden of the Lord in beauty and fertility, becomes
a desolation—a place never to be inhabited from gene-
ration to generation—a valley of desolation and of
death, where the wandering Arab shall never dare to
pitch his tent nor the shepherd to make his fold—a
haunted and horrible region, doleful in reality, and

clothed with additional terrors by gloomy superstitions and evil imaginations.

And God made this great desolation in his own beautiful and glorious work because the sin of Sodom was great and the cry of its iniquity had come up to heaven. The last night was as serene and beautiful as ever hung its starry curtain over a sleeping world. And when the golden dawn broke into day the rising sun had not seen a fairer city than Sodom in all the "gorgeous East." In one moment her last cry went up to heaven amid tempests of fire that rained down from above and fountains of fire that burst up from the deep. And Sodom has become a name of infamy for all generations; and its awful doom stands forth as a perpetual sign that God's patience with sin has a bound beyond which it will not go.

The Scriptures expressly declare that the fiery fate of this doomed city in ancient time is set forth as an example, to warn men in all subsequent ages against leading ungodly lives. The lurid flame of this great act of the divine justice sends its warning light through all the centuries of human history, to show that there is a God in heaven, before whom the cry of man's iniquity goes up day and night. The things that are told of Sodom may be said of many a city that has not shared in Sodom's doom. The prophet Ezekiel says that the sin of that city was "pride and fullness of bread and abundance of idleness." Millions would count it happiness to revel in abundance and have nothing to do. Thus far in the world's history the highest rank in human society has been conceded to those who have the greatest revenues secured to them without effort on their part, and who never touch the common burdens of humanity with one of their fingers. And we all know how naturally pride enthrones it-self as the master-passion in the heart, when once all fear of want and all necessity to work are taken away.

The sin of Sodom, however gross in reputation and in reality, was the offspring of wealth and leisure—the two things which the worldly heart most desires, and of which, when possessed, the worldly heart is most proud. If men could have all that they desire of both, how hard it would be for them to think or care at all for the life to come. Many are ashamed of work—all are afraid of want. And yet it is work which makes worth in men, and the deepest sense of want is the be-ginning of immortal life in the soul.

This awful lesson in sacred history may be all summed up in two words: One is from man and the world—the other is from heaven and God. One says to the careless and the worldly, "Tarry, be at ease, enjoy yourself while you can." The other says, " Es-cape for thy life." One says, "Wait, be not alarmed: make yourself comfortable where you are." The other says, "Haste, look not behind thee, flee to the moun-tain, lest thou be consumed." One says, "Soul, take thine ease, eat, drink and be merry." The other says, "Thou fool! this night thy soul may be required of thee."

The question which every one must answer for himself is always this, Which of these two voices shall I obey? Shall I sit down in that seductive and false security which is all absorbed in earthly things and fears no evil, because at present there is no appearance of danger? Or shall I obey the voice from heaven, which commands me to arise and shake off the dangerous lethargy of the world and escape for my life? Shall I listen to the voice of earth, which cries peace and safety, or the voice of heaven, which says that destruction lies in the path of souls that are at ease without God?

To many it seems like mockery to talk of danger to the young and the gay, the healthful and the happy. But who was the mocker on the peaceful night when the cities of the plain rioted in pleasure for the last time—the righteous man, Lot, who exposed himself to the jeers of the mob and made his way through the darkened streets to warn his sons-in-law and fled himself for his life, or the sons-in-law themselves, who laughed at the warning and perished in the flames?

All the seductions and falsehoods of temptation, and all the dangers and sorrows of perdition, are bound up in that one word—*wait*. The voice of love speaks to the careless in terms of terror and alarm. God's patience will not always last. The day of grace must have an end. And with many it is much shorter than they expect. The God who rained a fiery tempest upon the cities of the plain, and destroyed them, is the God who holds oui everlasting destiny in his hands. He will not always be mocked. He will not long be trifled with.

And the loving and compassionate Jesus himself declares that there is a greater sin than that for which Sodom and Gomorrah were overthrown. It is the sin of those who hear the gospel call to repentance and heed it not. It is the sin of those who see the Son of God agonizing in the garden and dying on the cross for their salvation, and who still refuse to give him their hearts. It is the sin of those who have been many times warned and entreated, and who nevertheless spend their lives in waiting for a more convenient season to repent and turn to God. It is the sin of those who put off the first great work of life to the dying hour, and death finds them with the work all undone. It shall be more tolerable for Sodom and Gomorrah in the day of judgment than for those who spend their lives in such utter neglect of the great salvation.

The blessed and compassionate Jesus gave forth that solemn warning to the neglecters and despisers in his day, that the echo of his voice might resound through all time, and that all who hear might be saved from such a doom. His most awful threatening involves and includes an invitation of equal extent. He would awaken fear that he may kindle hope. He commands

effort that he may save from despair. He draws back
the veil from the pit of darkness that we may be con-
strained to look up when he unfolds the glories of
paradise.

The angels hastened Lot while he lingered and was
loth to go. The voices of the divine mercy are ever
repeating the cry to the heedless and the hesitating—
HASTE, ESCAPE FOR THY LIFE. Wait not for better
opportunities to begin a better life. Any opportunity
to secure infinite and eternal ·blessing is a good one.
And a better one than the present may never come.
Look not behind to see what will become of worldly
pleasures and vanities. When the soul is in peril, no
earthly interest can be a sufficient reason for an hour's
delay. The solemn monitions of conscience, the uncer-
tain tenure of all earthly possessions, the embittered
and transitory nature of all earthly joys, the admoni-
tions of divine providence in affliction and death, the
sweet and mighty constraint of the love of Christ, and
all the perils and sorrows and necessities of the soul,
continually say to the hesitating and the halting, Haste
thee; escape for thy life. Make sure thy flight to the
stronghold of hope before the voice of mercy shall
cease to call, and the wrath that is ready to burn,
burst in an endless storm.

Abraham's Night Vision at Beersheba.

And it came to pass after these things, that God did tempt Abraham, and said unto him, Abraham: and he said, Behold, here I am. And he said, Take now thy son, thine only son Isaac, whom thou lovest, and get thee into the land of Moriah; and offer him there for a burnt-offering upon one of the mountains which I will tell thee of.—GEN. xxii. 1, 2.

II.

ABRAHAM'S NIGHT VISION AT BEERSHEBA.

BRAHAM was an hundred and twenty years old when he received the strange and startling command to offer his only and beloved son Isaac for a burnt offering, upon an unknown mountain in the land of Moriah. The message came to him in a vision of the night, in his quiet home in Beersheba. We can well imagine that there would be no more sleep for him that night, after he had heard that mysterious and awful voice which spoke only to him, and which himself only could hear.

He already passed for an aged man, even upon the longer average of human life in his time. His heart had lost much of the fervid and hopeful feeling of youth. It was no longer easy for him to bend before the storm of affliction, and rise with renewed strength when the blow was past. It would be a bitter thing for him now to be made to drink more deeply of the cup of sorrow than he ever had done in the days of his young manhood.

It is easy to face the storm while the heart is fresh and full of hope, and we can rise up from every dis-

45

appointment strong in the purpose and promise to reap the fruits of success and repose in after years. But it is very hard for an old man to find that the sorest trial is reserved for the last, when the burden of age is heavy upon his shoulders and the fire of youth is dim in his eye. Fifty years before, when Abraham left the land of his fathers, the love of adventure, the impulse of curiosity, the prospect of a long life yet to be enjoyed, would help him in his first great act of obedience to the Divine command.

But now he needed repose. His quiet home in Beersheba had been sought as a place of rest. There he had planted the sacred grove and reared a living temple for the worship of the Most High. There he had set up an altar and called on the name of Jehovah, the everlasting God. There he had sunk deep wells in the solid rock, opening perpetual fountains of living water upon the borders of the desert. The Arab's camels bend their course across the burning sands to-day, to drink at the same spot where Abraham and his flocks refreshed themselves thirty-eight centuries ago. There he had gathered round him a great household, even hundreds of servants and herdsmen, and thousands of camels, and sheep, and goats, and cattle. His flocks and tents covered all the grassy plains between the deserts of Arabia and the hills and mountains of Judea. There Abraham had become very rich in silver and gold, and he was already greatest among all the men of the East. And there was fulfilled unto him the Divine promise in the gift of Isaac, the son of his hopes and his heart. His trials and conflicts all over, his desires all fulfilled, his faith confirmed, what had he now to expect but a serene and cheerful old age and a peaceful close of his long and eventful life?

He had left father and mother, kindred and country, at the Divine command. He had lived a pilgrim and a stranger in a land not his own. He had clung to the Divine promise, when, to all human judgment its fulfillment seemed a contradiction and an impossibility. He had borne all the bitterness of a father's grief in sending forth Ishmael to wander in the wilderness. And, after all these trials of faith and submission, could there be in store yet another and greater to wring his aged heart when he was least able to bear it?

The announcement of the voice in the night vision at Beersheba must have fallen upon Abraham like a peal of thunder from a cloudless sky. And the terms in which the terrible command is expressed seem as if they were intentionally chosen to harrow up his soul. Every word is a dagger to pierce the father's heart. Four times over, the emphasis falls just where it would give him the deepest pain: Take *now*, thy *son*, thine *only* son, Isaac whom thou *lovest*, and offer him for a burnt-offering. It would have been enough to break an old man's heart to lose such a son by the ordinary course of sickness and death. Then he could be watched and comforted, and his last hours soothed by the acts of parental tenderness and affection. But how could a father shed the life-blood of that son with his own hand? How could he heap on the fuel and the fire that must burn his body to ashes in his own sight?

It makes the home desolate, and it casts a deep shadow upon all the subsequent pathway of life, for an aged father to lose one of many sons. How much more must the loss of all in one make the remainder of life but as the bitterness of death, and bring down the gray hairs of age with sorrow to the grave.

If Isaac had been a profligate and disobedient son; if he had made himself such a grief to his parents that they had even sometimes thought it would be a relief to see his face no more—still in that case they would have wept in all the bitterness of parental sorrow over his new grave. How much more would such grief be called forth by the violent and unnatural death of one so gentle, so amiable, so deeply and tenderly loved as was Isaac!

If Abraham had been a selfish, cold-hearted man, caring little for the ordinary attachments of kindred and home, never concerning himself to know who should bear his name when he was gone, it would have been a sad day for him when he found himself childless and alone in the world. How much darker must that day be to the kind, generous and affectionate old father! How cruel, how inhuman must have seemed to him the voice which commanded him, with his own hand, to extinguish the life in which he himself lived anew in his old age! How contradictory for him to put out the light which had been kindled to enlighten all nations, to lead all wanderers into the right way.

If it had been his silver and gold, his flocks and herds, his servants and herdsmen, his promised land and peaceful home that he was to give up—if he had only been commanded to spend the remainder of his life in poverty, and wandering, and exile—it would have been a hard lot for an old man. But it would have been nothing compared with the command to sacrifice his only son with his own hand. Nay, more, it would not have seemed so strange, so terrible, so contradictory—it would not have cost the father's heart such a pang—if it had been himself that was demanded for the sacrifice.

We know not what passed in the patriarch's mind when he received the message. But we almost seem to hear him say in an agony of surprise and sorrow: "Oh, my son, my son! would God I could die for thee! I am old and withered, and in a few years, at most, I must be gathered to my fathers. Let the remainder of my days be accepted as a free-will offering, that the sole joy of my heart and the hope of my family may not utterly perish in the death of my son."

Then, again, the seeming contradiction between this new command, and all the instructions and promises which had already been given to Abraham, must have added perplexity to his mind and agony to his heart. The voice came in a vision of the night. Strange, terrible and unaccountable it must have seemed to him at first, as if he had dreamed, or as if some tempting and tormenting demon had assumed to speak in the name of the Lord. Restless and alarmed, he rises up early, that the cool air of the morning may arrest the feverish dream, if it were only a dream, that had disturbed the peaceful sleep of the night. As he passes silently from the inner to the outer apartment of the tent, and looks upon the calm face of his sleeping son, he feels for the moment as if the blood of the dreadful sacrifice were already upon his hands. He shudders as the awful scene, upon some unknown mountain, flashes upon his mind. The repose of that peaceful countenance, dimly seen when the curtain door is lifted, makes the father groan in spirit when he thinks of the terrible secret in his own heart.

He steps forth silently into the open air and looks up. The coming dawn has just begun to tip the edge of the eastern hills with light. Above him the clear blue dome of Arabian skies is all ablaze with the fiery hosts of stars. He remembers that his fathers worshiped those peaceful orbs " beyond the flood," and that no such message ever came to them from the silent depths of the firmament. He remembers that the Divine voice which called him out of Chaldea fifty years before, had once said to him, " Look now toward heaven and tell the stars, if thou be able to number them ; so shall thy seed be." And can it be that now that same voice has commanded him to slay his only son ?

The morning breeze from the mountains of Judah raises a cloud of dust as it sweeps across the broad sandy paths where his vast herds are wont to come down to the wells of water. And again he remembers the words of the Divine voice, "I will make thy seed as the dust of the earth, so that if a man can number the dust of the earth, then shall thy seed also be numbered." And now has that same voice commanded him to slay his only son? And shall he believe both, when one contradicts the other, and so, at last, an old man go childless and in sorrow to the grave?

He looks away northward and eastward, and he sees the baleful light of altar-fires blazing upon the hill-tops. And he well knows that on those high places the heathen inhabitants of the land offer their own children in sacrifice to Moloch and Baal and Chemosh. And shall the worshiper of the true God become like one of them and stain his hand with the blood of his own son?

The wind moans through the sacred grove of terebinth, as if in sympathy with his great sorrow. He walks beneath the widespreading branches of the oaks, where he had many times met angels face to face. He listens and strains his eye in every direction through the gloom of the waning night, if peradventure he may descry some celestial messenger coming to relieve his perplexity. He bows at the foot of the altar which he has reared unto Jehovah, in an agony of prayer for more light But his mind grows darker as the night wanes. Every sound seems to echo the dreadful word: " Take thy son, thine only son, Isaac, whom thou lovest."

The dawn comes slowly up the eastern heavens, and now he can hear the lowing of his flocks gathered by thousands in distant folds, and eager to be led forth while the air is cool and the grass is fresh with dew. The full day and the fiery noon will soon come on. If the journey be undertaken at all, there is no time for delay. If the command be from God, and it must be obeyed, the quickest obedience will be found the easiest and the best. Abraham knows all this, and the father of the faithful is not a man to dally and shuffle with excuses and tamper with his own con- science when once the way of duty, however hard, is plain.

So Abraham goes silently to one of the tents where his servants sleep. Of the hundreds at his command, he selects two. They prepare the wood for the sacri- fice and lay it upon the beast of burden, and the aged father, with a tender and tremulous voice, calls his son. When Isaac wakes and starts to his feet, the old man turns away his face. He cannot meet the innocent and unsuspecting look of the victim named in the voice of the night. Shall the father tell the son where he is going and what is the object of the journey? Oh, how can he conceal it?—how can he tell it? Not now—not here. There will be a better time to break the awful secret to the son when they are far away upon the long and lonely journey. But shall not the son be permitted to take leave of his mother? It would be cruel not to do so. And yet how can it be done? It would cause alarm and confess the whole object of the journey, and perhaps make it impossible for Abraham to obey the Divine command. He himself could not witness the parting.

And yet, shall not the fond old mother be told that she is to see the face of her beloved and only son no more? Must that son, that only son, die a bloody death, and by the father's own hand, and she not be consulted—she not know it till all is done? Shall she be denied the bitter consolation of giving him one parting word? If the sacrifice must be made, may she not share with the father in the great act of faith and obedience? She must know it in the end. Will it be right, will it be honorable, will it be kind to tell her only when it is all over? Must the grief of never having one word of farewell, must the bitter feeling that her only son was *stolen* from her and slain, be added to her worse than orphan's woe?

All these questions and many more must have passed through the mind of Abraham as he started from Beersheba in the dim light of the early morning, with Isaac and the two young men. It must have been a sore task for his wonted serenity and self-possession, to go forth from his home, shutting up in his own generous and magnanimous heart the dark and dreadful secret of the voice which he had heard in the night, and of the sacrifice which he had been commanded to make.

The natural features of the road from Beersheba to Hebron, Bethlehem and Jerusalem, are the same now that they were in the days of Abraham. Passing over the ground now, we see much that the patriarch saw. The first day's journey is over grassy plains and slightly undulating hills, with no forest or mountain or shadowy rock to diversify the scene or to afford a shelter from the noonday heat. On goes the little company, solitary as a single cloud in a clear sky, companionless as a ship alone in mid-ocean, traversing a sea of verdure emblazoned in every direction with millions of bright flowers mingled with the green and waving grass. The air murmurs slightly with the hum of bees feeding upon the honeyed blossoms, and with the twitter of small birds that build their nests upon the ground. But no other sound mingles with the footfalls of the travelers as they pursue their journey. Occasionally a solitary camel or the dark waving line of a caravan appears in the distance and then passes out of view, as ships seen by voyagers at sea seem to hang for a while in the horizon and then melt away in the misty air.

The very solitude of the first day's journey must have been oppressive to Abraham. In company with his only son, to whom he had ever confided everything that concerned himself and the family, he now travels all day by his side with a secret in his heart, which touches his very life and all the dearest hopes of the family, and he dare not tell him of it. He thought when he started that he could talk with him when alone. But now he can only look at his open and unsuspecting face, and turn away lest the son shall see the starting tear and the heaving breast. A hundred times in the day he begins to speak, designing gently to unfold the awful purpose of the journey. A hundred times his struggling emotions become too strong for words, and he stops, leaving his son to wonder at the father's excessive feeling and to inquire vainly for the cause. He feels as if it were deception and mockery to talk with Isaac of anything else than the object of the journey; and yet he walks all day long by his side, and does not tell him of the dreadful deed that must be done when they reach the mountain.

Abraham must have felt relieved when night came on and they all lay down upon the bare earth, and Isaac and the young men slept. Then the agonizing father, wearied with the long torture, could withdraw himself from the company, and pour out the sorrows of his breaking heart under cover of the darkness, even as a greater Sufferer prayed in his agony, "Oh, if it be possible let this cup pass from me!" The countless host of stars come out again in all their burning ranks upon the plains of heaven, only to pierce the soul of the patriarch as with a sword, while they remind him so clearly of that Divine promise, " As the number of the stars, so shall thy seed be;" and he is on his way to sacrifice his only son.   All night long he waits, if peradventure that voice which gave the terrible command will speak again and tell him that his faith has been sufficiently tried—his son may live.   But no such message comes.

The hours of darkness are always long to a sleepless man with the bare earth for his bed.   But the morning comes too soon to Abraham; for it brings him the summons to renew his journey and hasten on to the bloody sacrifice.   And now he approaches the hills, to every one of which he looks with trembling, lest he shall see the sign of the place where the sacrifice must be made.   He passes the oaks of Mamre, where he interceded so fervently for guilty Sodom.   But no angels appear to hear his petition for his only son. He ascends the heights afterward named Kirjath-arba, and Hebron, and Bethlehem, and every outlook upon the surrounding country only reminds him that all this fair land, westward to the sea, and northward to Lebanon, and south to the desert, was to have been the possession of his posterity.   And now, with his own hand and by Divine command, he must cut off his name and inheritance from the earth.

Another day passes as they journey among hills and valleys and streams; and when night comes on, Abraham lies down with the rest upon the bare earth, wearied and ready to perish with having carried the terrible secret of his errand so much longer shut up in his heart.   Isaac sleeps, as the lamb sleeps the nigh before the sacrifice. And the wakeful father only suffers the more keenly when he looks upon the calm repose of his son. Sleeping and waking, he is all the while listening and longing to hear the Divine voice speak once more and say, "It is enough; thy son shall live, and thy paternal heart shall be spared this dreadful pang." But the night passes and the morning of the third day begins to break, and no such message comes. And Abraham must renew the journey with the full expectation that before another evening closes round him the bloody sacrifice will be completed. When another morning breaks, he will be on his way back, childless and broken-hearted, to bear the dreadful tidings of what he had done to his stricken and desolate home.

"Had he not better go back now and never breathe the object of this mysterious journey to any living soul? So his son shall live, and he shall be the staff and joy of his old age. And in time it may be found that this supposed voice in the night vision at Beersheba was all a mistake, a false and feverish dream, growing out of his very anxiety to preserve the life of his only son."

If Abraham had been anything less than the father of the faithful, it would have been easy for him to yield to such fond and parental misgivings, and so he would have lost the fulfillment of the Divine promise through his fears, and the world would have lost the rich inheritance of his great and victorious faith.

We all know the conclusion. The journey of the third day is begun. Soon the mysterious sign, doubtless like the flame of the burning bush or the glory of the tabernacle, appears upon a distant height. Now it is settled beyond all question in Abraham's mind that the voice in the night vision at Beersheba was a reality, the command was Divine, the sacrifice must be made. He girds up his soul anew with desperate and agonizing firmness to complete the great act of faith.

He lays the wood for the offering upon the one that must be burned. With a trembling hand and a breaking heart he takes the fire and the knife, and goes silently up the steep alone with his son. Isaac wonders where the victim for the sacrifice is to be found, but the father cannot tell him yet. The altar is built by the hands of both; the wood is placed in order for the fire; the last dreadful moment has come, and no delivering angel appears—no Divine voice speaks to stay the sacrifice. The father must tell the son the awful message which he has carried in his own bleeding heart through all the long journey. Isaac himself must be slain, and by the father's hand. It must be with his own consent if he is offered at all. For he is a full-grown man, twenty-five years of age, and he can easily resist or escape the hand of his father, who has a hundred more years upon his shoulders.

We do not know what feelings, what expressions the startling announcement brought forth from Isaac. We are not told what surprise, what horror, what fear, what distrust, what agony he manifested. Had he seen something wild and strange in the look of his father all the way? And does he now conclude that the old man has become insane on the subject of sacrifice? Or does he reason, does he remonstrate, does he resist? Does he claim that the father can have no right to take the life of the son, and that the vision or voice which commands such a dreadful deed cannot be from God?

We do not know what was said, thought or felt by Isaac when he heard from his father that he must be the victim. But we do know what surpasses all our comprehension—we know that Isaac in the end submitted to the sacrifice. He consented to be bound, as he had seen the lamb bound, and laid upon the altar. He gave up life, hope, everything, just because his father told him, there, on that lonely mount, that it must be so. He looked, as he thought, for the last time upon the face of his father, and then silently waited for the stroke of the knife that was already in the father's hand. Which was most to be pitied it were hard to tell—the father, who must inflict the fatal blow, or the son who submits in silence to be slain. If the sacrifice must be made, the sorrowing father will certainly endure a longer and a deeper agony than the dying son.

Abraham turns away his face, that he may not see when the blood follows the blow. Isaac, with fortitude equal to his father's faith, bids him strike. But now,

at length, it is enough. The voice from heaven comes
at last. The faith of the father and the submission of
the son are sufficiently tried. The delivering angel
of the covenant cries aloud, " Now I know that thou
fearest God, seeing thou hast not withheld thy son,
thine only son, from me."

And this great act of faith, which made Abraham
the father of the faithful, shines forth like the sun
amid the darkness of far-distant times. It teaches the
great lesson of confidence in the Divine word and sur-
render to the Divine will in such a way as most deeply
touches the heart. Nothing is too precious for us to
give to God. We never secure the full value of any
possession until we give it all to Him. Give Him
your money, and you will get more of all that money
is good for than you will by keeping it all to yourself.
Give Him your time, and a day spent in his service
will be better than a thousand spent in " pleasurable
sin." Give Him your talents, your efforts, your toil,
and every act of duty done in His name shall receive
an exceeding great reward. Give Him your children,
and they will never be so dear to you as when they
are wholly dedicated to God. Give Him your heart,
and the blessedness of heaven will begin in your soul
the moment you fix your supreme affection on Him
who alone is altogether lovely. Give Him all—heart,
soul, life, everything—and then Christ is yours, heaven
is yours, eternal life, eternal joy is yours—all things
are yours.

Nothing is too precious for God to give to us. Abraham's offering of Isaac was appointed to foreshadow a greater and more awful sacrifice, which was complete when the Almighty Father actually gave His only-begotten Son to death that we might live. All the sorrows that wrung the heart of Abraham during the three days of his dark and dreadful trial were imposed on him to help us understand how real, how deep, how unutterable was the self-denial of the infinite God in giving His own Son to death for our salvation. No trial, no mental torture could possibly have been greater to Abraham than that which he bore in obeying the command to sacrifice his son. God actually surrendered His well-beloved Son to the slow and dreadful agony of crucifixion. No voice from heaven commanded to stay the sacrifice when once He had been nailed to the cross. Legions of angels were in waiting, but they were not permitted to interpose for His relief, The torture and the mockery went on till he bowed His head in death. And all for our sake! Surely the Infinite One himself can give us no greater proof that He sincerely desires our salvation. And as the free gift of His love to us is infinite, His claim upon our faith, our services and our affections must be correspondently complete and extreme. If we withhold from God, we are infinite debtors, though we answer every other claim. If we give ourselves to God, we shall be acquitted of every charge—we shall be accepted in every prayer.

Prompt and unquestioning obedience to God is the easiest and the best. Abraham rose up early, and was on his way to perform the fearful duty assigned him before the cares of the day could divert his attention or the interference of others could shake his resolution. We should not allow ourselves for once to look in the face of a present and an acknowledged duty, and delay to meet its demand. It darkens the mind, it perverts the judgment, it hardens the heart, it wastes precious opportunities, it weakens all good purposes, to hold ourselves back from doing anything which, to us now, is clearly and unquestionably right. It does not require a long process of reasoning to convince any honest, candid, truth-seeking mind that the whole heart and soul should be given at once and cheerfully to Him who loved us and gave himself for us.

The hindrances that hold us back from obedience to God are indeed many and subtle and strong. We must make it a study to cut off every influence, to break up every habit, to sunder every tie that keeps us from the most free, open and hearty committal of our whole heart and soul to God. We cannot be too strongly or too openly bound to any course that is right. The greatest difficulties melt and vanish before a full and earnest purpose to do God's will. Light shines out of darkness for those who, in trial and perplexity, look only to Christ and wait for the words, " Follow me!"

Jacob's Night at Bethel

And he lighted upon a certain place, and tarried there all night, because the sun was set: and he took of the stones of that place, and put them for his pillows, and lay down in that place to sleep.—GEN. xxviii. 11.

JACOB'S NIGHT AT BETHEL

JACOB'S NIGHT AT BETHEL.

THE journey upon which Jacob went forth from his father's home at Beersheba was both perilous and long. He must go without a guide and he must start without delay. He had provoked his wild and passionate brother Esau to anger, and his life was no longer safe in his father's tent. He must pass through a country where there was no law for the protection of travelers; no courtesy or hospitality was thought to be due to strangers, except within the limits of tribe and family. He himself did not belong to the native occupants of the land; he could not invoke the name of chieftain or clan for his protection. There would be none to revenge the wrong if he should be robbed or murdered on the way.

What made the matter worse, Jacob himself was to blame in the sad quarrel that had broken out between him and his brother. In the long and lonely journey before him he must have the worst company a defenceless traveler can ever have—a guilty conscience. Hard roads, and scanty fare, and bad weather, and exposure to accident and sickness, and robbers and assassins all the way, are quite enough to remind the weary wanderer that there is no place like home. But altogether they cannot do so much to make a long journey miserable as that secret whisper in the soul which says, "I have brought all this upon myself by my wrong-doing."

And, besides, Jacob was naturally a cautious and a timid man. He had never, like his brother, sought the fierce and wild delight of traversing the mountains and the desert with the hunter's tireless step or the warrior's eager hate. He had never roused up the lion in the chase or met his fellow-man in the fray. He had never learned to go homeless and hungry through the livelong day, and to lie down upon the bare earth for a bed, with the open sky for a covering by night.

He had been nourished from his earliest youth with all the tenderness and solicitude of an indulgent and doting mother's love. As he grew up to mature years, he became a man of plain and peaceful life. He preferred the quiet occupation of a herdsman to the hazards and uncertainties that Esau loved. From boyhood he had been subjected to caution and restraint in the presence of his boisterous and daring brother.

Human nature is apt to take to its opposites. We like that which is most unlike ourselves. We are drawn to one who possesses the qualities in which we feel ourselves most deficient. The quiet and meditative old man, Isaac was greatly taken with the reckless and self-reliant hardihood of his wild and vagrant son Esau. And Jacob always appeared to a disadvantage in comparison with the dashing and outspoken bearing of the wild man of the desert and the wilderness. His modesty was taken for meanness of spirit, his correctness of deportment for coldness of heart, his attention to the wants and feelings of others for servility and cowardice. The fond and peace-loving old father thought the rudeness of Esau manly, his boastful and irreverent language courteous, and his recklessness in giving and forgetting to pay generous and noble-hearted in the extreme. Jacob's services were all taken as a matter of course, because they were so constant and faithful. Esau's were received with gratitude and praise, because they were seldom bestowed and never could be relied upon. Jacob, always at home, always attentive to his father's wishes, was looked upon as a dependant and a drudge. His filial obedience was rewarded with few thanks and less affection.

The father's heart was with the son who seldom showed himself in the paternal tent, and who, when he did appear, made everybody tremble with fear and everything yield to his rude and boisterous manners. Isaac himself was afraid of him, and never could be quite at ease when he heard the ringing and rollicking voice of his wild son coming in from the chase, with the smell of the forest in his garments and the lightness of the roe in his step. But no sooner was he gone than the fond old father wished him back. And Jacob's filial attention to his father's wants for weeks and months could only draw forth from the old man's heart the constant and querulous inquiry, " When would Esau come again ? "

So the fond parent will often receive coldly and as a matter of course the faithful attentions of a son or daughter at home, while all the parental affections and anxieties are expended upon some absent child, who is a burden rather than a blessing to the parent's declining years. So do we all make little of daily and common blessings, just because they come of course. And we imagine we should be so happy if we could always command pleasures which soon weary us when they come, and which are esteemed more highly just because they are rare and remote. A single cup of cold water will call forth more gratitude from lips parched with fever, a single beam of sunshine will be received with more thankfulness by the prisoner in his dungeon, than rivers of water and a universe of sunlight bestowed in the ordinary course of free and healthful daily life.

Strange as it may seem to us, Jacob lived the dependent life of a child with his parents until he was seventy-seven years of age. He had had little opportunity to cultivate the more noble, generous and self-reliant traits of character. Held in subordination to the will of others, he was in danger of becoming timid, cautious, crafty, distrustful of others, and not safe to be trusted himself.

The mode in which he provoked the outbreak between himself and his brother Esau shows that he had gone far toward the formation of such a character. He knew very well the Divine promise that the inheritance of the ancestral name and the fulfillment of the covenant with Abraham should fall to him. And he should have been content to trust that immutable word, without resorting to deceitful devices to secure and to hasten its fulfillment.

But the timid and subtle supplanter had not faith enough to wait, or to leave Divine Providence to accomplish its own ends in its own way. Once upon a time, when Esau came in from the chase, weary and dispirited, faint and fretful, he said, in his usual rash and extravagant manner, that he was at the point of death with hunger, and that he must have food at any cost. Jacob artfully took him at his word, and told him that he would relieve his hunger at once if he would give up to him his birth-right claim to.the inheritance and the honor of precedence in his father's family. The reckless and roving hunter cared little for a claim which would tie him down to his father's quiet and peaceful life. Tired, impatient and hungry, he only wants something to eat to-day, and the mountains and the wilderness, with his quiver and bow, shall be his birth-right and inheritance to-morrow.

And so he carelessly said, and confirmed the rash

word with an oath, that Jacob might have all such claims of his and welcome, if only he would bring him the plainest dish and let him eat and go back to his hunting-grounds again. And thus the bargain was made between the two brothers, the cautious and timid herdsman getting the advantage, because the brave and improvident hunter was hungry, tired and fretful, and cared little what he promised if only his appetite for the time could be appeased.

Alas! how many even now, with more light and instruction than Esau had, throw away health, character, life, and their very soul's salvation just for a brief and trifling gratification! How many, in an unguarded and fretful moment, let words pass the lips which no tears or after-regrets can recall! How easy it is to do in a moment of enticement or provocation what one would give his right hand to change when done, but which can never be blotted from the book of memory! And it is always a bad bargain for one to barter away a good conscience, a pure heart and the hope of heaven for any amount of sensual gratification or earthly advantage.

Esau is elsewhere, in the Scriptures, called a " profane person," a man who made light of sacred things, and would invoke the most awful curses upon himself and others just to gratify an irritable and ungoverned temper. And of all persons in the world the profane man throws away the greatest good for the least gratification. He dooms himself and others to everlasting exclusion from the Divine favor, just for the pride or the passion of uttering "great swelling words of blasphemy." He commits the most senseless and shocking sin against God and his own soul, under an inducement so slight that only a rude and irreverent mind can feel that it is any inducement at all.

When Isaac was old and blind, and desired to pronounce his final blessing upon his favorite Esau, it was agreed between the two that the wild hunter should bring venison from the field and make savory meat, such as the old man loved, and that under the stimulus of his favorite dish his soul should bless his first-born before he died. The arrangement was overheard and cunningly defeated by Jacob and his mother. While the hunter was out in pursuit of game they took advantage of the old man's blindness, and drew from him the blessing which had been promised to the absent brother. Undoubtedly, Jacob sincerely believed that the birth-right was due to him, both by purchase and by Divine promise. But nothing could justify him for attempting to secure even what he thought was his right by gross deception and repeated falsehood.

He put on the garments of his hairy brother, and covered his hands and neck with goat-skins to make the disguise complete. He said plainly to his doubting father, I am Esau, thy first-born. He said he had done as his father had bidden him, when he had done no such thing. He offered him the flesh of kids, disguised by the cunning cookery of his mother, and said

it was venison.   He said the Lord had given him suc-
cess in the chase, when he had not been to the chase at
all.   He came near his blind father, and confirmed the
lie of his lips by exposing to the blind old man's touch
the hairy covering of his hands and neck.   He said
again to his still doubting father, "I am Esau, thy
first-born."   And he sealed the whole tissue of im-
posture upon the lips of his father with a lying kiss.
And he did all this, not in the heat and thoughtlessness
of youth, but when he was a mature man, seventy-seven
years of age.   And he did it to make sure of an in-
heritance which he knew had been promised him by
the word of the immutable God.

However sacred and venerable became the name of
Jacob in subsequent years, we must admit that all this
was flagrantly and inexcusably wrong.   Such conduct
manifested a very strange mixture of deceit and devo-
tion—of anxiety to obtain the Divine blessing, and of
reliance upon fraud and falsehood to secure it.   A man
who could do such things would have to be subjected
to some very sore discipline before he would become
frank and straightforward in his dealings with his
fellow-men, truthful and upright toward God.   And
it was of the Lord to bring such discipline upon Jacob
as a direct consequence of his own distrustful and dis-
honorable policy.

Instead of establishing himself at once as the head
of a rich and honorable family by his duplicity, he
was obliged to flee for his life, with nothing but his staff

In his hand. He must go on foot and alone four hundred and fifty miles through a wild and inhospitable country. If he takes servants or beasts of burden, his course can be too easily traced, and he will be pursued and overtaken by his impetuous and angry brother. If he takes money, he may be robbed the first night. If he goes without it, he must beg of such roving bands as he may meet on the way, or live with the beasts of the forest and field. He must depend upon his poverty for protection, and upon his destitution for the supply of his wants.

The journey was as long and perilous as that of young Washington from Virginia to Fort Duquesne in the early history of this country, and for accomplishing which he received the admiration of the civilized world. Washington was twenty-two years of age—Jacob was seventy-seven. Making all due allowance for the greater duration of human life and bodily vigor in Jacob's time, it would take a man at his age twenty days to travel so far on foot alone, in a strange country, without roads, bridges, landmarks or houses of entertainment on the way.

Going with such a prospect of danger and suffering before him, he must have left his father's home with a heavy heart. He starts out in the silence and the gloom of the morning before the day, and he passes on over the rolling grassy plain toward the distant hills, afraid to be alone, and yet more afraid of such company as he is most likely to meet. On the ascent of every ridge his quick eye surveys the whole length of the landscape before and behind, and every unusual object is sure to arrest his attention. Passing through the hollow places of the plain, he keeps watch right and left, lest some robber should rush down suddenly upon him from the higher ground. Here and there he sees a solitary shepherd keeping his flocks, or a single traveler like himself hurrying across the houseless waste, or the long file of pilgrims and merchantmen making their way from the hill-country toward Egypt. But he is afraid of all, and takes the utmost pains to keep himself from being seen, while he hurries on all day toward the distant hills. He takes the same path that his father Isaac traveled many years before when going with Abraham to be offered in sacrifice upon the mountain of Moriah. But he is far from having the peace and strength of Isaac's faith to comfort him on his journey.

On the evening of the second or third day he finds himself in a solitary place, some fifty miles from his father's home. The path before him leads up a wild, rocky hill, on the top of which is a rude walled town. He can hear the voices of the villagers floating out upon the evening air. He can see families upon the housetops and lights moving to and fro. But he dares not approach the gates and ask for hospitality. Tired and timid and heart-stricken as he is, he would rather lie down among the stones of the naked hill and get such sleep as he can with wolves and jackals howling round him all night.

Weary, hungry, homesick, he feels that the God of his fathers has forsaken him, and that all this danger and desolation have been brought upon him by his own folly. The darkness in his soul is deeper than the shades of night, and the utter loneliness of the bleak and barren hill is in sympathy with the feeling of solitude and desertion that weighs upon his heart. He seems to himself like an outcast and an unblessed creature in the howling waste of the wilderness. The proximity of the town, which he dares not approach, intensifies the sense of abandonment and despair in his soul. The hardships of the day and the horrors of the night are multiplied and aggravated by a fearful heart and an excited imagination. When the darkness becomes complete, and the sound of voices ceases to be heard from the hill, he selects a stone for a pillow and lies down upon the bare ledge to sleep or wake and wait for the day. And now he feels, as he never had done in his father's tent, the need of protection from an Eye that never sleeps and a Hand that never grows weary.

Oh how much it would be worth to the lonely fugitive to be assured in this desolate place that God has not forsaken him! How much lighter would be the burden upon his weary heart if he did not know that his own wrong-doing had driven him forth upon this lonely and perilous wandering! But there is no servant of God to whom he can turn for counsel—no written word of God from which he can draw precept or promise to sustain his sinking hope. The blessing which he was so anxious to secure has only made him an outcast, and he lies down to sleep with the despairing conviction that the God of Abraham has cast him off.

But when man loses all confidence in himself, it is God's time to help. When he sees and deplores the folly of all worldly and selfish devices, it is God's time to give light and hope from above. And so the Almighty Father had compassion on this unhappy wanderer in the desert. In the dreams of that memorable night he received Divine assurance that the God of Abraham and Isaac was with him in his wandering, not less than in the patriarchal home at Beersheba. The covenant of infinite mercy should be fulfilled in his behalf; his promised inheritance of everlasting blessing should remain secure.

In the inspired vision of that night the sleeping exile saw the pathway of communication between earth and heaven, glorious as the gates of the morning, broad and firm as the everlasting mountains, open and free as the boundless realm of air. He saw the shining staircase, going up with steps of light from the desolate ground where he slept, and reaching to the highest heaven. Living messengers were passing up and down the terraced steep, as if it were the special ministry of God's host to wait on him in his wanderings! Where the successive gradations of ascending heights were lost in the surpassing splendor of a throne great and high, the glory of Jehovah appeared and gave forth a voice, renewing the promise of mercy, of protection and of ever-lasting blessing.

When the astonished sleeper woke, and thought within himself what this strange vision might mean, he felt and believed that the promise and the protection of the Almighty God were his best reliance. He learned that the most lonely and desolate spot on earth could become a holy place to the heart that turns with longing and with hope to the living God. He saw that the pathway between earth and heaven was ever open and free, and that angelic messengers of mercy were ever coming and going. To him, that bleak and barren hill, strewn with jagged rocks and haunted all night by howling beasts of prey, was the most sacred spot he had ever found on earth. It was none other than the house of God and the gate of heaven.

And when the wandering Jacob, in the depths of his sorrow and danger, was thus especially assured of God's unfailing love, his heart was won. He dismissed his doubts and fears, and he determined to make that vision at Bethel to him the beginning of a new and a better life. He made a solemn covenant with his own soul that thenceforth he would trust and obey the God of his fathers for evermore. He set up a memorial of that covenant. And in the subsequent years of his life, with only such imperfections and shortcomings as are common to man, he was faithful to that vow.

And this sacred story of Jacob's night at Bethel may serve to teach us that in our darkest and most desolate moments God may be using our trouble and despondency as a means of drawing our hearts to him. We may find him nearest when we thought him farthest off. What the world would call the greatest misfortune may be found to have been sent in the greatest mercy. There is no such word as chance or accident in the inspired vocabulary of faith. Nobody but a skeptic or a misanthrope would say of himself—

> "I am as a weed,
> Flung from the rock on ocean's foam to sail
> Where'er the surge may sweep, the tempest's breath prevail."

All places are safe, all losses are profitable, all things work together for good to them that love God.

Every experience of the unsatisfactory nature of earthly things should direct us to the stronghold of hope. Every pang caused by an uneasy conscience should awaken within us a more intense longing for the peace which passeth all understanding. Every unanswered desire, every disappointed expectation, every unhappy hour should lead us to seek for true and permanent rest for the soul. Whoever would grow in Divine knowledge, whoever would find out the secret of happiness here and the seal of promised salvation hereafter, must heed the voice with which Divine Providence speaks in the common events of life.

When the aims of human ambition are frustrated, the objects of earthly affection are removed, the sources of worldly pleasure, desire and effort fail to satisfy the soul, then the voice of God is calling to trust in him; then the heavenly Father is coming forth to invite the wanderer home. Like Jacob in his desolate pilgrimage, we should obey that voice with gratitude and with vows of consecration. We should rejoice that the Divine compassion can follow us in our wandering, even when we have forgotten our duty and forsaken our God.

To the eye of Christian faith tne skies are always clear, the pathway of ascent from earth to heaven is always open, and angels of blessing are ever coming and going upon errands of mercy. The great inheritance, the glorious home, is not far away nor hidden in thick clouds. God's presence makes heaven, and he is with us everywhere. His banner over us is light and love. His angels are our guardians and companions. In every place where there is a human heart longing for Divine consolation there is God's house, there is heaven's gate, there are infinite sources of hope and peace.

Out in mid-ocean there is a ship tossing on the waves. The night is dark, the winds are high. The angry elements rage and howl as if determined to tear the shattered vessel in pieces or sink it in the deep. A sailor-boy has just climbed down from the swinging mast and crept into his narrow locker, wet and cold, to get a little rest.   He sleeps unconscious of the howl of the storm and the roll of the groaning ship.   His heart is far away in that quiet home which he left for a roving life on the seas.   He hears again the voice of evening prayer offered from the parental lips, and one fervent, tender petition bears his own name to 'the throne of the infinite mercy.   The Sabbath bell calls, and he goes in the light of memory, with his youthful companions, along the green walks and beneath the shade of ancient trees to the village church.   He hears the blessed words of Christ, " Come unto me."   God is speaking to that wanderer upon the seas as he spoke to Jacob at Bethel in the dreams of the night.   And that vision of home and voice of prayer is sent to that sailor-boy to make the tossing ship to him the house of God and gate of heaven.   When he wakes from that brief and troubled sleep, he has only to answer the call of Heaven, as Jacob 'did, with the gift of his heart, and that night of tossing on the lonely seas shall be to him the beginning of a new and a better life.

Far away, among the mountains of Nevada, where of old God's creative hand locked up veins of gold in the fissures of the rock, the weary miner lies down in his cheerless cabin to sleep.   It is the evening of the blessed Sabbath, and yet to him it has not been a day of rest.   Work, work, work, with hammer and spade and drill, from morn to eve, through all the week, has been his life for months and years.   His calloused hands and stiffened frame and weary step tell of hardships such as few can bear and live. And he has borne them all with heat and cold, and rain and drought, and famine and fever, that he might fill his hands with gold. And now, in this wakeful and lonely hour, something impels him to ask himself what all the treasures of the mountains would be worth to him if he has not found rest for his soul. To that tired, Sabbathless worker in his solitude comes a gentle influence as if it were an angel's whisper, to tell him of riches that never perish, and of a home were the weary are at rest.

And so all round the earth—on the sea and the land, in the city and the wilderness, by night and by day—God is calling wanderers home. He is speaking from his high and glorious throne to the desolate and weary and disappointed, saying, as he said to Abraham, "I am thy shield and thy exceeding great reward."

And man can be guilty of no greater infatuation than to refuse to hear when God speaks to him by his providence or his word. Destruction must certainly lie in the path of him who pushes away from himself the everlasting arms of love which surround him every moment for his protection and salvation. Sad and hopeless must be the life of the man who chooses to plod on his weary way, groping in the dust, clinging to the earth, refusing to look up when there are voices of God continually calling to him from above, and wings of ministering angels hovering around him, alluring to brighter worlds and leading the way.

Blessed and glorious is the lot of him who can find Bethel every day in the journey of life, the house of God in every home, the gate of heaven in every hour of need. All the waste places of the world will become sanctuaries, and the light of paradise will shine in every human dwelling, when every eye can see the pathway from earth to heaven bright with the procession of angels, and the ransomed millions of earth going up to the heavenly Zion with songs and everlasting joy upon their heads.

Jacob's Night of Wrestling with the Angel.

And he lodged there that same night. . . . And Jacob was left alone, and there wrestled a man with him until the breaking of the day.— GEN. xxxii. 13, 24.

IV.

JACOB'S NIGHT OF WRESTLING WITH THE ANGEL.

THE night vision of Bethel was the first great era in Jacob's eventful life. The second was his night of wrestling with the angel on his return from Padan-aram. The scene of this mysterious and memorable adventure was on the banks of the river Jabbok. It is a wild rocky stream, that comes roaring down from the mountains of Gilead and Bashan, and joins the Jordan on the east, midway between the Sea of Galilee and the Dead Sea. In the upper part of its course, among the highlands, it is a dry bed for half the year. The hot sun of the Syrian heavens burns down upon bare rocks and glimmering sand with such fervor that its deep channel seems like the heated shaft of a mine.

In the rainy season the main stream and all its branches are transformed into foaming and furious torrents, that fill the hills and valleys with their voices. The lower portion of the river runs with a swift and strong current through the whole year. The banks are high and precipitous, with here and there a green

85

and level recess of a few rods' width between the base of the hills and the water's edge. The neighboring country is wild, and piled up into broken ridges and rounded peaks. The descent to the Jordan is so steep that the smooth current of the stream is often interrupted by shooting rapids and silvery cascades. The Ganges falls four inches in a mile, and it flows five miles in an hour. The Jabbok falls twelve hundred inches in a mile, and it must have a current correspondently swift.

The neighboring heights are studded with picturesque ruins of castles and strongholds, once held by robber chieftains, and still haunted by the memory of their dark and bloody deeds. The narrow borders between the stream and the base of the high and rocky banks are covered with thickets of cane and oleander, and the blaze of bright flowers in spring makes the bed of the ravine look as if it were all on fire, and the river had been turned in to put out the flame. The high table-lands are covered with dark green forests of oak and pine, which appear the more fresh and beautiful from contrast with a rocky peak or a barren ridge occasionally lifting itself above the billowy sea of verdure.

To this wild river Jabbok, not far from its junction with the Jordan, the patriarch Jacob had come with his family and flocks, a great company, on his return from Padan-aram. Twenty years before, in his flight from his father's home, he had crossed the same stream a lonely fugitive, with his staff in his hand, carrying a'l his earthly possessions in a shepherd's bag. Now, in his return, he had become so rich that he could select from his vast herds five hundred and fifty sheep, goats, camels and oxen for a present to his brother Esau, and yet have so many left that the multitude of his flocks filled the valleys as they went. The long and lonely exile in the strange land had done more to enlarge his possessions than seventy years of filial service in his father's house. He was feeble, timid and poor when he went forth upon his wanderings alone. When he came back, trial had made him strong and misfortune had made him rich. So evermore does God bring light out of darkness, and joy out of sorrow, and great peace out of conflict, for those whom he is leading in the Divine life and preparing for the blessed rest.

Jacob had left Padan-aram and started upon his return to his native country in obedience to a Divine command. The day before, while coming down from the heights of Gilead to the fords of the Jabbok, he had received a strange and startling assurance of the Divine protection. While his flocks were moving slowly, like fleecy clouds, along the grassy hill-sides and over the wild pasture-lands, Jacob lifted up his eyes and saw in open day, as if encamped in the air, two hosts of angels encompassing him behind and before and moving with him for his protection. He remembered the vision of Bethel, and he rejoiced that the heavenly guardians who cheered him on his departure twenty years before were ready to welcome him on his return.

And we who live in this matter-of-fact and mechanical age are apt to think that it was a wrapt and wondrous life which the patriarch led in that old time, when he could meet God's host among the hills, and he could see convoys of bright angels like the burning clouds of sunset hovering round him in the solitudes of the mountains. But God's host is always nearer than we are apt to suppose in the dark hours of trial and conflict. The angels have not yet forsaken the earth, nor have they ceased to protect the homes and journeys of good men. Heaven and earth are nearer each other now than they were when Jacob saw God's host in the broad day and Abraham entertained the Divine messengers under the shadow of the oak at noon. The spiritual world is all around us, and its living inhabitants are our fellow-servants and companions in all our work for God and for our own salvation. The inhabitants of heaven find more friends and acquaintances on earth now than they did in ancient times. It is not from any want of interest in the affairs of men that they do not now meet us in the daily walks of life or speak to us in the dreams of the night.

We must not think that God was more interested in the world in ancient times, when he spoke by miracles and prophets and apostles, than he is now when he speaks by his written word and by his holy providence.

The heart of the Infinite Father never yearned toward his earthly children with a deeper or more tender compassion than now. No burden rests upon our shoulders, no pain touches our hearts, without our Father. If we do not see angels come and take us by the hand and lead us out of danger, as they led Lot out of Sodom, it is not because they have ceased to come, or because they fail to guard us when we need protection.

There never was a time when God was doing more to govern, to instruct and to save the world than he is doing now. To those who look for him the tokens of his presence are manifest everywhere; the voice of his providence is in every wind; every path of life is covered with the overshadowings of his glory. To the devout mind this world, which has been consecrated by the sacrificial blood of the cross, is only the outer court of the everlasting temple in which God sits enthroned, with the worshiping hosts of the blessed around him.

We need only a pure heart to see God as much in the world now as he was when he talked with men face to face. He speaks in all the discoveries of science, in all the inventions of art, in all the progress of the centuries, in everything which enriches life and enlarges the resources of men. All the great conflicts and agitations of society prove that God is on the field. We need only add the faith of the patriarchs to the science of the philosophers, and we shall find

Bethels in the city and in the solitude, Mahanaims in every day's march in the journey of life.

Jacob greatly needed such encouragement as "God's host" gave him on the heights of Mahanaim. He had heard that his offended brother Esau was coming out of Mount Seir to meet him with four hundred men as wild and warlike as himself. What could he do against such a roving and reckless band, who lived by plunder, and who could easily make an old grudge of twenty years' standing an excuse for any amount of violence, of bloodshed and of robbery. It would only be a daily custom and a fierce delight with them to swoop down upon Jacob's herds from the hills, like the eagle from his eyry, destroy the keepers and drive off the cattle to their own mountains beyond the Jordan.

Jacob is not a man of war. He has no skill in the use of the spear or bow. He has no guard of soldiers or armed herdsmen to protect his family and his flocks as they move along the unoccupied pastures of the wilderness. But he sets himself to prepare for the encounter in the best way he can.

First of all, he feels that this new peril has been sent to call his past life to remembrance; and he receives it as a Divine admonition to see that all is right between him and God. He has learned by sad experience that an accusing conscience is the worst companion in the hour of danger. And he begins his preparation for the great trial before him by adjusting the solemn account between him and his father's God. He makes humble confession of his many sins and shortcomings in duty. He pleads the Divine promise that God would deal well with him in his return to his native country. He prays for guidance and protection in the coming peril.

Men who never pray in health and safety will sometimes call upon God with great earnestness when danger and death are near. And God sometimes opens the pit of destruction in the path of the disobedient and wandering, that they may be induced to cry to him for help. Sometimes it is the last and greatest act of God's mercy to a prayerless and worldly man to lay so many pains and afflictions and losses upon him that he feels compelled to cry out in agony of soul, "Lord, help me!"

And there is no good thing in the world which a man cannot afford to lose, if the sacrifice and the suffering will only teach him to call upon God in humble and fervent prayer. Jesus taught that men ought always to pray ; that they *must needs* pray, just because they are men, having the nature, necessities and privileges that belong to men in this world. And if any man thinks he has not time to pray, let him ask who gives what time he has, and whether in fact he has time for anything else so long as prayer is neglected. Let him see to it, lest God shall give him time to fail in business, to be sick, to suffer and die, and not leave him the choice so to use the time given or not. Then whose shall all those things be that he has been so busy in seeking as not to have time for prayer? If any man says he has no fitting form of words for prayer, let him observe in what way the little child asks for food when hungry, and then make the earnestness and the simplicity of that petition his own when asking his heavenly Father for the bread of life. If we fully understood the greatness of the privilege of prayer, we should say at once that it were better to die than not to pray.

After Jacob had performed the first duty of seeking help from God, he adopted such other measures for his protection as a wise and thoughtful man would have chosen in his circumstances. He divided his people and his flocks and herds into two companies, that one at least might escape should either be attacked by the robbers. Next he selects and sends forward five hundred and fifty from his vast herds as a present to his brother Esau. Then, when the weary day was closed, and night had come down upon the dark hills, and the bleating of his herds had ceased among the valleys, he passed his own family silently across the ford of the river, and went back himself to spend a sleepless night on the northern side of the stream alone. He could not bear to have his family see his distress or to break their slumbers with his cries and supplications. In the great conflict before him he would rather be alone with God. So he left them sleeping, and went back to the other side of the river, as

Jesus, on the night of his great agony, left his disciples and went away into the darkness to pray alone.

To come up to the fullest and loftiest exercise of the privilege of prayer, we must feel that the world and everything else is shut out and we are alone with God. Nothing can make our souls so pure and strong, nothing can arm us so completely for the great conflicts of life, as to be alone for one hour with infinite Truth and infinite Love; to lay open all the secret places of the heart to the search of the infinite Eye, and to put forth all the strength of the soul in grasping the hand of infinite Power. Even Jesus himself, when preparing for some new and great trial, would steal away to the solitude of the mountains and spend the whole night in prayer to God.

And there is no joy or duty or conflict or sorrow of life for which we cannot be better prepared by prayer. If the child would be kept from the paths of the destroyer while his heart is tender and his mind is not skilled to discern between good and evil, let him pray. If the young man would pass in safety through the dark scenes of trial and temptation, let him pray. If the weary, anxious, hard-working man of business would not be wholly given up to a life of earthly care and endless disappointment, let him pray. If the aged pilgrim would find the last days of life the best and enter the valley of the shadow of death in peace, let him pray. If any one does not know by personal experience how much of heaven's promised rest can be secured for the soul even now by prayer, he had better leave every other lesson of life unlearned till he has mastered that.

Jacob was alone, and it was night. Nothing broke the silence save the roar of the mountain river and the occasional call of herdsmen keeping his own flocks in the distance. In thirty-six hundred years there has not been a time when a solitary man could spend the night where Jacob was without peril to his life. There is now an intense desire to explore the country of Gilead and Bashan, and great honor would be conferred upon one who should traverse the whole region and tell the story of his wanderings. And yet we could count on our fingers all the travelers who have been there to any purpose within the last hundred years. In Jacob's time, robbery and murder were even more common in all that country than they are now. And then, too, the lion couched for his prey, and the bear wandered at night on the banks of the Jabbok.

In such a place this troubled and fear-stricken man bows down to the earth in his great agony and weeps and prays in darkness and alone. Suddenly he feels the grasp of a strong hand laid upon him, and he is sure that in such a place, at such an hour, it must be the hand of an enemy. He springs to his feet, grapples his unknown antagonist, and struggles with all his might to fling him to the ground. He does not succeed in overcoming his silent and mysterious assailant, but he maintains his hold upon him, and the wrestle goes on for hours, a real hand-to-hand grapple in which neither party speaks a word, and neither prevails against the other.

Nothing in the sacred narrative hints or warrants the supposition that this wrestling of Jacob took place only in a "dream" or "vision" or state of "ecstasy." The struggle was as real and corporeal as the halting and the lameness that followed. Jacob himself took it for granted that his antagonist was a real, living man, and he did not dare to loose his hold or relax the contest for a moment, for fear he should be thrown to the earth and killed or utterly disabled. At last, when the day began to break and the contest still went on, the mysterious Stranger put forth his reserved power and brought the struggle to a close. He touched and paralyzed the seat of strength in Jacob's frame, and the man, so strong and unmasterable a moment before, could only hang, a crippled and weeping suppliant, upon the neck of his Divine antagonist, and gain by prayer and tears a victory which his human power and skill had failed to win.

Now it was all plain that Jacob, in seeking his own safety, had been contending against God. In the darkness of the night, and in the deeper darkness that clouded his mind, he had taken his best friend and surest protector for an enemy. The mysterious Stranger with whom he wrestled so long and so vainly was the Divine Angel of the Covenant, the incarnate Son of God. That mighty helper had condescended to take on himself a human form and enter into a bodily struggle with his own servant Jacob, to teach him and millions of others that man's greatest victory is gained by self-surrender and supplication.

Jacob had nothing but fear and weariness and pain so long as he sought to prevail by his own strength and skill. When he found himself utterly prostrate and helpless, and he poured forth the wrestlings of his soul in strong supplications and tears, then he became a prince in power and he prevailed with God. In the end of the struggle the revealed Angel of the Covenant condescends to entreat his human antagonist and say, "Let me go, for the day breaketh." And the poor, stricken and suffering man has the boldness to reply, "I will not let thee go except thou bless me."

The mightiest man on earth is the man who has most power with God. For God is almighty and man is omnipotent for the accomplishment of his purpose when he has the promise of all needed help from the Most High. The hiding of the power which determines the destiny of nations is not in the cabinets of kings or the heavy battalions of war, but in the closets of praying men, who have been raised by faith to the exalted rank of princes with God. The conflict which gained the greatest victory for Scotland, and gave her such freedom and intelligence as she enjoys to-day, did not originate in Holyrood Palace, nor was it waged upon the high places of the field, but in the solitary chamber of the man who prayed all night, crying in the agony and desperation of faith, " Give me Scotland or I die !"

We are all encompassed with hazards and uncertainties. We must struggle and endure even to live. Life itself is a continued struggle against both real and imaginary foes. The powers of light and darkness are ever set in array against each other. The most quiet home on earth must be shaken every day ·by the shock of the contending forces. We must all take part in this ceaseless struggle.

See to it, young man, that you are not found wrestling against God. In some dark and dangerous hour God will lay his strong hand upon you to pull you out of temptation. Beware, lest you think it the hand of an enemy and try to shake it off!

When you give yourself up to be chained and imprisoned by debasing appetites and worldly passions, God's angel will come in and smite you, as he smote Peter in the prison-house, with a swift and smarting stroke, and he will bid you rise up quickly and go forth with him into the paths of a pure, earnest, self-denying life. That delivering angel may come in the cloud of a great conflict, in the stroke of a sudden disappointment, in the deep night of a sore affliction. However startling the voice with which he speaks, however dark the aspect which he puts on, do not think him an enemy. Anything which delivers from bondage to a low, worldly, self-seeking life should be received as a blessing.

In your hours of retirement and meditation God's Spirit will wrestle with you and make you feel utterly worthless and helpless in yourself. Strange and startling light will flash in upon your soul, and you will wish you could hide yourself from the sight of your own vileness and impurity. When that feeling of wretchedness and dissatisfaction is deepest and most depressing, be sure that, like Jacob, you make supplication unto the Divine Comforter, and cease not till you prevail and are blessed.

There are deep mysteries in the word of God—unsearchable mysteries in Divine Providence—mysteries past finding out in the plan of redemption—mysteries not less deep and dark in our own souls. And sometimes, when you try most earnestly to solve these dark things for the satisfaction of your own faith, it may seem to you that the night is deepest around you and that the day will never break. But remember that God is very near you in the darkness. He comes in the very mystery which troubles and saddens you most, to lay his hand upon you and to bless you.

God comes to men now as he came to Moses on the mountain, in the thick cloud. His way is in the whirlwind and the storm, and out of the deep darkness he brings forth revelations of light and of love. Many a time you may be sure that the arm of his strength is around you for your protection when you think it the grapple of an enemy. God's children often say that they have received the brightest revela·

tions of their Father's love when the night of affliction and trouble and mental conflict was deepest around them. In the very moment when you could say with a sad heart, "Things never looked so dark to me as now," God is hiding the secret of his presence in the very darkness which surrounds you, and you have only to long and look for his blessing and he will bring you the bright day.

God's providence is the school in which he is ever setting before us the true aims of life. The term of instruction takes in all our earthly days. None are too young, none are too old to learn, if only they heed the Divine Teacher who "guides with his eye," and who whispers to the wanderer, "This is the way—walk ye in it." And there is no hope for the man who will not give attention when God sets before him the great lessons of life, of duty and of happiness.

It is a sad mistake to neglect the hard lessons, and count nothing interesting save that which is learned without effort and forgotten as soon as learned. Peace is attained through conflict. When God comes to a man to give him a new life, the poor child of earth is apt to think that some secret power is taking away all his joy. He wishes he could shake off the grasp that is laid upon him, and that makes his thoughts dark and full of trouble. He takes his best friend for an enemy, and he pushes away the hand that is put forth to save him from his greatest peril.

Let him cease from such vain and blind resistance.

Let him yield himself penitently and trustingly to the strivings of the Divine Spirit and the leadings of the Divine Providence, and he will gain the first great victory of life by surrender. .His weakness shall be clothed with immortal strength and victory. He shall become a prince unto God. Having acquired power with the Almighty, he shall have power with everything else. Power over temptation; power over the hearts of men; power over the means and sources of happiness; power over all the troubles and afflictions of life; power over all the pains and terrors of death, shall be his who ceases to wrestle against God and submits, and makes supplication and has faith to say, " I will not let thee go except thou bless me!"

God's blessing is what we all have most reason to seek and desire. It is the only thing which we cannot afford to surrender at any price. The deepest poverty with God's blessing is better than all riches without it. The darkest dungeon with God's blessing is better than thrones and palaces without it. The chamber of sickness and the house of mourning with God's blessing are better than the halls of gayety and the haunts of pleasure without it. God's blessing gives the chief value to everything that we possess, and it makes us rich and happy, whatever we may lose or suffer in the discharge of duty.

It would dry up all the fountains of human sorrow and set everything right in this world if men could be persuaded to seek and pray for God's blessing more earnestly than for anything else. The young would never be seduced into the ways of death if they acted upon the resolution never to enter any path save that upon which they could ask God's blessing. It would sanctify all the relations of home and business and society if none would allow themselves to live a single day without asking God to go with them and bless them in all that they do. Living thus, we should all find many places which, like Jacob, we could name Peniel, "For here have I seen God face to face, and my life is preserved!" To us also would belong the name of Israel, for as princes we should "have power with God and prevail."

Bethel, Mahanaim, Peniel—house of God, host of God, face of God—these are the three steps of progress in Jacob's spiritual life. First he saw in dreams darkly a pathway of light reaching from earth to heaven. But the glory of Jehovah was above and far away, and the path was too high and steep for human feet to climb. He could only look up from his stony pillow and rejoice that even in that desert place the voice of Jehovah could still be heard, and the angels of light were continually coming and going between the throne of heaven and his lowly bed. Again at Mahanaim he saw the bright battalions of the guardian host attending him before and behind. And this was no longer a dream of the night, but a clear and calm view in open day. The angel-band were not now coming and going in brief and occasional visitations. They were stationed in air to guard him in his perilous journey, with "double camp" before and behind. They kept him safe, but they stood apart and beyond his reach. He did not feel the touch of a living hand, nor hear the beating of another heart close to his own. At Peniel the Jehovah-angel came near, as man approaches his fellow-man. With mingled terror and joy, Jacob found himself in the embrace of an Almighty arm; he was both conquered and crowned by infinite strength. The revelation of the Divine love to him was now complete. The weeping and wrestling man saw God face to face and did live.

And such is still the law of advance in the Divine life. Our steps toward heaven must be taken one by one. The path of the just begins with the faint dawn and shines more and more unto the perfect day. The transformation into the image of Christ is from glory to glory.

Israel's Last Night in Egypt.

It is a night to be much observed unto the Lord, for bringing them out from the land of Egypt: this is that night of the Lord to be observed of all the children of Israel in their generations.—Ex. xii. 42.

V.

THE LAST NIGHT OF ISRAEL IN EGYPT.

THE last night of Israel in Egypt was the birth-night of a nation; the beginning of a history that shall flow with a continuous current through all time; the fountain of a stream that shall carry life and blessing to all the nations of the earth. On that memorable night, God himself appeared on the field as the great arbiter in human events, beginning a series of providences which is still going on, and which, in its completion, shall fill the whole earth with his glory.

When the sun went down, the descendants of Abraham were sojourners and slaves, toiling under the lash of the taskmaster and in a land not their own. When the morning broke, they were a great people on the march, with an army six hundred thousand strong, and with the God of hosts for their guide. This enslaved and despised race came forth from the house of bondage and took their place among the great historic nations as suddenly as an Eastern dawn breaks into the full day.

Rome began with a score or two of shepherds and robbers, drawn together in a miserable cluster of mud cabins, and it was seven hundred years in reaching the summit of its greatness. The Hebrews numbered three millions the first day of their life as a nation. They started upon their eventful career, as the river Rhone springs, full-voiced and strong, from the foot of the glacier.

The Egyptians, the Babylonians, the Assyrians, all the great conquering nations of ancient times, have utterly passed away from the earth. They have now no representatives to bear their name or to glory in their history. It is impossible to trace their influence in the life of the world to-day. The inscriptions upon their monuments tell us so little that we dare not trust the correctness of our reading. We see their greatness only in their ruins.

The Hebrews, in all their wanderings and dispersions, are Hebrews still. The descendants of the three millions who marched out of Egypt under Moses may be found on all the continents and in all the great cities of the earth, yet everywhere a people apart by themselves, a peculiar and an inextinguishable race.

When the Egyptians were carving riddles upon their monuments to baffle and to blind the inquirers of all succeeding ages, Moses, a thousand years before the father of profane history, was writing the first, clear, simple, life-like record of Divine Providence and human events for the instruction of all times. This nation of slaves, that passed from bondage to freedom in a single night, has become the teacher and emancipator of the human race. Their own peculiar history, their Divine laws, their sacred principles of morality, their inspired modes of thought, their God-given faith, their individual character, the biographies of their representative men, exert more influence upon the cultivated and ruling mind of the world to-day than all the other nations of antiquity taken together.

We are warranted, then, in saying that the birthnight of the Hebrew nation was the great era of ancient times—the first advance of forces that are still on the march for the conquest of the world. Let us reverently study the events of that night, that we may learn in what way God gives force to individual character and pours unconquerable life into the heart of a nation. Let us suppose ourselves carried back to that ancient time, and standing by, as silent and thoughtful spectators, while the great movements of God's providence are going on before our eyes.

It is night throughout all the land of Egypt. In that rainless clime there is no cloud to darken the blue serenity of heaven. The bright full moon moves in queenly majesty among the princely stars, and the lesser orbs of the heavenly host are hidden only by the excess of light. The feathery palms are motionless in the still air along the banks and branches of the Nile, and the canals and water-courses shine like threads of silver among the silent fields. The gardens and vineyards bordering the river, the temples and obelisks and palaces and the barren ridge of the distant hills, east and west, can be clearly seen in the broad moonlight, and the night seems "a softer day."

It is night in the twenty thousand cities and villages that line the banks of the Nile. The laborers have come in from the fields; the yoke is lifted from the beasts of burden; the boats are moored to the banks of the river. The princes of Pharaoh are asleep in their porphyry halls. The house-slaves are asleep on the stone floors and flat roofs of lordly mansions. The bondsmen of the field and brick-kiln are asleep in their mud-cabins and slime-pits.

It is night in the proud capital of Pharaoh. The mighty monarch has said that the man Moses shall see his face no more. He has sworn by the life of Pharaoh that the hated Hebrew shall die the moment he appears at the palace gates with his impertinent and troublesome petitions for his people again.

For many a day and week the inspired fugitive from the deserts of Sinai has haunted the halls and tracked the steps of the proud king. His shepherd's staff has become more powerful in Egypt than the sceptre of Pharaoh. He has excited the slaves to rebellion. The taskmasters complain that labor upon the public works and in the field has been neglected. The wise men of the realm and the priests of the national gods have been confounded and put to shame by the strange power of this one solitary man from the desert. The subjects of Pharaoh have been plagued with tempests and locusts and darkness. The water of the sacred river has been changed to blood, the cattle have been smitten in the field, and all unclean and creeping things have come up into the houses and sanctuaries of the land at his bidding. And the haughty monarch has determined that he will endure insult and insurrection no longer. He has forbidden the Hebrew agitator, on pain of death, to appear in his presence again.

And now Pharaoh congratulates himself and his people that at last the land shall have rest. The devouring locusts have been swept away into the sea. The people have recovered from the boils and blains that burned into their flesh. The flax and barley that were beaten down by the hail have been replaced with harvests of wheat. The blood-stained waters of the Nile have become fresh and pure. The thick and palpable darkness has passed away, and to-night the queenly moon walks with her wonted brightness through a clear and cloudless sky.

The weary monarch sleeps, forgetful of the mysterious and awful threat which Moses threw out in great anger when he left his palace gates for the last time. Surely nothing can come from words spoken by an excited and angry man, who had himself been threatened with death.

The priests are asleep under the palms and in the corridors of their countless temples. They, too, have congratulated themselves that they shall be confronted with the hated Hebrew in the presence of Pharaoh no more. The shrines and sacred places are all still as the stony eyes of the sphynx that guards the temple gates. The worshipers of Apis and Osiris and Anubis, the servitors and pensioners of the "bleating gods" of Egypt, no longer fear that the mightier God of Moses will put them to shame.

There is rest in all the houses of the Egyptians and there is silence in the streets of the capital of Pharaoh as the midnight hour of doom draws near. The oppressors have gone to sleep with the assurance that they shall hear no more of this excitement about the release of their slaves. Moses having been compelled to let the people alone, the dependent bondmen themselves will be glad to resume their old habits of toil and submission. And, besides, every master sleeps with the fond belief that his own slaves are so content and happy in his service that nothing could persuade them to forsake their homes and start off upon a wild and fanatical journey of three days into the deserts of Arabia. So in all the habitations of the Egyptians there is silence as of the grave—there is sleep as of death.

Not so in the cities and villages where the bondmen of the land live apart from the homes of their proud masters. In all the houses of the Hebrews every soul is awake and every eye upon the watch. The day had resounded with the din of some great and mysterious preparation. As the hours of the night move slowly on every heart is held in the suspense of eager and awful expectation. There is no stir in the streets. The families are all inside of their houses, and there is a mysterious blood-stain on the lintel and the two side-posts of every door. The anxious eye of parents runs frequently around the group to see that all are there. When the little child lays his hand upon the door, eager to open it and look out into the bright moonlight, the mother springs with terror in her countenance to arrest the movement and rebuke the dangerous curiosity. One face wears the look of resigned and trustful expectation, another of doubt and impatience, another of high and eager hope.

Their long, loose robes are gathered up and girt tightly around the loins. Their feet are shod with sandals for a journey. They have the shepherd's scrip upon their shoulders, filled with provisions for the way. Men and women stand with staffs in their hands ready to go forth when the sign shall be given for departure. The sacrificial lamb has been roasted, and each grasps a portion in his hand, seasoning the morsel with bitter herbs and eating in haste. No one dares to lay aside staff or scrip for a moment, lest the signal for departure should come and any should be found unprepared to go. Strong men turn pale and women weep, and little children cling to the hands of their parents; and the whole family group are so still that they can hear the beating of their own hearts as the awful moment of midnight approaches.

They have been told by Moses that about midnight the Lord will go out into the midst of Egypt, and his hand shall fall so heavy upon the homes of the oppressor that the princes of Pharaoh shall come to their Hebrew slaves with supplications entreating them to go forth free and in haste. The hour draws near. They must soon know whether the Divine Deliverer will actually come and break their bonds.

Hark! was it the step of the angel of death passing along the street and counting the doors with the sign of the blood-stain on the side posts and the lintel? No, it was only the light breath of air rustling the feathery fronds of the palm that overhangs the house.

Again! was not that the wail of a human voice wafted upon the still night from some distant home, where the messenger of wrath has breathed in the face of a sleeping child? No, it was but the lowing of the sacred Apis in some idol temple where men change the glory of the incorruptible God, into " birds and four-footed beasts and creeping things."

But now it comes in very deed at last—the great cry of which Moses spoke. Glory unto Jehovah! His right hand and holy arm hath gotten us the victory, and we are free. Glory unto Jehovah! for the dark days of bondage are ended, and the ransomed tribes shall go forth in triumph to their own land. Hark again, that wild and piercing cry, such as can come only from the untold depths of human woe—such as the heart sends forth when wrung with its greatest agony. Not from one stricken house alone, but from every Egyptian home, shrieks and howls break forth upon the stillness of the midnight air, as if the dead of all generations had burst their marble tombs with one universal wail. Village cries to village, and city answers back to city, and the mighty wave of midnight lamentation rolls over the whole " realm of impious Pharaoh" and fills all the land of Nile.

The death-angel has smitten the first born of every family with a single stroke, and there is not a house in which there is not one dead. There has been no such sudden, wild, frantic, universal cry of woe on this earth since man began his pilgrimage of pain and sorrow to the grave; for in one awful moment the angel of death has smitten every family in the whole nation with just that one stroke which must cause the deepest wound and the most crushing sorrow.

And this great cry goes up to Heaven from the palace of the king, from the halls and harems of the princes, from the courts and cloisters of the pagan temples, from the floorless huts of the peasants along the Nile, from the mud-hovels of the poor, and from the cruel dungeon of the prison-house. From every place where human hearts can be found to suffer or human eyes to weep, there goes forth the same exceeding great and bitter cry.

In the universal terror the king calls for the heir
8

of his throne, and the answer is death. Aged parents
turn to their stalwart son for protection, but his strong
arm will be lifted for their support no more. The
young mother wakes to find the babe in her bosom
dead. Affrighted neighbors rush to each other's
houses for consolation only to find that the dead are
there. The sacred beast in the temple is stretched
in death on the marble floor, amid the wail of wor-
shipers who come with incense and with offerings to
stay the universal plague. Jehovah is passing through
the land in vengeance at this midnight hour, accord-
ing to his word, smiting the first-born of both man and
beast, executing judgment upon all the princes and
gods of Egypt.

And this is the great cry for which the Hebrews are
waiting as the signal for their departure out of the
house of bondage. The stifled agonies of four hun-
dred years of servitude find utterance in that loud
lamentation which comes from the homes of the
oppressor. And now the proud monarch sends mes-
sengers in every direction to say, in his name with
every urgency and entreaty, to the Hebrews, " Rise
up, go forth from among us; take everything with you ;
only begone, and bless me, even me, in your departure."

And when the morning came, the Hebrews were
a free people on the march to their own land, with the
God of nations for their guide. A work of judgment
and of mercy had been done, to declare the name of
Jehovah throughout all the earth and to the end

of time. With that memorable night of departure out of Egypt began the providential history from which we still draw our deepest and wisest philosophy of human events. Reading the inspired narrative of Moses, we first begin to comprehend the prime fact that God is in all history, and that the moving and governing force behind the apparent order of things in this world is always the Divine Hand.

God is the great Emancipator of nations. The Son of God appeared incarnate on earth that he might set at liberty them that are bound. This great deliverance of a whole people in ancient time is a type of the rescue which Christ would accomplish for every human soul. He comes to call men out of bondage into liberty. To be a Christian is to be the honored and immortal freedman of the Lord. It is to shake off the dominion of evil appetites and passions, and stand forth in the glorious liberty wherewith God sets his chosen people free.

This spiritual and immortal emancipation is what man most needs. The world puts chains and fetters upon us all. It binds us in sore and exacting bondage to customs and prejudices, to fears and hopes, to cares and anxieties, to pleasures and sorrows, that should never have dominion over an immortal being. We all have capacities which can be fitly and fully employed only in overcoming the world, lifting ourselves above its pride and power, extending our hopes and plans and desires beyond the utmost reach of earth and time.

Christ comes to set us free from bondage to things that perish. He would give us the mastery over ourselves and over the world. He would give us strength to stand fast in the liberty wherewith he makes us free. He would give us freedom to use all our powers and opportunities in such a way as shall be most for our own honor, most for our present and our everlasting welfare. He would give us a complete and permanent superiority over all the powers and falsities and enticements of temptation. He would save us from the waste of our best endowments, and the bitter regrets that follow the mistakes and losses of an unwise and an unfaithful life.

Looking unto Jesus for guidance and hope, we leave the dark house of bondage behind—our faces are set toward the promised land of light and liberty. If we follow him, as the Hebrews followed the pillar of cloud and flame, the desert will yield us fountains of water, the Divine Hand will give us bread from heaven day by day. Whatever delays or afflictions we may have to meet on the way, our Divine Leader and Emancipator will be sure to bring us at last to the promised rest.

The follower of Christ alone has the promise of the life that now is and of that which is to come. He owns allegiance to no other power save that which is infinite and eternal. He can be content with no other inheritance save that which is boundless as the universe and lasting as eternity. He is exalted to the highest rank among all created beings by his gracious adoption into the family of which Jesus Christ is the head. The mightiest of the princes of the earth have nothing in their temporal estate to be compared in value with the freedom, the glory, the hope of the lowliest disciple of Jesus, the citizen of the heavenly Jerusalem, the joint heir with Him who is the first-born of every creature, the beginning of the creation of God.

This great inheritance of light and liberty is freely offered, in God's name, to the poor, the enslaved and the perishing. Whoever chooses this infinite possession shall be defended in his title against every opposing power, world without end. There is nothing left for a wise, considerate man to choose but the life of free, willing, happy devotion to Christ. In the discharge of Christian duty all the faculties of the mind and all the susceptibilities of the heart are called forth into the noblest, freest, happiest exercise. All the arguments of reason, all the creations of fancy, all the treasures of memory, all the anticipations of hope, all the raptures of love and devotion may enter into that true, exalted life which begins by faith on the Son of God and is continued by obedience to him.

When Moses came to the Hebrews to deliver them from bondage, they distrusted his commission and begged to be let alone, that they might serve the Egyptians. They hearkened not unto Moses, because the hard inheritance of bondage, transmitted from generation to generation, had so debased their spirits and deadened their hearts that for a while they could not be aroused by the offer of liberty.

And so it happens when Christ, the Divine Emancipator, comes to men who have long worn the inherited chain of bondage to sin. They have become so habituated to the hopes, the desires, the pleasures and expectations of a worldly life that they give no heed to Him who offers to break their chain and bring them forth into glorious and immortal liberty. It is the saddest thing ever seen in this world—the determination and obstinacy with which men cling to the bondage of Satan and refuse to be made free in Christ.

I have seen the caged eagle beating vainly against the iron bars of his prison, his plumes soiled and torn, his strong wings drooping, the light of his glorious eye dimmed, the pulse of his proud heart panting in vain for conflict with the careering clouds and the mountain blast. And I thought it a pitiable sight to see that kingly bird subjected to such bondage, just to be gazed at by the curious crowd. And I have seen the proud denizen of the air rejoicing in the freedom of his mountain home—

> "Clasping the crag with hooked hands,
> Close to the sun in lonely lands"—

basking in the noon's broad light, balancing with motionless wings in the high vault of heaven, or rushing forth like the thunderbolt to meet the clouds on the pathway of the blast. And I thought that that wild and cloud-cleaving bird would choose death, could the choice be his, rather than give up his free and joyous life to drag out a weary bondage in a narrow and stifling cage.

And yet I have seen a greater and sadder contrast than that. I have seen men, made in the image of the living God, endowed with the glorious and fearful gift of immortality, capable of becoming coequal companions with archangels, consenting to be caged and fenced around and fettered down by customs and cares and pleasures and pursuits, that only bind them to earth, make them slaves of things they despise and answer their noblest aspirations with disappointment. I have seen men, to whom God gave souls to become heirs of the universe and to outlive all ages, living as if this earth were their only home, and this fleeting life were the measure of their existence. I have seen men with hearts full of infinite longings, and with " thoughts that wander through eternity," laboring to confine the range of hope and desire within the narrow compass of earthly pleasures and occupations.

And if the eye of such an one should ever fall on this page and trace these lines, let him pause just here and ask himself why he need any longer lead such a life. Made to live for ever, why suppress and contradict the noblest aspirations of your nature by trying to live only for this world? Made to enjoy the glorious liberty of the children of God, why consent to be the slave of habits that you condemn and influences that you despise? Why imprison your immortal spirit within the narrow round of earthly cares and toils and pleasures, when you are invited to enter the palace of heaven's eternal King, and to associate on terms of freedom and equality with the princes and powers of the universe? The everlasting God desires to adopt you as a child and to make you heir of an inheritance that shall be great as his infinite love can give and your immortal powers can enjoy. The Creator of all worlds, the Giver of all blessing, desires you to possess and enjoy everything that can ennoble, expand and exalt your whole being, and fit you to dwell with him for ever.

I confess this is something I cannot describe, for it surpasses all thought, all description, all imagination. But I beg you to believe that it is a reality, and that you may learn what it is by experience and possess it for your own. And with such a great destiny open before you, surely you must not give yourself up to the cares and toils, the frivolities and pleasures of earth and time alone. With God and heaven and eternity to inspire your hopes and call forth your efforts, how can you be so unwise, so thoughtless, so unmindful of your true and proper destiny as to give yourself up entirely to things that perish, when your own existence has only just begun?

The Hebrews were required to prepare the Paschal lamb, to sprinkle the blood on the door-posts, to remain within their houses, to keep themselves awake with sandals on and staff in hand. But in the great and critical moment of passing from bondage to liberty, they were to trust and see the salvation of their God.

So every one of us, in securing our everlasting deliverance from the bondage of sin and death, have many things to do. We are to watch and to pray; we are to shun the path of the destroyer; we are to observe all the ordinances and instructions of God's house; we are to hold ourselves ready to obey every call of duty. But in the one infinite matter of securing our own personal salvation we have only to trust and receive the salvation of our God.

And if any feel or fear that that salvation is far remote or long in coming, I am commanded to say to you, in the name of the Lord of Hosts, that his salvation is very nigh. This is the great hour of the Lord for your deliverance from bondage. You are called to begin the glorious march to the heavenly Zion without delay. You are to make this very hour memorable for ever as the birth-hour of your immortal soul into the free and blessed life of love and obedience to God. Then, in the everlasting ages to come, you will count this day, or this night, one to be much observed unto the Lord as your great Passover, when the bondage of sin was broken and you came forth into the glorious liberty of the sons of God.

No one should hesitate to join the great emigration which Christ, the captain of salvation, is leading out of this woe-stricken world to the blessed home of

freedom and of rest. We are all living in the land
of bondage and of death. We are bound with chains
which are hard to wear, and which we find it impossi-
ble to break. The mind and the body groan together
under heavy burdens. The destroyer walks unseen
through every street. The angel of death stands
ready to enter every house. None are safe from a
worse death than befell the first-born of Egypt, save
those on whom are found the signs of the sacrificial
blood.

The Captain of salvation is leading forth a great
host. They are already on the march. Many are
passing in at the heavenly gate, and the angel-welcome
comes ringing down the shining ranks even to us,
"Whosoever will, let him come." The effort and the
desire of the heavenly host are not to shut any out,
but to gather all in. And let all that hear the invita-
tion take up the cry, and say to all that linger,
"Come." The Almighty Father is ever sending
messages of love and instruction to draw his wander-
ing children home. He throws open the doors of his
many-mansioned house, and he stands all day with
outstretched hands in merciful entreaty, inviting, and
beseeching all to come.

Parents, come, and bring your children with you.
Brothers and sisters, husbands and wives, join hands
and take your place in the ranks that are marching
toward heaven. Young men and maidens, set out for
the promised land, with the Prince of salvation for

your guide, and with all the fresh hopes and fiery zeal of youth to spur you on. We cannot any of us stay here, if we would: strength and beauty, and health and manhood must all fade. The world itself is fast passing away. To be safe, to be free, we must take the pilgrim's staff and set out for heaven. We must join the ranks of the great host that are marching to the better land.

Imagine some poor shipwrecked mariner cast ashore upon a lonely island in mid-ocean. The gallant vessel which had been his home upon the deep went down with all its precious freight before the fury of the storm. His fellow-voyagers all perished in the terrible conflict with the winds and the waves. He alone was cast alive on shore, to suffer more than the bitterness of death in sorrowing for his lost companions, and in longing for a return to his far distant home. The climate of the island is perpetual summer. Everything needed to sustain life springs from the earth without cultivation. Flowers blossom and fruits ripen through all the year. The forests are full of singing birds. Their bright plumage flashes like meteors in the shadows of the thick woods. The air is loaded with perfume. The plains are carpeted with verdure, the hills are covered with the feathery foliage of palms and all graceful trees. The skies are genial and the whole year is one continued season of growth and bloom.

But to the lonely shipwrecked mariner this seeming

paradise is a prison. He longs for his distant home beyond the melancholy main. The first thing in the morning and the last at evening he climbs the rocky height overlooking the sea, to search round the whole horizon for some friendly ship coming to deliver him from his watery prison. And when at last he sees a white sail hanging in the far horizon and growing larger as it approaches, it looks to him as if it were the white wing of an angel flying to his rescue. With eager and frantic joy he makes every possible signal to arrest the attention of the coming ship. And when his signals are answered and a boat is lowered to take him on board, he is ready to rush into the waves and swim out to meet his deliverers before they reach the land. And all his joy is excited by the hope of return to an earthly home, where he must still be exposed to pain and sorrow and death.

This earth is an island in the infinite ocean of space. It has abundance of riches and pleasures and occupations for a few, much toil and work and suffering for many, and it must be a temporary resting-place for all. But it has no home for the soul. The ship of salvation is sent over the ocean of eternity to take us to the land of rest. Shall we not look often and eagerly for its coming? And when it appears shall we not be ready and willing to go? Shall we try so to accustom ourselves to the ways of living on this island waste of earth that we shall be unfitted to live in a land where there is no death?

The Night Passage of the Sea.

It was a cloud and darkness to them, but it gave light by night to these so that the one came not near the other all the night.—Ex. xiv. 20.

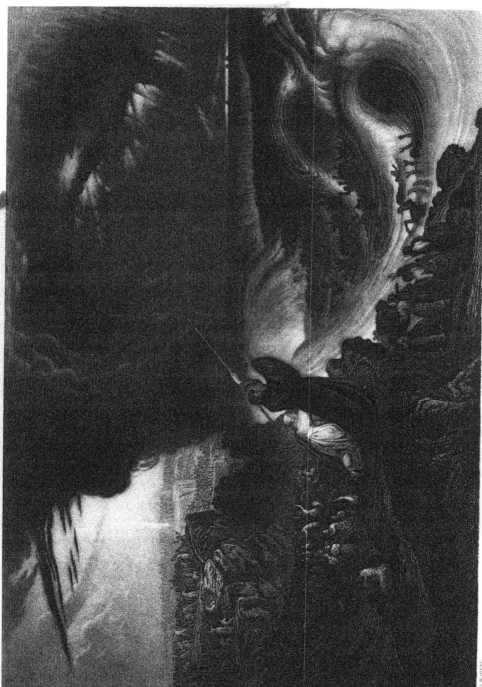

VI.

THE NIGHT PASSAGE OF THE SEA.

THE life of the Hebrew nation began with the departure out of Egypt. The first great landmark on the line of their progress as a people was the passage of the Red Sea. That one miraculous deliverance in the outset of their career established their character as a favored and providential people. It declared to the neighboring heathen nations that Divine power was ever ready to break forth in fire and flood for the protection of Israel. It carried on and completed the terrible and tenfold demonstration of the plagues in Egypt, that the mightiest elements in nature were the servants of Him who had chosen the Hebrew people for his own. It proclaimed aloud to the Israelites themselves that their greatness in subsequent time must depend not upon chariots and horses, and mighty hosts trained for war, but upon the help of the living God. The secret of their success, the hiding of their great power as a people in all after time, must be direct, personal, unwavering reliance upon the Most High.

This they were to learn as a first lesson. They

fice to Him that giveth showers and fruitful seasons, that their land might yield its increase and the harvest fail not. And when they went out to meet their enemies and they set the battle in array, army against army, still their most inspiring war-cry should be a prayer unto the God of Israel, " Arise, O Jehovah, and let thine enemies be scattered !"

All this will be apparent if we consider the scene and the circumstances described, with inspired calmness and simplicity, in the fourteenth chapter of Exodus. With a multitude of facts, theories and conjectures before me to choose from, I put the case to my own mind somewhat in this form.

I see before me an open plain, ten or twelve miles across, covered with low, gravelly ridges and hillocks of sand. On the eastern side is the sea; on the south and west a chain of mountains coming obliquely down to the sea, in a southeasterly direction, and giving the plain a triangular shape, with the apex at the southeast. Between the mountain and the sea there is space enough left for a great multitude to move in a disorderly march. Beyond this pass, between the mountain and the sea, is another plain, completely walled in north and south by mountains, on the east terminated by the sea, and the opening toward the west leading directly back to Egypt and the capital of Pharaoh.

The third day's march of the Hebrews after their departure out of Egypt was across this first plain and along the sandy pass between the projecting bluff and the sea. As the sun goes down, we find them encamping for the night on the second plain, walled in by ranges of mountains right and left, and with the sea in front. The next movement must be either to advance into the sea or turn westward and march directly toward the capital of Pharaoh, or go back the way they came.

Surely there is reason for the Egyptians to say, " They are entangled in the land—the wilderness hath shut them in." Their situation is strange and perplexing to the Hebrews themselves. They do not know where they are going or why they have been led into this inextricable net of difficulties, unless it be to hold them entrapped till their enraged masters can overtake them and drive them back to their former bondage. Of one thing, at least, they are sure. They are not on the way to the wilderness of Sinai, where it was proposed to go, nor to the land promised to their fathers. They have come down a whole day's march on the wrong side of the sea, and if they could pass the mountain which interrupts their advance, they would only be going still farther out of the way. If the army of Pharaoh should follow them up from behind, they would have no way of escape but to turn

9

westward, between the mountain ridges and flee directly toward the capital of the kingdom.

They are weary with the day's march across the sandy plain. Straggling companies have been coming in and joining the host ever since they started. Friends, neighbors and families have lost each other, and are striving to get together for the night. Old and young, women and children, flocks and herds, are all mingled, crowded, passing to and fro, and the dry plain is beaten into dust under their feet. The green pastures of Goshen, the waving palms, the blooming gardens, the shining water-courses of their forsaken homes, are now far away. The sun-burnt earth, the salt sea, the suffocating dust-cloud, the barren mountains, are all around. The piteous lowing of thirsty cattle, the cries of weary children, the frantic wails of women, are answered by loud calls and angry complaints and expressions of discouragement and fear.

The first joy of escape from bondage has subsided. The terrors of the desert, the mountains and the sea— the weariness, the hunger and the thirst of the long march over yielding sand and rolling stones—now make even a home in Egypt and a life of bondage seem attractive. This is not the way to the land promised unto their fathers. And it is impossible to go on in this direction if they would. Three days of freedom have been worse than all the woes of the house of bondage.

And besides, this great multitude of two or three

millions of people, with innumerable flocks and herds, cannot live upon this sandy plain another day. Just as little can they retrace their steps, pass over the ten or twelve miles of sand-ridges and gullies which they crossed yesterday and regain the course where they left it at the head of the sea. They are lost among barren hills and desert plains. The moaning sea sings the dirge of all their hopes. The desolate mountains seem like funeral monuments to mark the grave of the mighty host. It is a sad night to follow so soon after that glorious morning when they came out of Egypt, harnessed like men of war and exultant with high hope, while the wails and supplications of their proud masters besought them to go.

And now, to complete their despair, they lift up their eyes, and behold! the Egyptians are marching after them! The cloud of dust which had settled down upon their own track in the rear rises again in the distance, and over the ridges of drifted sand they see the flashing armor and the tossing plumes of the terrible chariots of Pharaoh. The advancing host is commanded by the proud and impious king himself. It is composed of the pride and power of Egypt, with all the advantage of weapons, armor and discipline on their side. They come on in orderly march, with the confidence of trained armies moving against an unarmed and panic-stricken mob.

They can ride down upon this disorderly multitude of fugitive slaves, encumbered with their families and flocks, as the eagle swoops upon the dove, as the lion springs upon the herd of deer. They see at once that the Hebrews are hemmed in on all sides, and that they can take their time to capture 'their prey. The sun has already set. The moon, which was full on the night of the departure out of Egypt, will not rise for three or four hours. The Egyptians· are themselves weary with the long and rapid march of the day. They resolve to encamp for the night and wait for the morning before they rush in upon the host of fugitives and destroy them there, or drive them back to their former bondage.

And now the cries of the Hebrews are wild and frantic, and all voices are lifted up in reproaches and imprecations upon the head of Moses. They forget the mighty miracles wrought by his hand in Egypt. They have no thought or hope that the rod which changed the sacred Nile to blood can smite the sea and make a dry path for the host through the waves.

When trouble and danger come, there are always some to say, " We knew it would be so, we told you so before." And Moses had millions to remind him, in this great extremity, that they told him of all this great peril before, and that it would have been better to live in bondage than to die of hunger and thirst in the desert, or to be ridden over by the iron chariots of war and trampled, torn and bleeding, into the sand.

With sublime faith and self-possession the great leader meets the reproaches and soothes the excitement of the multitude, even before he himself knows what will be the end. Of one thing he is sure—Jehovah, who gave him the commission to deliver his people, will not desert him while he is attempting to fulfil that command. He says calmly to the excited and clamorous multitude, "Fear not, stand still and see the salvation of the Lord, which he will show you to-day. The Lord shall fight for you, and ye shall hold your peace."

This was wise and faithful counsel for Moses to give, but to hold their peace was just the hardest thing for the excited and terrified host of the Hebrews to do. Two and a half millions of people of all ages in one vast crowd, mixed with as many cattle, and with all their worldly goods lying about them in the sand, are not easy to keep quiet under any circumstances, least of all when every one feels himself to have been suddenly brought into imminent peril of death.

Let twenty-five hundred persons, old and young, men, women and children, be gathered in one great hall, and let a cry be raised that the roof is falling or the building is on fire, and no voice can calm their fears; they will trample each other to death in the endeavor to get out. Here are a thousand times twenty-five hundred people, crowded into one vast assembly. They are ignorant, credulous and impulsive. They have never been accustomed to habits of order, reflection or self-command. A breath of excitement will sweep over the host as the hot wind sweeps the desert.

Let the chariots of Pharaoh rush upon them, and they will trample each other into the sand by thousands in the effort to escape. Weary, discouraged, terrified, in a desert place, with the darkness of night closing around them, they fill the air with wailing and cries and supplications, such as came from all the homes of the Egyptians when the destroying angel smote the first-born. They now fully expect to fall into the hands of their former taskmasters again, and to be held responsible for all the plagues and afflictions which their deliverance has brought upon Egypt. If the lash fell heavily before, it will become a scourge of scorpions when they go back to the brick-kilns and slime-pits again.

What had drawn them into that dark and perilous condition? Bound for the green hills and sunny plains of Palestine on the north, how came they to turn in the opposite direction and march, as if with blind infatuation, into this waste and howling wilderness of burning sand and barren mountains?

It was in this way. On the morning of the third day of their march, there appeared a strange, mysterious cloud in the van of the host, extending upward in a lofty column, like the smoke of some mighty sacrifice. It rose so high into heaven that it could be seen for miles by millions of people, scattered over a vast plain, and it came so near the ground that those who walked could follow it as a guide. It was not blown away by the wind. It did not melt into air like mists from the sea in the heat of the risen sun. All day long it moved slowly, majestically across the plain, and the Hebrews were commanded to follow where it led the way.

Thus they had been drawn silently, mysteriously out of their course into this secluded valley, hemmed in by the mountains and the sea. As the sun went down, the awful pillar of the cloud advanced eastward against the wind, and took its stand along the shore between the host and the sea. The Israelites had never seen any such appearance before. Their ignorance and superstition would easily lead them to fear that it was some malignant and misleading shadow raised by the magical arts of their enemies for their destruction. The strange and inexplicable course which they had been led, and the appearance of Pharaoh and his army at evening, would do much to confirm their fears.

But now, as darkness is coming on and the Egyptians are encamping in sight, and the wail of distracted myriads rises louder than the roar of the sea, this awful cloud lifts majestically into the air, passes over the heads of the Hebrew host, and settles down upon the earth between them and their pursuers, so as to hide the one from the other. There it stands, as darkness comes on, unmoved by the strong wind blowing from the sea, black as midnight to the Egyptians, and yet sending forth a cheering and glorious light over all the host of the Hebrews, calming their fears, quieting their lamentations, giving them the assurance that some great deliverance is yet in store for them.

And now the time has come for Jehovah himself to ride with chariots and horses of salvation through the sea. At the Divine command, Moses lifts up the wonder-working rod, and the waters are cloven down to the bare earth. The channels of the deep are seen before the brightness of the protecting cloud. A broad highway is made for millions to pass on foot and dryshod where the ancient sea had its bed. The command, "GO FORWARD!" passes through the great host of the Hebrews, and all night long the tramp of the mighty multitude goes on between the walls of waters, and the protecting cloud sends its strange light to show the way through the whole length of the channel to the other shore.

When the last of the fugitives have passed down the beach and entered upon the bed of the sea, the cloud itself moves slowly after them. The plain of the encampment is now bare. The light of the risen moon shines upon it, and the Egyptian sentinels, roused from the heavy sleep which had fallen upon them, give the alarm that the Hebrews are escaping. The trumpet sounds to arms. The chariots and horsemen are set in array. The whole force rush forward bewildered, hearing the march and the voices of the Hebrews in the distance, and yet seeing nothing but the cloud in the direction of the sea, and the plain·

where they were at sunset, all empty and silent beneath the light of the risen moon. They follow on in the rear of the moving cloud, thinking it only a mist, and not knowing that they are marching in the bed of the sea. On they press, driving their chariots heavily in the miry bed of the deep, yet determined to pursue and overtake and divide the spoil. They hear the murmur of the fugitive host—they trace the broad path of their march—they expect every moment to break through the retreating cloud and come upon their prey. And so all the remainder of the night, like men in a dream, the panting and toiling host of Pharaoh is just upon the point of coming up with the Hebrews, yet never succeeding.

At length, when the morning begins to dawn over the desert hills of Arabia, and the children of Israel have all passed safely through the channel of the divided sea, the awful cloud is suddenly changed to the Egyptians. It becomes a column of fire as high as heaven, shooting forth lightnings and shaking the earth with mighty thunders. To them it seems as if some awful eye were looking upon them out of the darkness, blazing with infinite anger and striking them through with strange fears. The chariot horses break the ranks and dash against each other in wild confusion. Wheels are entangled with wheels and torn off, while the frantic steeds drag the scythe-armed axles over dismounted charioteers and trample prostrate footmen alive into the mire. The archers and the spearmen are pierced with their own weapons. And while the lightning flames and the thunder rolls, and the host of men and horses are struggling together in fear and madness and agony,' two mighty waves come crashing over them from opposite directions, and when the shock has subsided and the sea is calm, Pharaoh and his host, the pride and power of Egypt, are no more. When the morning comes, the daughters of Israel sing the song of triumph with timbrels and dances, while the sea heaves the dead on shore at every surge.

And this mighty God who so delivered Israel in ancient time is our God for ever and ever. We have only to trust him and obey him, and he will be our guide and deliverer even in the deep waters of death. All might and dominion belong to him in heaven and in earth. We are all, every moment, girt with his power and surrounded with his presence as really as were the Israelites in the midst of the divided sea.

The walls and covering of our habitations are as truly upheld and kept from falling and crushing us to death, by the Divine hand, as were the walls of waters kept upright, like solid stone, by almighty power, while the Hebrews passed safely between. We say that it was miracle which protected them and laws of nature which protect us. But in both cases it is God. He is the one personal, uncreated, infinite Force, and all acts and existences are manifestations of power going forth from him. The deepest and truest philosophy of life

and faith for us is to bring ourselves into the most inti-
mate relations with the infinite God. The most pro-
found and accurate student of nature is he whose
eye is quickest to see the plan and purpose of an intel-
ligent, governing Mind in everything that exists.

What should we think of an Israelite walking
through the depths of the sea on dry ground, between
walls of water standing up like marble on either hand,
and yet not recognizing the intended and merciful dis-
play of the Divine power for his protection? What
should we think of a ransomed Hebrew standing on
the safe shore of the Red Sea on that memorable morn-
ing, and yet refusing to join in the song of thanks-
giving for the great deliverance of the night? The
same that we ought to think of one who lies down to
sleep at night in his own house, and goes to his daily
occupation in the morning, and never prays, never
offers thanksgiving to God for the mercy which re-
deems his life from destruction every moment.

In God we live and move and have our being.
Every use of our faculties, every sensation of pleasure,
every emotion of happiness, every possession, experi-
ence and hope that makes existence a blessing, is a wit-
ness to us of God's special, minute and ceaseless atten-
tion to our welfare We deceive ourselves with a form
of words when we separate nature, laws or life, in any of
their forms, from the immediate manifestations of Divine
power. A grateful, trustful, habitual recognition of
God lies at the foundation of all right conduct, all true

character. It were less ungrateful, less unreasonable. to forget every human friend we have in the world than to forget God.

No one should be ashamed to say, "Among all the calls of interest, of occupation and of pleasure, I put first and foremost my duty to God. Nobody shall ever make me afraid or ashamed to be known as the servant of God. The skeptic may doubt and the scoffer may rail, but neither the sophistry of the one nor the scorn of the other shall prevail on me to disown or dishonor my greatest and best Friend." This is no more than any man, having heart and conscience, should be willing to say. And whoever says it, and makes good his words by a correspondent life, will be able to walk through all the deeps of trial and temptation, and come forth at last upon the heavenly shore with songs of triumph and everlasting joy.

The command to "*go forward*" is the Christian watchword of duty and of safety in all ages. It is only because some have faith and fortitude to advance in the face of difficulties, dangers and uncertainties that the life of the world does not stagnate and every good cause die. To stand still, when the voice of God's providence cries go forward, quenches the light of hope in the heart and opens every avenue of the soul for the incoming of the powers of darkness. Sometimes it does a man good to be brought into such a strait that he must choose one of two courses immediately and for ever—either an absolute and abject submission to the enemies of his soul or a bold and open declaration of himself as a servant of God, a follower of Jesus Christ. In the days of persecution, the threat of immediate martyrdom has induced some to stand up for Jesus, when they might have lived and died without making the choice, had they supposed they could have a long and peaceful life time to choose in.

It may be that these lines will be read by some one who, at the moment of reading, is ready to say with a sad heart, "The way of duty never seemed so hard and dark to me as now." Yet even to such an one would I say, in God's name, *Go forward!* Do your duty at whatever cost. Obey the Divine command with a ready mind and cheerful heart. The sea of troubles will open before you and show you a safe path through. The trials and hindrances which you now fear will all vanish before the first firm and resolute step in the right path. This may be the very hour when you are to decide once and for ever whether you will follow Christ and be saved, or hesitate and falter until you are swallowed up by the waves of worldliness and temptation.

If the Hebrews had not advanced—weary, terrified, afflicted as they were—when Moses gave the word to go forward, we have no reason to suppose that the waters would have divided, or that they would have escaped a return to worse bondage than they had ever suffered before in Egypt. And the difficulties that hinder the discharge of duty, the clouds that darken the path of faith, do not disappear before the halting and the doubting just because they stand still and refuse to go forward when commanded to do so in the name of the Lord.

Go forward is the watchword of progress for the world and of salvation for the soul. Obedience to that command makes all the difference between success and failure, triumph and defeat, salvation and perdition. It climbs the dangerous steep, bridges the mighty stream, opens fountains in the desert, makes the wilderness blossom as the rose. It discovers and tames the most terrible forces in nature and puts them into iron harness to work for man. It lifts the cloud of ignorance from the human mind, scares away the horrid spectres of fear and superstition, stretches the iron nerve for the electric thrill of thought to pass with lightning speed over the mountains and across the continents, and under the ocean, and all round the globe. All the generations that have gone before us send back the cry, along all their ranks, from century to century, *Go forward!* The uncounted millions that are soon to fill our places are pressing on from behind with the same cry. From every source, from every age and from every creature comes the repeated and earnest cry, "*Go forward!* press toward the mark; forgetting the things behind, reach forth to those before. Do your duty now, for the time is short, and opportunities once lost may never return. When the prize to be secured by an immediate advance in the face of difficulties is eternal salvation, it is impossible to assign a justifying reason for a moment's delay."

There were two hosts in the Red Sea, and the cloud which moved between them was light to one and darkness to the other. So it is now. So it is always. I go to one home of poverty and affliction. There is trouble and sorrow enough there to break one's heart. And yet I hear nothing but expressions of cheerfulness and gratitude and hope. I go to another, and the wretched abode is full of murmuring and impatience and wrath. The same cloud of affliction has settled down upon the two homes. To one it brings light and peace, to the other darkness and despair. God's afflictive providence is a cloud full of light to the meek, the humble and the obedient, but it is very dark to the proud, the impatient and the unthankful. Light is sure to break, sooner or later, upon the path of those who hold themselves ready to go wherever Christ leads the way. Every step in the life of faith, of love and of consecration is an advance toward the light. And to those who thus live the darkest night of fear and trouble and affliction will soon break into the morning of joy and triumph.

The time is not far distant when we shall all stand upon the shore of the great sea of death. We shall not be able to pause at the brink or to return when once our feet are set in the cold flood. There is but one Guide who can take our hand and lead us safely through to the bright and blessed shore. That Divine

Guide has come all the way across the flood to meet us here, that we may not fail to find him when we need him most.   He is willing to walk with us through all the journey of life, that we may not be found alone and helpless when the hour of our greatest peril comes.   Pilgrim in a desert world, traveler to the unknown regions of eternity! will you hesitate to receive such a Guide now?   Would you rather wait till your feet are set in the cold waters and the cloud of death is around you, hoping to grope about in the darkness, and find even then the guiding Hand which now you will not take?

Saul's Night at Endor.

10

And Saul disguised himself, and put on other raiment, and he went, and two men with him, and they came to the woman by night -1 SAM. xxviii. 8.

T. MORAN

S. SARTAIN.

SAUL'S NIGHT AT ENDOR

147

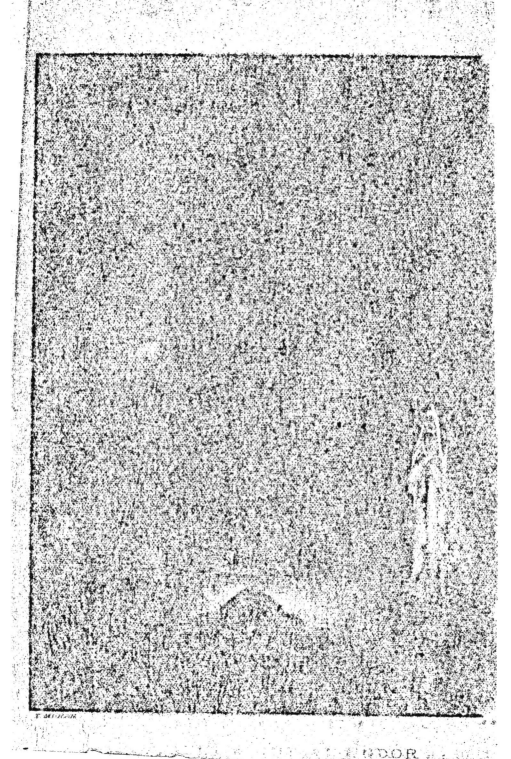

VII.

SAUL'S NIGHT AT ENDOR.

THE history of Saul, from his first appearance as king of Israel to his death, reads like an inspired tragedy. His brilliant achievements in war and his melancholy end were celebrated by the greatest of the Hebrew Psalmists in his own age. In modern times, poetry, painting, music and sculpture have clothed his history with the fascination of genius and the spell of romance. It is near three thousand years since he fell down slain upon Mount Gilboa, and still one of the great masters of musical composition in modern times can find no better theme for the display of his wondrous power in giving utterance to the sorrows of stricken hearts. Ninety generations of men have appeared and passed away from the earth since the beauty of Israel was slain upon the high places of the field. And still the most mournful march to which. funeral processions move in modern times is known by the name of Saul.

There is so much of good and bad, strength and weakness, success and failure, in the man, that we are drawn to him when we do not like him. We pity him when

147

we feel that he deserves to be punished.   Like David, we lament his fall when we know that it would have been a calamity to his people and the world if he had continued to reign.   We go back and read the history of his call to the kingdom for the hundredth time with something like hope that he will fulfill the fair promise of his manly frame and his modest deportment.   We close the record with the same repeated disappointment, that one on whom Nature and Providence had conferred all gifts and graces to make a "king of men," should fail through his own fault and die in dishonor for his own transgression.

His character combined the most opposite qualities, and his life abounded in startling contradictions.   At different times he exhibited the rustic simplicity of Cincinnatus, the unnatural sternness of the elder Brutus, the clemency of the first Cæsar, the cruelty of Nero, the superstition of Wallenstein, the jealousy of Philip the Second, the irresolution and remorse of Macbeth, the madness of Lear.   He was rash in danger and cautious in safety.   He had the courage of a hero and the timidity of a coward.   He spared his worst enemy and he would have put to death his best friend. He prophesied himself and he destroyed the prophets of the Lord.   He cut off the diviners and necromancers out of the land, and on the last night of his life he traveled ten miles, in great peril and fatigue and distress of mind, to inquire for himself of a woman that had a familiar spirit.

He named his own children just as the mood of faith, superstition or mockery happened to move him at the time—Jonathan from Jehovah, Melchishua from Moloch, Eshbaal from Baal, Mephibosheth from contempt of all faith. When brought under the influence of sacred music and song and religious worship, he would catch the spirit of devotion and pour forth the most fervid expressions of praise and prayer. He would become so carried away with religious ecstasy as to give himself neither rest nor food, day nor night, until his strength failed and he fell upon the ground faint and exhausted. And then, when the paroxysm of wild and stormy zeal had passed, his old moody and implacable disposition would break out with greater violence than ever.

He would pursue the object of his jealousy with the hate and fury of a demon, and then he would melt into tenderness and weep like a child when some act of generosity had touched his heart. Thus kindness and cruelty, manliness and meanness, superstition and faith, firmness and indecision, were combined with fearful extremes in this one man. And so this mad monarch of Israel, with the good and evil angel ever struggling in his soul, was swept on in his stormy reign to the dark day when he was encamped with three hundred thousand men upon the northern ridge of Gilboa, with the greater host of the Philistines in sight at Shunem, five miles away on the other side of the valley.

It was a place of great historic interest to the tribes of Israel. It overlooked and bordered upon the great plain of Esdraelon, the most fertile and famous plain in all Palestine, even then, as it has been ever since for three thousand years—from Joshua to Napoleon— the battle-field of nations. On the same bare, bleak and jagged ridge where Saul was encamped, Gideon had hidden his three hundred men among the rocks two hundred years before, when the Midianites filled the valley beneath, as grasshoppers and as the sand of the sea for multitude. Down the face of those dark limestone cliffs Gideon and his servant Phurah had slid silently by night and had crept stealthily along through the wild grass and giant thistles "unto the outside of the armed men," and there had overheard a wakeful soldier telling his companion the dream of a barley loaf rolling into the camp of the host and over-turning a tent. In that valley, on the same night, the brave three hundred, divided into three companies, broke their pitchers, making a sound like the clash of arms, brandished their lamps like the signal-lights of a great army, blew their trumpets and cried, "The sword of the Lord and of Gideon," until the heights of Hermon and Gilboa echoed the shout and the peal. From that spot the countless host of the Midianites rushed in disorderly rout and wild dismay toward the passes of the Jordan, while Gideon and his chosen three hundred chased and cut them down from behind.

Saul was encamped by the very spring of Harod

where Gideon's Spartan band drank hastily, lifting the water to their lips in the hollow of their hands. Saul had a thousand times as many men as Gideon, better armed and disciplined for war, and the place was one to inspire hope and courage.

But the unhappy king was not in a state of mind to secure the advantage or meet the peril of the hour. Misfortunes had multiplied upon him in consequence of his perverse and passionate temper, and the gloomy clouds that had long lowered upon his guilty path were now ready to burst forth in one final and destructive storm.

The tribes on the east of the Jordan had nearly renounced allegiance to his sceptre. His own fiery little tribe of Benjamin and the champion tribe of Judah had grown weary of his turbulent reign. Increasing numbers were daily turning their faces toward the rising star of David. Samuel was dead, and his last words to Saul were words of threatening. The prophets and the priests were slain. The oracle of the Lord gave him no answer. There was no voice nor sound of harp that could charm away the tormenting demon from the dark soul of the king. With the heart of a hero in his bosom, he looked across the valley to the camp of enemies that he had often routed, and his mighty frame trembled exceedingly with fear.

In an age when physical strength was the best title to sovereignty, there was no man in all the host of

Israel to be compared with him for the greatness and
beauty of his stature.   Above them all he stood,

> " With Atlantean shoulders fit to bear
> The weight of mightiest monarchies."

And his trembling was the more apparent and pitiable
because, in every limb and look of his mighty frame,
he seemed made for a king and a hero.   With three
hundred thousand warriors entrenched around him
upon heights that the chariots and horses of the Philis-
tines could not climb, Saul felt himself to be defence-
less and alone, because God had forsaken him.

Alas! there is no path so dark and desolate for
human feet to tread as that chosen by the man who re-
sists and grieves away all holy influences from his heart,
until he feels that God has given him up.   The worst
thing that can ever happen to a willful and disobedient
man like Saul is for God to let him have his own
way.   It is the darkest hour of life and the beginning
of the shadow of death to such a man when he is left to
follow the bent of his own blind passion, and to fall
into the pit which his own folly has digged.

The sun went down behind the oak-crowned ridge
of Carmel, and the shadows of evening covered the
great battle-plain, while the sleepless king watched the
kindling of the camp-fires, and heard the murmur of
the mighty host of the Philistines rising, like the roar
of the sea, on the other side of the valley.   His distress
of mind increased as the darkness deepened around
him, and he " bitterly thought of the morrow." ·He

needed rest, but he could not sleep. He needed coun-
sel of God, but he had so often rejected it when given
that it was no longer offered. When men give up
their faith in God, God gives them up to believe a lie.

So this unhappy king, having shut his eyes to the
light that shines from heaven to guide all in the safe
way, resolved to seek counsel from beneath. He took
off his royal robes. He laid aside his buckler and his
battle-spear. He put on the garments of a common
peasant, took two trusty men with him and stole
silently out of the camp.

They pass silently down the steep sides of Gil-
boa into the valley to the east of the Philistines, and
then cross swiftly over the ridge of Little Hermon or
the Hill Moreh, watching every moment lest they
should fall upon some roving band or outpost of the
enemy. After having traveled some ten or twelve
miles across the grass-grown plain and the successive
ridges of lower hills, they come to a miserable little
cluster of mud and stone cabins, hanging on the
northern declivity of one of eight rounded peaks that
form the range of Little Hermon.

One of these wretched cabins, forming the entrance
of a rocky cavern on the mountain side, Saul and his
attendants seek out in the darkness and enter. In
that damp and diabolic den at midnight they find a
solitary hag, who receives their late intrusion with
mingled terror and cursing. Her fear is allayed by
the promise of secresy, and her wrath is appeased by

the offer of a rich reward. Her suspicions are doubt-less awakened as to the character of the intruders, both by the value of the present offered, and by the fact, generally known, that there was but one man in all the land of such gigantic and kingly stature as now stands before her.

In this wretched hamlet of Endor, with a heathen name and half-heathen population, this outcast woman of Israel has hidden herself away, that she may the more safely and profitably practice the profane impos-ture of divination. She pretends to the power of call-ing back the spirits of the departed and wresting the secrets from the unknown future. But she has no more power over the spirits of the dead than the Caffre rain-maker has over the clouds. She has no more knowledge of the future than the gypsy fortune-teller, who pretends to read the decrees of eternal destiny in the lines of the hand. Her spells, mutter-ings and incantations are only cunning devices with which to distract attention and deceive the credulous. Her magical arts are wicked and forbidden, not because they have any power over spiritual agencies, good or evil, but because they are impositions and lies, and they lead men to withdraw their confidence from truth and the God of truth, and to believe in nothingness and vanity.

And it is to consult this low, cunning and abomina-ble creature, under the cover of midnight in a cavern of the mountains, that the anointed king of Israel comes in the hour of his great extremity. Trust in God and obedience to every word from the mouth of the Lord was the first article in the constitution of his kingdom, and the first condition of his continuing to reign. And here he is, on the night of imminent and terrible destiny to himself and his people, ten miles away from his great army, in the den of a sorceress, asking to be made the dupe of the vilest imposture. He might have had Omniscience for his guide and the strength of the Almighty for his shield; and he seeks light from a confederate of the prince of darkness—he craves a more intimate alliance with the powers that have already brought him to the very brink of destruction. The hours of the night are swiftly passing, and when the dawn appears the hills will shake with the battle-cry and the thundering charge of a half million warriors, and the consecrated king of Israel, who should rule the destinies of that day in the name of Jehovah, is away from the camp, wasting his strength and unnerving his heart by consulting with this wicked and worthless woman at Endor.

To such dreadful darkness and delusion are even great and strong and princely men given up, when they turn away from the only living and true God and trust in lying vanities. If you would meet the great battle of life with the courage of heroes and the faith of martyrs, do not ask counsel of those who pretend to be wise above what is written in God's revealed word. Do not turn away from the instructions and admonitions of holy men, who spake as they were moved by the Holy Ghost. Do not put yourself under the guidance of men and women whose wisdom is of the earth and whose inspiration is from beneath. Let the horrors of despair, which drove the wretched king of Israel in his perplexity to the darker cave of Endor for comfort, warn every one not to forsake the safe and plain path of trust and prayer and obedience to God.

" And the woman said to Saul, Whom shall I bring up unto thee? And Saul said, Bring me up Samuel." And before the woman had time to practise her arts for the deception of the king, behold, at the command of God, Samuel actually appeared. The woman herself had the least expectation of any such thing. She was so startled and terrified that she cried out with a shriek of horror. She was well fitted by her abandoued character and by the long practice of imposition to turn any unexpected occurrence to the credit of her divination. But the actual appearance of a living man from the spirit-world was too much for her courage and her self-possession. It was indeed just what she had long pretended to see and to do. But to her it was as great a surprise as it would have been had the stony idols come down from the sides of her cave and spoken with a human voice.

Her magical arts had no power to compel the great prophet to leave the society of Abraham and Moses and appear in that den of sorcery. The spirits of the mighty dead have something else to do than to answer the call of conjurors and clairvoyants in any age, in any land. And if they were to come down from their high seats in bliss; they would bring better messages and wiser counsels than the seers and mediums of modern times have reported in their name.

It was by the power and appointment of the infinite God that Samuel appeared to confound the arts of the sorcerer, and again to rebuke the rebellious king because he had not obeyed the voice of the Lord. It was no semblance or shadow, much less any confederate of the sorceress, any emissary of Satan. It was the same majestic and awful look that Samuel wore when Saul saw him at Ramah for the last time; the same voice which commanded the thunder and the rain in the day of the wheat harvest; the same mantle that Saul rent when Samuel told him that the Lord had rent the kingdom from him twenty-three years before. The same words of doom came again from the prophet's voice, with the addition that to-morrow all should be fulfilled.

And peradventure, too, this last sharp and terrible warning was sent in mercy, that the blinded and maddened monarch might have one more opportunity to repent of his fearful impiety in going to the den of the sorceress, when he should have called only upon the Lord in his distress, and prayed, if need be, all that night with strong crying and many tears unto the God of Israel for help. The unhappy king saw and heard, but no word of penitence or of hope came from his pale and trembling lip.

> " He heard and fell to earth as falls the oak,
>   At once, and blasted by the thunder-stroke."

Hungry, weary, terrified, conscience-smitten, he lay like one dead, with the full length of his giant frame prostrate upon the ground. And when he revived and rose up to go back upon the perilous night-journey to his army he went a doubly-doomed and despairing man.

When the morning came, the host of Philistines swept across the valley from Shunem and up the heights of Gilboa, as the earthquake at sea heaves a mountain-wave on shore. On the plain and up the hill-side were seven hundred thousand men, yelling and struggling with all the demoniac ferocity of a hand-to-hand conflict, and with no cloud of cannon-smoke to hide the infernal spectacle from the sun. The fountain of Jezreel ran blood all the way ten miles to the Jordan. The ranks of Israel were broken. The trampled grass of the plain and the rocky steep of Gilboa were piled with countless slain. Amid the discomfiture of his scattered host, the despairing Saul fell by his own hand, and still in his death-agony received, perhaps, a final stroke from the sword of one who had shared with him in his transgression against the Lord.

And this is the last sad memorial which the sacred

chronicler writes of Israel's first king: "So Saul died for his transgression, which he committed against the Lord, even against the word of the Lord, which he kept not, and also for asking counsel of one that had a familiar spirit to inquire of it, and inquired not of the Lord."

And out of this dark cave of Endor, and down from these blood-stained and curse-smitten heights of Gilboa, there comes a voice of warning and instruction even to us. It is this: In all the trials, perplexities and conflicts of life seek counsel first of all from God. All who go astray from him wander in darkness, and they know not at what they stumble. The path of obedience to God is as the shining light that shineth more and more unto the perfect day. The first step in duty makes the next easier. The higher you climb the difficult steep of faith and self-denial, the farther you leave the misleading clouds of doubt and temptation beneath you.

The first king of Israel was overwhelmed with disaster and blinded with delusion just because he failed to make obedience to God the first law of his kingdom and the first principle for the government of his own conduct. His life was a failure, and he died in dishonor and despair, just because he set up his own perverse and passionate will against God, and was bent upon having his own way.

And just as certainly will any man come to sorrow and disappointment who seeks the success and the joy of life in anything else than obedience to God. God has a special work for every one to do, just as truly as he had for Saul in calling him to the kingdom of Israel. It is the wisdom and glory of every one's life to do the work given him by God and to do it well. The only failure which we have reason to fear is failure to be found at our task and doing our work well, when called to give account of our trust.

There is no madness so dreadful, so hopeless as the madness of trying to live without God. These inspired histories of good and bad men in ancient times were written to impress upon our minds this one most practical lesson—that the fear of the Lord is the beginning of wisdom, and in the keeping of his commandments there is great reward. All the crowns and kingdoms of the earth would not be a sufficient compensation for one hour or one act of disobedience to God. It would be neither wise nor profitable to accept all that the tempter offered Jesus for the least concession to his evil power. Wickedness in all its forms is a waste; disobedience to God is both dishonor and disaster; temptation can never come in such a form as to make it safe or right to yield.

As the result of this night's study of sacred history, I would that some thoughtful reader might close the book with this solemn and unalterable purpose in his heart: "Henceforth I will live for God, and no earthly consideration shall persuade me to disown my Saviour and my King." The course of life is all plain and open before him who makes that resolution the start-ing-point of his career and the constant guide of his course. He is relieved from a thousand doubts and uncertainties and conflicts that harass the unresolved and uncommitted. He is satisfied with his choice, and nothing, by any possibility, can ever make him regret anything done or suffered for God. He has peace of conscience, and that gives him more real happiness than all the brief and deceptive indulgences of a worldly life. He has the hope of heaven, and that makes him richer than all earthly possessions could without it. He has the assurance of his heavenly Father's love, and that gives him light and joy in all the dark hours of affliction and trouble. He has the pardon of sin, and that takes away the sting of death and disarms the king of terrors.

Doubtless every one who will be at all likely to read this page means to serve God in some way, at some time. The critical question with many is this, *how, when,* shall that better life begin? I say, Do it with all the heart, do it openly, do it now. God has called many times; he is calling still. God has waited long; he is waiting still. The child should answer when the Father speaks. Take heed, lest you go so far away in the paths of worldliness that you cannot hear your Father's voice. Take heed, lest you stay without until the door of your Father's house is shut.

Loving and obedient children long to be near their father. The best evidence of a right disposition in us

11

is an ardent and irrepressible longing after God. The highest attainment of a holy and happy life is a serene and cheerful walk with God. In the loftiest and purest communion with him the strong desire of the heart will still go forth in the Christian song—

> "Nearer, my God, to thee,
> Nearer to thee;
> E'en though it be a cross
> That raiseth me,
> Still all my song shall be,
> Nearer, my God, to thee,
> Nearer to thee."

David's Night at the Jordan.

And the king, and all the people that were with him, came weary, and refreshed themselves there. . . . . Send quickly, and tell David, saying, Lodge not this night in the plains of the wilderness, but speedily pass over: lest the king be swallowed up, and all the people that are with him. . . . . Then David arose, and all the people that were with him, and they passed over Jordan: by the morning light there lacked not one of them that was not gone over Jordan.—2 SAM. xvi. 14· xvii 16, 22.

VIII.

DAVID'S NIGHT AT THE JORDAN.

THE Hebrew title of the third Psalm tells us that it was written by David when he fled from his son Absalom. The whole composition breathes forth a spirit of the most serene and sustained trust in God. And yet the author was at the time in the midst of the greatest peril and affliction. It was the first night after his hurried flight from Jerusalem. He had been driven from his throne and from the sanctuary of his God by a most cruel and unnatural rebellion. All the waves of trouble and sorrow had gone over him, and the pitiless sword of filial ingratitude had pierced his very soul.

He had spent the day in traversing the horrible wilderness of Judah, and the night encampment was on the banks of the Jordan. The bare earth was the bed on which he "laid him down and slept." The "waking," for which he thanked God, was caused by messengers rushing into the camp at midnight and giving the alarm that the usurper had been advised to pursue with a chosen force of twelve thousand men that night, and that all must arise and cross the swift and dangerous Jordan to save their lives before morning.

The conduct of David on this occasion supplies a lesson for the imperiled and afflicted at all times. It is well worth the while to inquire, even if it be merely as a study, by what means a man of quick and fiery impulses like him could maintain a firm and peaceful trust in God in the midst of so great excitement, weariness, peril and sorrow. With this end in view, let us glance at the history of the day preceding that night encampment by the Jordan.

Absalom had been planning a revolt for four years. He used all the blandishments of his personal beauty and winning address to alienate the hearts of the people from the king. He took his stand early in the morning at the gates of the city and at the very entrance to the palace, on purpose to make himself acquainted with all who went and came. If he had given himself to any good work with half the zeal and talent that he displayed in doing mischief, his name would have come down to us with honor, and the saddest chapter in the history of his sainted father had never been written.

His splendid bearing and courteous manners, his false and fascinating expressions of interest in everything and sympathy with everybody, drew all hearts to him, as pleasure draws passion and the serpent charms its prey. Added to these personal attentions to individuals, he appeared in public before the mass of the people with more pomp and splendor than the king himself. David, the old warrior-monarch, cared little for the parade and trappings of royalty. He moved about among his subjects in Jerusalem on foot, and he went out to the top of Olivet to worship without guards or attendants. Absalom rode through the streets and around the city in his chariot, attended by horsemen and foot-runners, who cleared the way before him with "the shout of a king." And so the vanity of the multitude was in every way tempted to wish that the brilliant and beautiful prince were in the place of their praying and psalm-singing sovereign.

All this was done under the eyes of the fond old father, who was too much blinded by his affections to suspect treason in his most indulged and fascinating son. Strange to say, the parent who is quick to read character in all others is sometimes the very last to know his own children. He will judge more accurately of the life and principles of one whom he meets only for an hour than of some who sit at his own table. The ruler, the statesman, whose word is law for the government of millions, may himself be the unconscious slave of a petted and passionate child in his own house.

When all was ripe for the long-plotted rebellion, Absalom disappeared, under some false pretext, from Jerusalem, and the next day, at evening, news came to David that his wild and wicked son was already crowned and proclaimed king, twenty miles away, at

Hebron. The intelligence was soon confirmed by messengers coming in from every direction, and saying, "The hearts of the men of Israel are after Absalom." David, by his own heroism and 'sagacity, had raised his people to the first rank among the great kingdoms of his time, and now, at the first breath of change, his subjects were ready to turn to the treacherous and parricidal son and cry, "God save the king!"

There was no time to be lost. The proud and impetuous rival for the throne was not a man to delay or to be trifled with for a moment. A few hours' march would bring him to the gates of Jerusalem, and once there he would not hesitate to add the murder of his own father to the many crimes which he had already committed.

Early the next morning the old king gave the order, "Arise, and let us flee! Make speed to depart, for we shall not else escape from Absalom." This is the darkest and most sorrowful day in the eventful life of David—the day that closed with the night encampment and the sacred psalm by the banks of the Jordan. The inspired historian tells us what was said and done with great fullness and touching simplicity.

The aged king went forth from his palace upon Mount Zion, and all his people with him. The members of his own household, the servants and officers of the royal court, the military captains and councillors of state, the heads of tribes and families, the body-guard of Philistines and the chosen six hundred who had shared in the perils and wanderings of the king before he came to the crown, their wives and children, the aged and the feeble—all went forth from the city in long and mournful procession on that memorable morning.

They descended the steep sides of Mount Zion into the Tyropæan valley, crossed over the northerly portion of the bare ridge of Moriah, on which the temple was subsequently built, and then went down into the deeper valley of the Kidron. They were all on foot, and the road which they were to travel was steep and difficult for the strong and unencumbered—much more for the feeble, the aged and the little ones—much more for those who carried in their hands food for the journey and whatever valuables or keepsakes they could snatch from their homes in their hurried departure.

At the last guard-house outside the city, before crossing the Kidron, the king paused and the sad procession of fugitives passed on before him. It touched the heart of the aged father deeply when he saw the little band of Philistines filing down the winding path and committing themselves to the fortunes of the fallen monarch, when his own son had conspired against his life. Such fidelity in a troop of foreign mercenaries was too much for David to see without some expression of admiration. Overcome with his feelings, he besought Ittai, the chief of the band, to go back and take his followers with him, and not commit himself and his peop'e unnecessarily to the fortunes of a dethroned and exiled monarch. But the generous and chivalric chieftain declared, with a solemn oath upon the name of Jehovah, his unalterable purpose to live or die with his adopted king.

So David and Ittai moved on together to the front of the procession, and the whole multitude lifted up their voices in wailing and loud lamentation, as they stood aside from the winding and stony path for the aged and broken-hearted monarch to pass, leaning upon the strong arm of the Philistine chief. The weeping and mourning of the multitude was so vehement and excessive that the sacred narrative says the very hills and valleys wept with a loud voice.

They had only just crossed the Kidron, and were beginning the ascent of Olivet, when they were over-taken by the priests and Levites bearing the ark of God. But David would not suffer them to subject that most sacred depository of the Divine covenant with Israel to the perils and conflicts that awaited him. If he was to be dethroned and exiled, he did not wish to have the constitution of the nation, written upon tablets of stone by the finger of God at Sinai, lost with him.

Some great men, when they fall, are ambitious to make the ruin as great as they can. They would have it appear that the world cannot go on without them—that everything sacred and precious depends upon their holding the reins of power and receiving the homage of the people. Not so David. He said to the priests, "Carry back the ark of God into the city. If I shall find favor in the eyes of the Lord, he will bring me again. But if he say, I have no delight in thee, behold, here am I. Let him do to me as seemeth good to him." In these words spoke out a great and generous soul that would not have others crushed with the weight of its own sorrows.

The ark was carried back to the city, and the heart-broken king began to lead the long procession of fugitives up the steep ascent of Olivet. It was a wild mountain path, with steps here and there cut in the ledges. It was strewn with loose pebbles and sharp-edged fragments of rock, and the king led the way barefoot, and covered his head to hide his grief. And when the people saw that the ark was gone and the king was leading off in the way to the wilderness, and faintness and weariness came over them at the beginning of the long march, they felt that the pledge of God's protection was taken from them, their conse-crated king was an outcast, themselves were sharers in his exile, and all was lost. They all covered their heads and broke out again in loud and piteous lamenta-tions, until it seemed as if the whole western slope of the mountain were covered with a funeral procession, and every mourner were going to the grave of his dearest earthly friend.

When the king came to the top of Mount Olivet, there had been so many delays that it was already noon, and there was fearful reason for haste, lest Absalom, who was on the march from Hebron, should arrive and cut off their retreat. But the afflicted monarch could not pass the olive grove, where he had been accustomed to worship God 'on the summit, without turning aside from the path and stopping to pray for Divine strength and guidance in all his affliction. He needed the calmness, the energy and the self-possession which come by prayer to meet the peril, the fatigue and the sorrow that awaited him. And when he rose up to renew the march, he was able to take a last look of his beloved Zion and turn his face toward the wilderness without a tear.

And now began the descent down the dreary, rocky road, among bare, desolate hills and wild ravines, which seem to have been made by rending in pieces the whole mountain range, and leaving the mighty fragments like a storm-tossed sea, to burn and blacken in the sun. The whole region through which David was passing on that saddest half-day of his life looks as if it had been scathed by volcanic fires and had never recovered from the fierce heat. Not a human dwelling nor a sign of cultivation nor a spot of green earth relieves the awful desolation. The road drops down the shelving ridges, sometimes buried in the bed of deep ravines, and sometimes hanging on the edge of precipices four or five hundred feet high.

Shimei, a man of the house of Saul, came out upon the edge of one of these ravines as the king passed below, and cast earth and stones upon the heads of the fugitives, and ran along on the heights from rock to rock, uttering the most vehement and terrible curses upon David. One of the men of war begged to be permitted to cross over the glen and stop the mouth of the reviler by taking off his head. But David counted the insult a slight matter compared with the grief which he bore upon his heart. He only said, " Let him alone, let him curse, for what are his *words*, when my son, my own son, for whom I could have died, seeketh my life?"

And so Shimei went on cursing and casting stones, until he tired himself out with cursing and went back, like a snarling dog that barks at travelers till he is tired with barking and then skulks back into his kennel. And silence is about the best answer to be given to an angry and spiteful man who curses in his anger. When he is tired of cursing and cooled of his anger, he may perhaps hear to reason, but not before.

The weary day passed slowly on, and the long line of straggling fugitives began to emerge from the wild mountain pass upon the hot plain of the Jordan toward evening. It was deep night before the hindmost of the company came in, weary, hungry and faint, and the small stock of provisions which had been given them on the way by a cunning and treacherous slave scarcely sufficed for those who had brought nothing. And then all lay down to sleep as best they could, without tent or covering, upon the level of hot sand and gravel bordering the river, or among the thickets of cane and oleander near the water's edge.

At midnight the alarm came that the forces of Absalom were at Jerusalem, that his spies were out in every direction, that the pursuit might be followed up any moment, and the only safety was to be sought in crossing the Jordan before morning. And so the fugitive king and his whole company of weary, heartbroken exiles were roused up from the first sleep after such a terrible and exhausting day as they had passed to renew their toil. But they woke and worked so promptly that when the dawn lifted the curtains of night from the mountains of Moab, the difficult and dangerous task of crossing the deep and swift river was accomplished.

Then David sang this psalm: "I laid me down and slept; I awaked, for the Lord sustained me. I cried unto the Lord with my voice, and he heard me out of his holy hill. I will not be afraid of ten thousands that have set themselves against me. Salvation belongeth unto the Lord. O God, thou art my God. Early will I seek thee. My soul thirsteth for thee, to see thy power and thy glory, so as I have seen thee in the sanctuary. Because thy loving-kindness is better than life, my lips shall praise thee. I will lift up my hands in thy name. My soul shall be satisfied. My mouth shall praise thee with joyful lips, when I meditate on thee in the night-watches."

Thus could the dethroned and exiled king David

pray and sing praises to God on the morning following
the saddest day and the darkest night in his life.
Yesterday, an absolute monarch, with millions of
subjects to obey his will. To-day, a fugitive and an
exile, with thousands upon his track to hunt him down
like an outlaw or a beast of prey. In the morning he
rose from a royal couch amid the splendors of kingly
state, with troops of servants at his command. At
night he slept upon the bare earth for a bed, sur-
rounded by a miserable multitude of fugitives, as
hungry, weary and sore with travel, though not as
heart-broken, as himself.

And this crushing weight of sorrow and suffering
was laid upon David when the white hairs of age had
silvered his brow and the fiery vigor of his young
manhood had left him for ever. He was a youthful
shepherd, with a step as light as the wild roe of the
mountains when he fled from the face of the demon-
haunted Saul. He could glory in danger, and he
heard the battle-cry of Israel with fierce delight when
he went forth to meet the giant in the valley of Elah.
He was a man to attack the lion with a shepherd's
staff, and to break a bow of steel with his hands when
he exposed himself among the lords of the Philistines
at the court of the king of Gath.

But it was a very different matter for a gray-headed
old king to be driven from his throne, and to find that
the fires of rebellion had been kindled by his own son.
And in estimating the force of the affliction and the

provocation which David suffered, we must remember that he was by nature a man of keen sensibilities, strong passions and impetuous temper. He had been accustomed for years to have the slightest intimation of his will received as supreme law by all around him. He lived in an age of violence, and he reigned over a people that had just emerged from a state of barbarism. He had the fullest confidence in his divine right to govern, and the power of life and death was in his hands. He was weary, insulted, wronged with the deepest and blackest ingratitude.

The great English dramatist, whose representations of human nature are wont to be received as of equal authority with Nature herself, has attempted to put fitting words into the mouth of an old king turned out of doors, but not, like David, conspired against for his destruction, by his unkind daughters. And Shakespeare makes the injured father say, among many other things too bitter and blasphemous to be quoted :

> " You see me here, you gods, a poor old man,
>   As full of grief as age ; wretched in both.
>   If it be you that stir these daughters' hearts
>   Against their father, fool me not so much
>   To bear it tamely ; touch me with noble anger ;
>   Oh, let not women's weapons, water-drops,
>   Stain my man's cheeks !—No, you unnatural hags,
>   I will have such revenges on you both
>   That all the world shall—I will do such things,—
>   What they are, yet I know not ; but they shall be
>   The terrors of the earth. You think, I'll weep ;
>   No, I'll not weep.

I have full cause of weeping; but this heart
Shall break into a hundred thousand flaws
Or ere I'll weep. Oh I shall go mad!
Ingratitude! thou marble-hearted fiend,
More hideous, when thou show'st thee in a child
Than the sea-monster.
How sharper than a serpent's tooth it is
To have a thankless child!
The untented woundings of a father's curse
Pierce every sense about thee!''

Thus, and with still more violent outbreaks of the wildest and most tempestuous passion, our English Shakespeare represents the natural effect upon an indulgent and fiery old king produced by the ingratitude of his children. And the critical and literary world extol the genius of the great dramatist as if it were a Divine inspiration for revealing the secret depths of the human heart.

But here, in actual history, was another old king, himself an absolute monarch, living in an age of violence, his whole being thrilling with passion, conspired against for his utter destruction by his most indulged, most beautiful son; and how does he attempt to express the unutterable things struggling in his soul? With what words does he pour out wrath and cursing upon the ingratitude which has deprived him of his crown, driven him into exile and is still seeking his very life?

We have read his words and they are full of trust and peace. In the very climax of his great grief he

12

exhibits a serene and cheerful confidence in God. He pours out his heart in praise and thanksgiving. He makes the silence of the night and the solitude of the wilderness resound with a psalm in which the afflicted of all times may fitly sing forth their sublime trust in God. The cry of his supplication and the longing of his heart are such as all human souls may use in coming before God. In the royal Psalmist the necessities of the man are greater than the affliction of the king. He can bear the loss of all that belonged to him as a monarch if he can still have that which he most needs as a man. And that is, the favor of God.

This is the lesson which David learned with the loss of his crown—a lesson worth more to us than the crown of all the earth. The infinite God alone can be a sufficient portion for the soul. The soul can be satisfied only when filled with all the fullness of God. It is not because one is a king or a slave, not because he is a millionaire or a beggar, not because he is prosperous or afflicted, that he needs the Divine favor. It is because he is a man—because he has a living, immortal soul to take hold on things infinite and eternal— that he cannot live safely or satisfactorily without God.

It is no more natural for the body to suffer hunger when deprived of food than it is for the soul to be unsatisfied and unhappy till it finds rest in God. If the most worldly man living would let his soul speak out—if he only dared to give voice to everything within him which thinks and feels and longs and hopes and fears—he would say, " I am unhappy, and I cannot help feeling and fearing that I am spending my life for naught."

Suppose I knew all science, art, literature, history— suppose I could range over earth and heaven with an angel's wing and visit the starry spaces with the speed of thought—what were all that power and knowledge to me compared with the faith which can look upon the universe of worlds and say, " Behold my Father's house ! He made them all. I am his child. His love is as great as his power, and I know that such a Father will never suffer his loving and obedient child to want for any good thing."

This great Being, who made all worlds, is a Father unto every one of us. It is our highest knowledge to know him. It will be the purest and truest manifestation of affection in us to love him. He meets us in every path of life with gifts in both hands, that he may win our hearts. He watches for the return of our gratitude as a mother watches for the first smile of intelligence and affection in her babe. That great and mighty One is ever bending over us with a deeper compassion than moves an earthly parent's heart toward a wayward and suffering child. He cries after us in all our wanderings, saying, " Return unto me and I will return unto you." And when we weary his patience and refuse to hear, he says with the relentings of infinite pity, " How can I give thee up?"

Every minister of the Gospel, every reclaimed and

forgiven child of God, is a messenger sent out in that patient, generous and loving Father's name, to say to every wanderer, "Brother, come home. Come back to your Father. He is waiting· with open arms to receive you. You cannot be happy without his love. Weary, wandering child, come back to your Father's house and find rest. Come back to your Father's heart and find forgiveness. Come home, and your brethren, who mourn over your departure, will join with the angels in singing songs of welcome and of joy."

We have seen David's calm and assured trust in God in the midst of all his troubles. His faith was proved to be the stronger because it had to contend with fierce impulses and fiery passions in his own natural temperament. If we would measure the full force of the trust that sustained him through the terrible night at the Jordan, we must glance at the sequel of this sad history. We must see how completely the heart of the father was bound up with misguided affection for his wayward and wicked son.

David was now in exile at Mahanaim, a city on the east of the Jordan, among the mountains of Gilead. The last decisive day had come, when he was to lose his son and regain his crown. He stood in the gate of the city, burdened with age and broken with grief, while the hundreds and thousands of his faithful troops filed before him, as they went out, in the glorious light of an Eastern dawn, to fight against Absalom. Beside him stood the iron-hearted warrior Joab and all the chiefs of the army.

He knew that the fate of his kingdom and his own life also, depended upon the defeat of the rebellious host. And yet, with the fondness of an indulgent father, he thought only of his wayward but still beloved son. That son had grown up to be an ambitious and wicked man—the worst man in the kingdom. But the fond old father thought only of the fair-haired boy who played before him in the innocence and beauty of childhood. In the hearing of the soldiers, as they passed, David kept charging the chiefs, saying, " *Gently, gently,* for my sake, with the boy Absalom."

To those stern and loyal chieftains, Absalom was nothing but an utterly bad and profligate man—the most dangerous man in all Israel. But to the father, carried away from his better judgment by his parental affection, Absalom was the same dear boy that his fond eyes doated upon in former years, when his glorious beauty was the wonder and praise of all Jerusalem. And as the fiery warrior Joab, the chief captain of the army, was impatient to mount and spur across the plain, and head the host that was already far on in the march and disappearing under the oaks of Bashan. David's last word to him at the gate of Mahanaim, was still the same, "*Gently, gently,* for my sake, with the boy Absalom !"

And now the day was far spent. The conflict was

over.   The trumpet of recall had been blown through
all the ranks of the victorious host.   Many thousands
who went forth with the morn to the fight, " burning
with high hope," were lying cold and dead on the
bloody field.   King David still sat in the gate of
Mahanaim, anxious most of all for the safety of the
unnatural son who had lifted up his hand against his
father's life.   The watchman stood on the tower above
the gate, looking down the winding descent of the hill-
side and far away across the distant plain for any
messenger that might come with tidings from the field.

At length, when the sun was almost set, a man was
seen coming out of the distant woods, and running
with great speed alone toward the gate of the city.
The watchman cried from the tower to tell the king.
And the king said, " If the man runs alone, he bring-
eth tidings."   The panting messenger came, and with
one gasping breath, cried, " *Shâlôm,*" *peace,* and fell
down to the earth upon his face before the king.   The
monarch had no inquiry to make for his army or his
people.   The father's heart broke forth in the one
eager and anxious question, "Is the young man Absa-
lom safe?"

And when the first messenger gave an evasive
answer, and the second came, the king had still no
other question to ask concerning the fortunes of the
critical day save the one in which he poured forth all
the passionate fervor of a father's love, "Is the young
man Absalom safe?"   And when the death of the

rebellious son was indirectly indicated by the second messenger, the man hinting what he durst not say, the king was too much agitated to restrain himself any longer. He groaned and shook as if a barbed arrow had pierced his aged heart. And then he went up slowly and tremblingly into the little chamber in the tower over the gate, covered his face with his robe, and as he walked to and fro poured forth that bitterest cry of parental anguish which the world has heard in three thousand years : "O my son Absalom, my son, my son Absalom ! would God I had died for thee ! O Absalom, my son, my son !"

And this mighty man of war, this hero-king, the greatest of all that sat on the throne of Israel, was greatest and mightiest in making his faith in God triumph at last over his vehement and passionate love for his unworthy and wicked son. In David, the man was greater than the monarch, both in faith and affection.

And let us not think too hardly of this aged king for seeming to forget his faithful people and his army in his anxiety for the safety of his rebellious son. Parental love is ever the same in all lands, in all times, among all people. It affects the monarch more than his crown. Even the hard life of bondage cannot crush it out from the heart of the slave. It lends the most profound interest to the daily life of home. It commands toil and study and treasure and suffering without end. It finds expression in rebukes and caresses, in tears and supplication, in wearisome labor by day and in wakeful hours by night. It is felt for the helpless babe, for the impulsive youth and for the full-grown man. It goes forth in unutterable longing and tenderness for the loving and the good, and also for the wayward and the wicked.

Children forget their parents and leave them homeless and comfortless in their old age. Brothers and sisters become alienated, so that they will not speak to each other. Bosom friends are changed to open enemies. Lovers are parted in hate. But it is against the deepest and mightiest principles of nature for parents to become indifferent to the welfare of children for whom they have toiled and suffered, over whom they have wept and prayed, on whom they have fixed their dearest hopes and fondest affections.

God teaches us all to call him our Father. He employs the natural, instinctive love of the parent for the child to show us how earnestly, tenderly, yearningly his heart goes out toward us in our afflictions and in our wanderings. He too is a King, and all our sin is committed against his high and adorable sovereignty. He never can forget or forego his right as a king. But in all his manifestations of mercy toward man we see more of the Father than of the sovereign. We hear the voice of compassion more frequently than the word of command. He loves because it is his nature to love. He desires our welfare because he cannot help it. When the ministers of chastisement and affliction are sent forth to reclaim the wandering and rebellious one, he says, " *Gently, gently,* for my sake, for it is my child that has sinned. It is mine own son that must suffer."

When children see the unceasing and tender anxiety of parents for their safety and happiness, they have only to listen and they will hear a voice from above, saying, " Like as a father pitieth his children, so the Lord pitieth them that fear him." When the messenger of death comes to the family and takes away an infant child, and the strong heart of manhood is melted into tenderness by the stroke, and woman's tears fall like rain upon the cherub brow in the little coffin, then the afflicted ones have only to turn to the covenant of God's everlasting love and they will find it written that the mother will sooner forget her own child than God will forget them.

Such is the paternal character of the everlasting God as revealed in the gospel, and learned by the growing experience of Christian faith. And, therefore, Christ in giving a form of prayer that should express all wants and be adapted to all ages, teaches us to say everywhere and every day—OUR FATHER.

This is the great and glorious revelation of the gospel—the Fatherhood of God humanized and appealing to our hearts in Christ the Son. Reason demonstrates his necessary and eternal existence. Science walks abroad with wonder and delight through the immensity of his works. Conscience makes us tremble at the thought of his awful justice and purity. Our own hearts tell us that every hiding-place of the soul is haunted by the omniscience of the Eternal Mind. From all these sources of knowledge we must turn to the words and life of Jesus to learn that the best and most acceptable name that we can give to this great and incomprehensible One is—Our Father, and that all the riches, glories, joys of his everlasting kingdom are open and accessible to him who comes as a LITTLE CHILD.

Elijah's Night in the Desert.

He himself went a day's journey into the wilderness, and came and sat down under a juniper tree: and he requested for himself that he might die; and said, It is enough; now, O Lord, take away my life.— 1 KINGS xix. 4.

IX.

ELIJAH'S NIGHT IN THE DESERT.

I T is night in the desert of Arabia. A day's journey out on the billowy sea of sand ridges and stony hills lies a living man, alone upon the bare earth, under the shelter of a low, scrawny tree. The scene is one of utter and melancholy solitude. If it were day, the distant shore of green fields and grazing flocks and human homes could be nowhere seen. And the aspect of loneliness and desolation is made more oppressive and painful by the presence of this weary, prostrate man in the midst of the arid and lifeless waste.

The sentinel stars are all out in fiery armor on the battlements of heaven, and the clear air is tremulous with their cold, twinkling light. The whole circuit of the horizon presents the same undulating sweep of bare earth and stony ridges, as monotonous and melancholy as the waste of waters seen from the deck of the ship in mid-ocean. There is no breeze, no sound of voice or footstep in the air. The desert is so silent that the weary wanderer can hear the beating of his

own heart and the flow of the life-stream in his own
brain.

Haggard and weary and travel-worn, the unhappy
fugitive has flung himself upon the ground in utter
despair, wishing that he might sleep in that solitude
and never wake again. Far from the homes of men
and the gentle charities of domestic life, he would
gladly give up his body to be covered by the drifting
sands and his bones to be bleached by the parching
winds of the desert. He has had enough of life, with
all its vain hopes and bitter disappointments. The
world is so given up to wrong and falsehood and
misery that to him it is no longer worth living in.
He would rather die in darkness and solitude than
ever see the face or hear the voice of his fellow-man
again. It is a dreadful thing for the human heart to
sink to such a depth of wretchedness and despair.
But who ever studied the great problem of life with a
reasoning mind and sensitive heart—who ever sur-
veyed and sounded the great ocean of human guilt
and misery, listening to its melancholy moan as it
comes down from far distant ages and rolls round all
the continents and islands of the peopled earth, and
heaves its dark waves of living wretchedness upon the
shores of eternity—who ever stood face to face with
these dark and dread realities without shrinking for
the moment from a share in such a mysterious and
awful thing as life? To those who have little thought
and less feeling, the order of things in this world and

the prospect for that which is to come may seem all plain. But to a great, generous, deeply sensitive soul, there will come hours when he will cease to wonder at the words which affliction and darkness wrung from the lips of the patient patriarch of old: "Let the day perish wherein I was born!"

And who is this weary and broken-spirited man daring to offer in bitterness of soul such a dreadful prayer in the desert? It is Elijah. It is the greatest and mightiest of all the prophets of Israel. After Moses, he was the one man who stamped the imprint of his own strong character most deeply upon the heart and hopes of the Hebrew nation. Up to the time of this strange flight into the desert he had seemed to be the very incarnation of courage, fire and energy. No threat or peril could put him in fear. No hardship could exhaust his endurance. No temptation could turn him aside from his duty. It will be interesting and profitable for us to learn, if we can, how so great and courageous and faithful a man could have given himself up to complaint and despondency and flight. The inquiry will lead us to review one or two points in his remarkable history.

At his first appearance in the sacred narrative he shows himself suddenly at Samaria, in the ivory palace of Ahab, the apostate king. He stands in the presence of the startled monarch with awful look and uplifted hand, and he solemnly swears by the living God that there shall be neither rain nor dew in the land of

Israel, for years to come, except according to his word.

It was a time of rebuke and blasphemy, and the inspired reprover of the nation's sins seemed like an embodiment of the Divine anger which they had provoked. He bursts upon the scene of action as suddenly as a meteor blazing forth from the midnight heavens. He delivers his word of doom and then disappears, as a solitary peal of thunder sometimes crashes through the clouds of a winter storm. The message which he brings is as abrupt and awful as the appearance of the messenger. Everything mysterious, and everything known of the man and of his history, conspire to invest his name with the most profound and fascinating interest. The greatest of the prophets, he steps forth upon the scene of action full grown from the darkness of the past, and he disappears, at the close of his career, in a chariot of fire.

The sacred chroniclers, who are so careful in genealogies, tell us nothing of the parentage of Elijah. His name is announced without father or mother, without beginning of days or end of life. It is now twenty-eight hundred years since he disappeared without dying, and the devout in Israel to this day still expect his return. They still place a seat for him in their solemn feasts, and set the door open for the prophet to come in.

The word Tishbite, so often applied to his name, gives us no information, for nobody knows what it

means. Of one thing only can we be certain in respect
to his origin. He came from the wild and mountain-
ous land of Gilead. From the abrupt western wall of
its pasture-grounds the shepherd looked down three
thousand feet into the twisted and terrible gorge of
the Jordan. Eastward it rose in rounded peaks and
broken ridges, like the frozen billows of a stormy sea.
The whole region was tossed into such wild and fan-
tastic forms as to seem as if it had been the battle-field
of giants, where

"hills encountered hills,
Hurled to and fro with jaculation dire."

The strongholds of robber chieftains crowned the
heights; the wandering shepherds pitched their tents
in the valleys. The native inhabitants lived as if in a
hostile country, and the herdsmen kept their flocks
with spear and bow day and night. They knew noth-
ing of towns or villages, cultivated fields or gardens.
As they roamed from valley to valley, in search of
pasturage, the plunderer might swoop down upon
them like the eagle from the heights, or spring upon
them like the couchant lion from the jungle. Vigi-
lance was the price of safety, and the strong arm was
the only law. The wolf and the bear made their dens
among the crags; the lion came up to prey upon the
fold from the swellings of Jordan.

In one of these wild gorges, where a furious torrent
comes leaping down the rocky terraces of the highlands,
Jacob wrestled all night with the mysterious stranger

13

on his return from Padan-aram. In these haunted and terrible solitudes, the Spirit of the Lord came upon Jephthah, and made him the deliverer of Israel in the days of the judges. In this wild region of exiles and outlaws, David took refuge from the unnatural rebellion of his son Absalom. The whole country was repeatedly overrun by raids from the east, the north and the west, and no sooner had the scattered inhabitants satisfied the rapacity of one plunderer than they were exposed to the exactions of another.

Whether Elijah lived as an exile or a native among such a people we do not know. But he shared their home and learned their habits of living. He had been accustomed to the savage and solitary life of herdsmen and mountaineers. He had met the roving bands of robbers on their raids, and the beasts of prey in their native haunts. He had watched all night upon the lonely hill-tops, and he had slept where deadly serpents made their dens. The fierce sun of the Syrian heavens had bronzed his brow, and poured its burning fires into his dark eye, till he became a man for kings and warriors to look upon and tremble. He had climbed rocky heights and battled with storms, and traversed the wilderness till his frame was like iron. He could walk with a firm step upon the dizzy brink of cliffs where the wild goats could not climb. He could run before the chariots without resting, and lead the way for the horsemen on foot until horse and rider were weary of the race. He would have been remembered as a Hercules or a Samson in strength, if he had not been the first of the prophets in faith and inspiration.

On the evening of a day of exhausting toil and terrible excitement, he trenched the earth and piled up the twelve stones of a great altar and offered a whole bullock in sacrifice, and slew eight hundred and fifty priests of Baal with his own hand, and offered in the solitude of the mountain his seven times repeated supplications for rain, and then ran before the flying chariot of Ahab fifteen miles from Carmel to Jezreel over a slippery, miry road, in the midst of a tremendous storm. He could traverse the desert like an Arab, sleep on the bare earth where the night found him without a covering, lodge for months in the rocky bed of a dry torrent, live as a fugitive and an outlaw in the wilderness until the ravens became his daily visitors and the wild beasts were more familiar than the face of man.

And yet in the deep loneliness of such a life, Elijah looked on himself as standing ever in the presence of the Lord of hosts. Amid all the perils and hardships to which he was exposed, he never forgot his sacred commission as the servant of the Most High. Everybody knew him when he made his sudden and startling appearances in the desert, on the hill-top, in the highway or by the Great Sea. The awful solemnity of his look made men fear that he had come as an avenging angel to call their sins to remembrance. But no one could tell whence he came, where he hid himself, or how his life was sustained. The inspired instructor and reprover of apostate Israel was trained for his mission amid awful solitudes. He was kept apart from the gentle charities and tender affections of domestic life. He was wet with the dews of night, girt with the terrors of the wilderness, beaten by storms and burnt by the sun. He was made familiar with the sublimities and glories of nature, that he might the better assert the power and majesty of Jehovah in his works, and thus rebuke the Nature-worship of his time and confound all false gods.

No silver-tongued rhetorician, skilled in all the graces of speech and courtesy of manner, could fitly bring the word of the Lord to the proud and pagan queen, to the weak and wicked king. The time and the mission demanded a sterner speech, a more startling and defiant address, a more awful and commanding authority. And in Elijah the message found the man.

In all times of great public exigency, God raises up men and fits them to do his work. Sometimes the age most needs an earnest and alarming voice that shall cry day and night in the city and the wilderness, "Prepare ye the way of the Lord!" Sometimes there are wanted men of action, whose silent and ceaseless energy is the voice with which they arouse and shake the nations. Sometimes there is need of men with the courage of heroes and the faith of martyrs to hew down the thrones and temples of iniquity with the stroke of battle-axes, and to meet the armed forces of wrong on the bloody field. Sometimes the world's great want is the embodiment of active benevolence, the incarnation of pity and humanity, to carry light into the dark homes of sorrow, to speak peace and pardon in the dens and dungeons of vice and crime. Whatever the want of any age, God is sure to find men to meet its demands. It should be our great study to know what work he has for us to do, and to do it well.

Fresh and fearless from the mountains of Gilead, Elijah remembered the history which Israel had forgotten. The deliverance from Egypt by a strong hand; the march through the waves of the divided sea; the guiding pillar of cloud and fire that went before the countless host; the bread from heaven that failed not for forty years; the mount of the law veiled in darkness and girt with its coronet of fire; the allotment of Canaan to the conquering tribes; the pomp and solemnity of the tabernacle and temple worship; the oracular responses from the mercy-seat; the brightness of the Shechinah shining in the Holy Place; the Divine messages that had been given to Samuel and David and Solomon,—Elijah knew them all. And he believed that the apostate house of Ahab and of all Israel was as much in the hand of the living God as were their fathers in the wilderness.

The priests of Baal had set up the worship of Nature

on every high place and under every green tree. The heathen Jezebel had imported the lascivious rites of Ashtaroth, the Sidonian Venus, from her home by the Great Sea. The people had been taught that these pagan deities ruled the elements of earth and fire and water by their mystic spells. But Elijah still believed that the sun and the clouds, the hills and valleys, the streams and the fountains were in the hands of Jehovah, the God of Israel, as they were when Moses smote the rock in the wilderness and living waters gushed out—as they were when Joshua commanded and the sun stayed from going down, and Samuel prayed and the Lord sent thunder and rain in the time of harvest.

Now at length a trial of terrible severity and of long continuance must be made. The wicked sovereign and the deceived people must be brought to recognize the power and sovereignty of their fathers' God. There must be a distinct and positive committal of the word of the prophet, that all may know by whose authority he speaks. For this purpose Elijah suddenly presents himself before Ahab. His court dress is the shaggy sheepskin mantle which had been his covering day and night, in storm and sunshine, among the mountains of Gilead. His flowing locks are such as had given him the name of the "hairy man" when seen striding, with wild and rapid pace, over the hills and along the solitary footpaths, attracting the wondering gaze of shepherds and villagers as he passed. He stands before the passionate and guilty king, and he utters a word of woe which we should suppose would doom him to instant death: "As the Lord God of Israel liveth, before whom I stand, there shall not be dew nor rain these years but according to my word."

The suddenness and the audacity of the declaration secure a momentary protection for the prophet. The startled monarch has not recovered from his surprise sufficiently to order his arrest, before the dread minister of the Divine vengeance has disappeared and can be nowhere found. This awful man, who can chain the clouds and imprison the winds and make the heavens as brass, has come out of his solitude into the ivory palace of Samaria, and spoken a word of vengeance which shall fall like consuming fire upon every family in the nation. Having delivered his message, he has passed on unchallenged, unmolested, leaving the king dumb and paralyzed with astonishment. Elijah has locked up the treasures in the whole kingdom of nature, and "carried off the key."

And now let apostate Ahab and pagan Jezebel make full proof of the power of their gods to unsay the prophet's word. They have altars and priests and sacrifices to the sun and moon and all the host of heaven. They have consecrated temples and groves and shrines and images to the brooks and rivers, to the falling rain and the gentle dew, to the fruits of the earth, the revolving seasons and all the secret powers of nature. They are many, and against them all the bare word of Elijah stands alone. Let them take their time.

The prophet of Jehovah is safe and he can wait.   If
they can make the heavens give rain, or if the ordi-
nary course of nature goes on of itself, then the word of
the Lord has not come by Elijah.   If Baal can clothe
the fields with verdure, if he can bring forth the har-
vest in its season, then let the king worship him and
let all the people say he is God.

Elijah must have been a man of great faith to be
willing to stake his very life upon the truthfulness of
what he had spoken.   Still, he was a man of like pas-
sions with us.   In him were all the human elements
of fear and doubt and infirmity which we find in our-
selves.   The inspiration of the Most High did not take
from him all temptation to suppress or reserve or
qualify the message.   It was easy for him to question
whether it could be the word of the Lord which com-
manded him to threaten such an awful calamity upon
the people of Israel.   He could see many natural indi-
cations to the contrary.

Coming over from Gilead to Samaria, he passed
Salim and Enon with their gushing fountains of water.
He crossed the fertilizing brooks and the marshy plains
of Beth-shan.   Looking forth from the palace of Ahab,
he could survey the green hills of Samaria, and the
excellency of wooded Carmel, and the teeming plain
of Jezreel, and the flowery fens of the Kishon.   On
the north and east were Little Hermon and Tabor and
Gilboa, fountains of perpetual streams.   Every wind-
ing brook and every green hill, every grove on the

heights and every cloud on the distant sea, would say to his doubting heart: "No, this land cannot be burned with drought nor wasted with famine. No word of thine can forbid the heavens to give showers or the earth to bring forth fruit. It cannot be the word of the Lord which puts the rain and the dew in thy power. Speak it not, lest evil come upon thee and the wicked mock at thy delusion."

So would Elijah's doubting heart say to him all the way as he came down from Mount Gilead into the gorge of the Jordan, and then climbed up the western hills and passed over into the luxuriant vale of Jezreel, to speak the word of the Lord to Ahab. So might he doubt whether his prayer of imprecation could shut up the heavens and change that garden into a desert. But he resisted the doubt. He obeyed the Divine voice which sent him forth at the peril of his life to stand before Ahab. If it cost him his life, he would show his apostate people that Jehovah was God in Israel, and all the gods of Jezebel and Zidon were vanity.

And the word of the Lord which enjoins a great and perilous duty is the one which we are most likely to receive with doubts and fears. We must not defer our obedience till every shadow of uncertainty and every possibility of mistake is removed. The doubt that demands perfect knowledge will never yield to faith, for faith rests upon probability, not demonstration. There is no scientific ground of faith, simply because what has become science is taken out of the sphere of faith. We must obey the voice of duty when there are many other voices crying against it, and it requires earnest heed to distinguish the one which speaks for God. We must cherish the impulse of conscience in the moment when it urges us to action, lest it cease from its promptings and we be left to the blind guidance of appetite and passion.

The word of the Lord comes to us all, and it is a message of light and of salvation. If we wait for louder calls or better opportunities, the light may be withdrawn and our path left to us in darkness. No man can tell how much he may lose by once neglecting to comply with the call of God's Spirit and word commanding him to perform some great and sacred duty. Many would give everything they have in the world only to be put back for a moment to hear again the call which they once heard and neglected. The argument which almost convinces to-day, if rejected, may have less force to-morrow. To have better opportunities in the future we must improve the opportunities of the present with prompt and willing hearts.

Nothing will help us more in the discharge of duty than the feeling which made Elijah always speak of himself as standing before the Lord of hosts. Among the mountains of Gilead, in the deserts of Arabia, on the heights of Carmel, in the valley of the Jordan and in the palace of Ahab, he felt himself to be equally in the presence of Jehovah, and he would not do what would offend the eyes of the Eternal King. He had no fear before a human monarch, because his mind was holden by the more awful presence of a Sovereign whose empire is the universe and who holds in his hand the destinies of time and eternity. To him the cave of Cherith was a holy place. The humble dwelling of the widow of Zarephath was a sanctuary. The solitudes of Horeb were vocal with praise. The long journey, barefoot and alone, over burning deserts and barren mountains, was a walk with God. In every place he felt himself to be the servant of the Most High, doing the bidding of a Sovereign higher than all the kings of the earth.

Let us in like manner cultivate the feeling that in every place we stand before the Lord, in every plan and work we are doing the will of the Most High, in every trial we are upheld by his hand, in every affliction we are comforted by his word; and then the whole of life will have a meaning and a sacredness which earthly honors can never give and worldly loss can never take away.

Everything is just and honorable which God commands to be done. Every service, every sacrifice which he requires is its own reward. The thoughts of the heart and the words of the lip, and all the acts of the outward life, will be most worthy and appropriate when the presence of the Infinite One is most deeply felt.

The first murderer " went out from the presence of

the Lord." All wrong-doing is a departure from God.
The wayward child leaves his father's house and is
lost amid the temptations of the world. The gay and
thoughtless forsake God's sanctuary and find no rest
in the pursuit of earthly joy. The fool says in his
heart, "There is no God," and he is left to believe the
falsehood which he wishes were truth. So all evil in
life and character follows as a consequence when man
forgets that he is ever in the presence of the Lord of
hosts. The pure in heart see him and are safe. The
believing have confidence in his help and are strong.
The righteous shelter themselves beneath the shadow
of his throne in the day of trouble, and so abide the
fury of the storm.

Go not out from the presence of the Lord. In
every place let your adoring heart be ready to say,
"Lo! God is here." So shall your earthly home
become the audience-chamber of the King of kings.
Every walk in life shall be made as pure for you as
the path of light on which the ministering spirit flies
forth from the Eternal throne. In all the toils and
joys and afflictions of the world, you will be ready to
take up the wondering and adoring ascription of
heaven, "Holy, holy, holy, Lord God of hosts, heaven
and earth are full of thy glory!"

We left Elijah at the beginning of the years of
drought and famine. He has uttered his word of woe
in the presence of the wicked king, and gone. Ahab

tells his pagan queen Jezebel what he said, and she
only wishes that she had heard him too. She would
have seen to it that he should never utter any more
threats in Samaria. The priests of Baal hear of it,
and they curse the prophet of Jehovah by all the gods
of Tyre and Sidon. It is told all over the land, and
it awakens mingled emotions of fear and wrath, dis-
trust and expectation.

By and by, the shepherd finds that the brooks are
getting lower among the hills. The ploughman is
startled to see the earth dry in the bottom of his
furrow. The vintager looks at his vines, and turns to
the sky with increasing anxiety every morning. A
whole year passes and another begins, and there is no
rain. A second and a third is completed, and the
inexorable sky is still covered day and night with the
same dry and dusty haze, out of which no clouds form
and no dew falls. The sun grows red and dim as it
descends the western sky, and disappears an hour
before it reaches the horizon. The brightest stars
make only a faint blur of light here and there in the
zenith, and the outline of the distant hills is lost in the
lurid air. The flames of sacrifice burn red on all the
high places around Samaria and Jezreel, and the
priests of Baal make the night hideous with their cries.
But the clouds refuse to form, and no spells of the false
prophets can unsay Elijah's word.

The parched earth is all burnt over as with fire.
The once fruitful field becomes like ashes from the

furnace. The hot wind drains the moisture from the green leaf and the living flesh, and the suffocating dust-storm sweeps along the hills and highways like the simoom of the desert. The grass withers on the hill-sides and in the valleys. The harvest turns to stubble before it is half grown. The groves give no shade, and the trees of the forest stretch their skeleton arms in mute supplication to the pitiless sky. The weary and heart-broken shepherd leads his panting herd from valley to valley in search of water, and daily the bleating of flocks grows fainter among the hills.

The famine enters the homes of men. The feeble and the friendless die first, and the living in their despair have neither heart nor strength to bury the dead. The traveler drags his weary frame, fainting and slow, along the highway, without heeding the haggard and hollow-eyed victims of famine crying for food or murmuring of fountains and feasts in the delirium of death, beside his path. The mother turns with horror from the pinched and shrunken face of her once beautiful babe, and the father feels a bitter satisfaction when he returns from the field and finds that the mouths for which he has brought no food will cry no more. The cruel drought dries up all the fountains of feeling, and the fierce instinct of self-preservation sunders all ties, crushes all pity, and makes men meet each other with the hungry and haggard look of the wolf haunting the fold or the lion ravening for his prey.

And all this terrible calamity was brought upon Israel in mercy to save them from the worse evil of denying and forsaking their fathers' God. Healthful seasons and abundant harvests can do little for individuals or nations, when once they have lost faith in truth, in duty and in man's eternal responsibility to his Maker. Whatever it may cost them to recover that faith, they had better suffer it all than live without God and prosper for a time in wickedness and unbelief.

There is something worse for individuals and nations than drought and famine. It is a worse thing to lose faith in God, in truth, in duty. It is a worse thing to be given up to the love of money, and the indulgence of ease and a life of pleasure. It is a worse thing never to possess those treasures which can be given only to the benevolent, the self-denying and the pure in heart. If only our consciences are clean and our hearts right before God, earthly calamity will prove a blessing—trial and suffering will make us strong. It is the ruin of too many that they set their hearts upon having all their good things in their lifetime. Truth, principle, conscience are the best things to possess—the favor of God is the best thing to enjoy.

So Elijah believed, and strong in that faith he waited through the long and terrible years of the famine for the heart of his apostate people to be turned back again by affliction. "And it came to pass after many days that the word of the Lord came to Elijah in the third year, saying, Go show thyself unto Ahab; and I will send rain upon the earth."

With him, to receive the word of the Lord was to obey. He had been outlawed and hated and hunted down by all the power of the king for three years, and the whole nation had been put under oath that the prophet could be nowhere found. And now, unbidden by the king, without explanation or apology, Elijah comes forth from his seclusion. Himself assuming to be the monarch, he sends a messenger to say, " Behold! Elijah is here." If Ahab wants to see him, he can come. The prophet will not go to him. And when the king makes haste to come, Elijah demands a solemn convocation of all Israel and of the prophets of Baal at Carmel. For three years Ahab had been sending spies through all the land of Israel and the neighboring kingdoms to find Elijah, that he might put him to death ; and now that he meets him face to face the passionate king is so awed and unmanned by the presence of the prophet that he only obeys at once when commanded, as if Elijah were king and Ahab were the subject and slave.

Swift couriers are sent throughout all the kingdom with the summons, and every village and family gladly sends its representative to the great assembly. All who have strength for the journey are in haste to answer the call of Elijah and the word of the king. The place of gathering was already sacred, and it was in sight of a large portion of the kingdom. The highways and the footpaths among the hills are alive with people moving in one direction. Clouds of dust arise and darken the sultry air, as the long lines of the gathering multitude stream across the great plain of Jezreel toward the wooded heights of Carmel. Jezebel's eight hundred and fifty prophets of Baal and Astarte march out in one body from their great temple, like a regiment of soldiers moving to battle, with banners flying and flushed with the hope of victory. At last a blaze of bright spears and burnished shields flashes across the plain, and the dust-cloud rolls as if caught in a whirlwind where the chariot of Ahab passes swiftly, with panting footmen running before and galloping horsemen riding behind. And when the sun goes down, an innumerable multitude are encamped on the eastern slope of the wooded mountain, waiting some great and awful decision on the morrow.

When the day is fully come, and the morning sun struggles through the murky air on the east, a sudden murmur runs through the great encampment—there is a flowing in of the straggling multitude toward one central position—for, behold! Elijah, with awful look and shaggy mantle, is there. The one man on whom a whole kingdom had laid the weight of its desolation and its agony, stands before them unterrified, defenceless, alone!

On the highest ridge of the mountain, where the altar of Jehovah had once stood and had been thrown down, in full view of the great plain and the temple

14

of Baal at Jezreel, and the high places of idolatrous worship around Samaria, the prophet comes forth and takes his stand. All down the wooded slope of the mountain, under the shade of oaks and olive trees, in orchards and gardens are gathered the thousands of the people, waiting with breathless awe and expectation to catch the first word from the lips of the man who ever spoke as in the presence of the Lord of hosts. Nearer, and hemmed in by the multitude around a fountain of water which flows to this day, are the false prophets and their patron king.

In the open light of day, under the broad canopy of heaven, with eager thousands to see and to hear, Elijah cries aloud, "How long halt ye between two opinions? If Jehovah be God, follow him: but if Baal, then follow him." But there is not one in all the multitude that dares to utter an approving word or give a sign of assent to a proposition so plain. Again the lonely prophet of Jehovah speaks, and challenges the priests of Baal to join with him in rearing two altars and laying on the sacrifice, and each calling upon their own object of worship, and the God that answereth by fire let him be God. And now the people are emboldened to answer, "The word is good."

The priests of Baal cannot escape the trial. They rear their own altar, lay on the wood and the victim, and then they begin to chant and howl, in the wild orgies of idolatrous worship, until the whole forest of Carmel resounds with their cries, "Oh Baal, hear us!"

They surround their altar like a legion of demons, with a whirling and giddy dance, leaping up and down, tossing and tearing their many-colored and fantastic robes, growing more rapid and furious in their motions and more wild and frantic in their cries as the slow hours of the morning pass on and the sultry noon comes and there is no voice nor any that answers. It is past midday, and still, hoping to gain time and find some device or sleight of hand by which the fire can be kindled, they continue their cries, cutting their flesh, leaping over the altar, staining their faces and their garments with their blood, howling and foaming with frantic excitement, making the whole mountain resound with the demoniac chorus of eight hundred hoarse and screaming voices, mingling curses with their prayers to their pitiless sun-god for the answer of fire, and still it does not come.

All the while Elijah stands alone, waiting and knowing full well that if by any deceit or cunning they should kindle the altar the people will join with them in tearing him in pieces on the spot. He even provokes and goads them on, telling them to call louder that their god may be awaked. But all in vain for the frantic and fainting priests of Baal. There is none to answer nor any that regards. The people are weary of the vain repetitions and terrible demonism of idolatry.

And now it is time for Elijah to take his turn. Again he lifts up his voice, and the people crowd to hear. The maddened priests of Baal, reeking with blood, exhausted with their own frenzy, sink in silence on the ground. With calm and solemn deportment, Elijah rebuilds the altar of Jehovah with twelve stones, according to the number of the tribes of Israel, lays on the wood and the victim for the sacrifice, and then causes it to be flooded with water three times over. And then, at the hour of the evening sacrifice, the prophet stands forth alone and calls upon the name of Jehovah, the everlasting God. The great multitude are pale and breathless with awful expectation while he speaks. His calm and simple prayer and his peaceful deportment are more impressive than the foaming fury and the wild cries of a thousand priests of Baal.

No sooner has he spoken than the rushing flame descends from the clear heavens like the lightning's flash, and the very stones of the altar are burnt up with the devouring fire. The sudden blaze blinds the eyes of the multitude and illumines the whole slope of the mountain with a light above the brightness of the sun. The people watching afar off, on the house-tops in Jezreel and Samaria, and on the hills of Ephraim and Galilee, are startled at the sight. It seems to them as if the pillar of fire that led their fathers in the desert had descended upon Carmel. The multitude on the mountain fall on their faces to the ground, unable to look upon the great light, and they cry with one voice, "Jehovah is God! Jehovah is God!" In the wild excitement of the moment they rush upon the false prophets with one accord, drag them down to the river Kishon, and there Elijah himself, the terrible and strong servant of Jehovah, slays them with his own hand, according as it had been commanded in the law of Moses. The ancient Kishon ran blood all the way to the sea, and the slain worshipers of Baal were piled in heaps higher than all the altars they had reared to their false god.

And now that the people have confessed their father's God and the false prophets are slain, it is time for the rain to come and for the parched earth to revive again with returning life. Elijah goes up from the terrible sacrifice to the top of the mount in such a mood that he can still pray. He continues his supplications until his servant has come six times from his outlook over the sea to say that there was nothing in sight but the glassy, heaving wave and the coppery, cloudless sky where the sun had gone down. At the seventh time, he can only say that there is a handful of mist hanging on the horizon, as if a sea-bird had shaken the spray from her wing in the air. But it is enough. Elijah, to whom all signs and aspects of the clouds and sky have been familiar from his youth, can already hear the sound of the coming tempest.

And now the prophet warns Ahab to hasten down to the plain and mount his chariot and drive swiftly, lest the blinding storm and the swollen stream of the Kishon make it impossible for him to reach Jezreel

that night.   And then, after all the terrible excitement
and exhausting toil of that day, this strange and strong
man, Elijah, girt his rough mantle close about his loins,
took his stand before the chariot of the king, and ran
all the way, fifteen miles, across the plain, through
darkness and wind and mire and a deluge of rain,
before the flying horses of the king, to the gate of the
city, and then, like an Arab of modern times, he would
not go in, but stayed outside the walls and cast himself
upon the bare earth, in the midst of the storm, for his
night's repose.   The prophet had put the king to
shame before his people at Carmel, and he ran before
his chariot as an act of homage to show that he still
acknowledged him as his sovereign.   He who could
call down fire from heaven, and bring the clouds and
the rain, was still willing to perform the menial ser-
vice of running in the rain and darkness before the
chariot of his king.

We should suppose that no threat or violence could
terrify such a man in the least.   After having faced
the king, the false prophets and the people, and com-
pletely triumphed over them all in a contest of life
and death, we should suppose that he would be just
the man to awe the furious queen in her own palace
and rebuild the altar of Jehovah in the capital of the
kingdom.

But no.   That very night, in the midst of the
darkness and the storm, a messenger came out from
the city gate, roused the weary prophet from his first

slumber, and shouted into his ear the oath of Jezebel, sworn by all the gods of Tyre and Sidon, that before another sun had set she would do unto him as he had done unto the prophets of Baal. We wait to hear in what terms this iron-hearted saint and hero will hurl back his defiance upon the queen in the name of the Lord of hosts.

But instead of that he rises like one terrified by a dream and not yet fully awake. Wet, cold, begrimed with mud and his garments still dabbled with gore, he springs to his feet, looks this way and that for a moment and then flees for his life. Over the hills of Samaria and the mountains of Ephraim, up and down the stony paths of Bethel and Gibeon, along the bed of the wild valleys west of Jerusalem and Bethlehem, and then out upon the plain of Sharon to Beersheba, he hurries like some conscience-smitten murderer who sees the avenger of blood behind him in every shadow.

Nor does he dare to rest, even in the farthest town of the kingdom of Judah. Leaving his only attendant behind him, without guide or provision for the way, he starts out in the early morning upon the waste and lifeless desert. All day long he toils over the broken hills and barren plains of yellow sand and bare earth. The dead uniformity of desolation stretches in every direction to the horizon. No living thing moves upon the earth or flies in the hot and glimmering air. Now and then a suffocating blast sweeps over the horrible wilderness, and the shining sand rises and whirls in waves and columns of fire. And still he presses silently on till the sun goes down and the stars come out in the sky. Then, finding a low, solitary bush of desert-broom, he casts himself beneath it, weary, hungry, and in such complete despair that he would rather die than live.

Such is the reaction which not unfrequently follows the most daring effort and the most dazzling success. Such is the despondency that sometimes presses hard upon the most sublime and heroic faith in the purest and noblest minds.

Peter drew his sword against a multitude in defence of his Master, and the next hour he was frightened out of all faith and courage by the scornful finger of a little maid.

Paul was caught up to the third heaven in visions of glory and Paradise, and he heard words of wondrous and ineffable meaning, such as cannot be spoken to ears of flesh and blood; and then, soon after, the same favored apostle was praying with thrice-repeated and beseeching supplication to be delivered from some common and petty annoyance, such as tries the temper and disturbs the peace of every one of us every day of life.

The Christian Pilgrim, in Bunyan's truthful and ingenious allegory, lodged in the palace Beautiful and slept in the chamber called Peace. In the morning he saw the Delectable Mountains and Immanuel's land from the housetop. He started forth upon his journey harnessed from head to foot in armor of proof. And yet he had gone but a little way before "he began to be afraid, and to cast in his mind whether to go back or to press on." The beautiful vision and the fair prospect of the morning were followed by the valley of Humiliation and the most desperate and agonizing conflict with Apollyon.

The young disciple of Christ rejoices in the freshness of his first love, and he feels that he would gladly go to the ends of the earth for his new Master. Frank and fearless in his faith and zeal, he is ready to speak out his overflowing joy to everybody, and only wonders that all others should not feel just as he does. By and by he meets a repulse from an unexpected quarter. His feelings suddenly change; he distrusts his best convictions, and his despondency becomes as extreme as were his hope and joy.

In the high day of health and prosperity a Christian man of business gives his money and time and effort with cheerfulness and constancy for the cause of Christ. He has many friends; his look is full of sunshine; he infuses hope and life into everything he undertakes. By and by he loses health, loses property, loses his vivacity and hopefulness. Then his friends fall off; he slides out of his former social connections; he ceases to be recognized by some who once eagerly sought his friendship. Then he desponds, takes gloomy views of everything, judges others with severity, blames his best friends, is still more dissatisfied with himself, and finally falls into the habit of saying that he has nothing to live for.

In the ardor of youth and the tireless energy of manhood the Christian soldier enlists under the standard of the cross. He storms the strongholds of sin; he inspires others with his own burning zeal; he gains great victories; he has many to bless him for their rescue from the bondage of sin and death. But he does not accomplish all that he would. Many times he finds the forces of the enemy too strong for him. Many times he is left to bear the brunt of the conflict alone, and when his noblest efforts fail of success he is blamed by his best friends. By and by, he loses his ardor, his hope, his courage. He becomes cautious, conservative, distrustful, suspicious, and finally settles down into inactivity and complaint.

A gifted and faithful minister of the gospel labors on with great energy and success for many years, while his health is firm, and his mind active, and his feelings warm, and his imagination teems with glowing imagery, and his iron frame never complains of exhaustion or work or pain. As long as he can do all that, he is full of hope—he has troops of friends—he can meet them all with a smile. But by and by, his step begins to falter, his eye grows dim, the wheels of life move heavily, the mind loses something of its vivacity and invention, the voice does not ring out as clear and clarion-like as it once did; he cannot catch the salient and soul-stirring forms of appeal, as he once could.

And now he sees plainly that he is losing the magnetic power of drawing people to him. His friends fall away from him one by one, and others do not come to fill their place. The attention that was once bestowed on him is given to others. He must stand aside and somebody else must fill his place. He must submit to see others increase and himself decrease. He must be blamed because he is not prompt enough in taking himself out of the way. And not unfrequently that trial proves too great for one who has been the very foremost among his brethren for every excellence of mind and heart. He whom everybody loved and admired in his prime finds it hard to be only pitied and forsaken in his infirmity and age. The closing years of life are darkened with despondency, and many times before he is called away he says, with Elijah, " It is enough. I have ceased to be of any use in the world. It is better that I should die than live."

So the sick, the weary the worn-out, the aged, the disappointed are in danger of feeling, even if they do not allow themselves so to speak. And we must prepare ourselves for such experiences beforehand, that we may meet them with patience and serenity when they are sent upon us. Elijah's despondency was the more violent and depressing just because he seemed to be upon the point of overthrowing idolatry and revolutionizing the nation, and then soon found himself a fugitive and ready to die in the desert. And all failure is bitter and hard to bear when it follows close on the reality or the great hope of success. The man who has worked hardest and done most in the service of God is the one who finds it hardest to be laid aside by age or sickness or the diversion of public attention to, others.

We must make up our minds to this, that the world can go on without us, and that God's work will prosper better when we are out of the way than it ever did in our hands. However much his cause may lose by the removal of one and another, it is destined to wax stronger and stronger. The little vacancy made in the ranks of the living by our departure will be filled before it is felt. But as long as God keeps us in the world it is for a great and a good purpose, and he will always give us something to do. We have never done enough so long as there remains anything to be done. God has work for the aged, the afflicted, the suffering, the disappointed, the helpless, the poor. The greatest work ever done in this world was done by One who was called a man of sorrows, and who had not where to lay his head. The greatest success ever gained in this world was called a failure at the time, and the greatest victory was thought by men to be an utter and shameful defeat.

When we are most weary and discouraged, and the world seems a desert, God's angel may be on the wing to bring us messages of mercy from the throne. Whatever seeming failures and disappointments we may experience, it is never time for us to fling ourselves down in despair and say, " It is enough." What we call failure may be Divine success with God, and our sorest defeat may be the preparation for the most glorious triumph. Elijah's night of despair in the desert, and his long contest with an apostate king and backsliding people, made him the man to be taken to heaven in a chariot of fire.

It is not the chief end of man to achieve what the world will applaud as success. It is our main business in life to show ourselves true men, loving righteousness, hating evil, and willing to take such measure of present happiness and success as flows from obedience to the truth. There is unconquerable strength which begins with the confession of weakness. There is a serene and lofty repose of soul which is reached alone through conflicts and through scars. There is a pure and sacred joy which springs from the deepest sorrow and suffering. The great loss which we have most need to deplore is the loss of earnestness to do right, the loss of strength to resist temptation, the loss of faith in the everlasting principles of truth and duty. The poorest man in the world has something to live and to die for so long as he preserves the integrity of his own conscience. The most successful man in the world is the man who gives himself most earnestly to the cause of God and truth, and who never bates one jot of heart or hope in his good work, whatever difficulties and delays he may have to meet.

Take courage, then, when the burden is heavy and the work moves slow, and the temptations and conflicts to be met are many and strong. Never say "It is enough," long as you have one wrong disposition in your own heart to subdue—long as there is one soul to be benefited by your effort or example—long as patience and faith and love and devotion to duty are the great lessons to be taught and learned—long as God says he will never forsake the soul that trusts in him and seeks his aid—long as the crown of life is offered only to him that overcometh. Never say it is enough! But toil on, pray on, hope on, and always believe that while life lasts there is something to do to prepare yourself and others for the better life to come.

Jonah's Night at Nineveh.

So Jonah went out of the city, and sat on the east side of the city, and there made him a booth, and sat under it in the shadow, till he might see what would become of the city. . . . And it came to pass, when the sun did arise, tha God prepared a vehement east wind; and the sun beat upon the head of Jonah, that he fainted, and wished in himself to die, and said, It is better for me to die, than to live.—Jonah iv. 5, 8.

X.

JONAH'S NIGHT AT NINEVEH.

THE prophet Jonah lived in the time of Jeroboam the Second, about 850 years before Christ. The book which bears his name in the Bible was doubtless written by the man himself. It sets the faults of his character before us in the most glaring light, and it takes no pains to explain or excuse his conduct. Such a record could have come only from one who was honest enough to confess his own errors, and sincere enough to desire that others might profit by his mistakes.

The one prophecy of his which has been preserved twenty-seven centuries for our instruction is embraced in the single sentence: " Yet forty days and Nineveh shall be overthrown." He was commanded to arise and go a perilous and weary journey of five hundred miles, over rugged mountains, through pathless wildernesses, across burning deserts, on foot, defenceless and alone, and to deliver that awful message in the name of Jehovah, the God of Israel, in the very streets of the doomed and idolatrous city itself. In obeying that command, he must cross rivers without a bridge or a boat; he must find his way through mountain passes without a map or a guide; he must travel in the track and sleep in the haunts of robbers and wandering tribes, without a present to buy their protection or a guard to resist their violence. He must climb the cedar-crowned Lebanon and face the chilling blasts from the snowy heights of Hermon. His sandaled feet must sink in the mire of the marsh, and his fevered brow must burn in the hot wind of the desert. He must follow the march of armies on the highway of nations, and he must trace the path of the wolf and the bear in the jungle.

And when all the toils and dangers of the long journey are escaped, he must show himself with his "one rough garment of haircloth," and with the strange accents of a foreign tongue within the walls of that vast Eastern capital, which the prophet Nahum describes as a great and bloody city, full of lies and robbery; in the streets of which the chariots rage like flaming torches, and jostle against each other in the broad ways and run like the lightnings; that great city, within whose walls the speechless babes that know not the right hand from the left count a hundred and twenty thousand; that rich and proud city whose merchants are multiplied above the stars, and whose princes and captains and warriors are like the swarming locusts in number; that violent and cruel city, by whose myriad population the stranger prophet from Palestine may be trodden down in the streets and his body cast from the gates as a prey for the jackals of night, and no one ask who he was or what was the object of his coming.

In the midst of that proud and conquering people, whose wickedness has come up before Jehovah, must this lonely messenger appear with no fiery sword of attending angels for his guard, no avenging thunder at his command to confirm his word ; and he must declare, without the least reserve or equivocation, that within forty days the imperial city shall be overthrown. In so short a time shall the glory of kingdoms, the tyrant and the terror of vanquished millions, be made a mockery ; her princes and nobles brought down to the dust ; her people scattered upon the mountains or buried in her ruins ; and the delivered nations shall clap their hands over her fall with mingled contempt and congratulation.

" Alas !" we seem to hear the prophet exclaim in terror and anguish of spirit—" Alas ! that this awful word of the Lord should come to me ! Let him send by whom he will send, I cannot bear the message." And so, for once in all the sacred record, we have a recreant prophet, fleeing from the call of duty, as Jonah rises up to go to Tarshish from the presence of the Lord. Fainting with fear and wild with anguish of spirit, he hurries from his home in distant Galilee, a journey of seventy miles, to Joppa, that he may there take ship and call to his aid the wings of the wind, and hide himself at the utmost extremity of the Great

Sea from Him from whose face the beams of the morning cannot fly—whose presence would still be with him though he should make his bed in hell.

When a little babe, nestling in his mother's bosom, she named him her "Dove," as if with a prophetic intimation of his subsequent character. And now a man, like that timorous bird he flees from the distant sound of danger, and he seeks some covert in which to hide himself till it is past. Alas! unhappy man, though a prophet of the Most High, he has yet to learn that the universe has not a hiding-place for the concealment of the fugitive from duty and from God. It will take the terrors of the sea and the thunders of the storm to teach him that lesson. He must go down to the bottoms of the mountains, and for three days and nights lie buried alive in the belly of hell, with all the billows of the great deep rolling over him, before he will be satisfied that the claim of duty is omnipresent like God, and that to flee from its voice is to rush upon destruction.

We justly blame the disobedient prophet for the moral cowardice which made him encounter worse dangers in fleeing from duty, than he would have met in facing its demands. But how many in our time, with far better opportunities, have not yet mastered the simple lesson which it cost Jonah so much to learn? The word of the Lord comes to multitudes in our day, and it is as a fire in their bones, and as a hammer upon their hearts, breaking the flinty rock in pieces.

It calls upon them to surrender all for Christ and to take up their cross and follow him. And they think it a hard message and they cannot receive it.

And so they flee from the sanctuary and shun the society of God's servants, and stifle their convictions in their shut and suffering hearts. The Christian life, as taught in the Divine message of the Gospel, seems to them a hard journey through parched deserts and over cold mountains, and with no congenial company by the way. And they dare not venture upon it. The word of the Lord must bring a lighter message, or they will seek some one to prophesy smooth things, or they will flee away in the hope to find some refuge where there is no bleeding Christ to burden them with his cross—no call of duty commanding them to suffer and to sacrifice all for his sake. They would face the sea and the storm, to find some Tarshish of pleasure, or business, or indolence, where the troublesome word of the Lord will never more awaken their fears, rebuke their sins or enforce their obligations.

Alas! mistaken men, they little think that there are no dangers so much to be dreaded as those which must be met in attempting to flee from duty. There is nothing in the universe to be feared by him who binds duty as a law upon his heart. But the tempests and the billows of perdition are in the path of him who would escape from God.

And so unhappy Jonah found it, while yet the desired refuge of Tarshish was a great way off, and

was never to be reached. He did indeed find a strong
ship, and he paid the fare for the long voyage in
advance, and he frankly told the shipmen why he was
going, that they might refuse him passage if they were
afraid to carry a fugitive from duty. And then he
went down and hid himself in the hold, and there,
wearied with his journey and stupefied with trouble, he
soon fell fast asleep. But no sooner is the ship started
upon its voyage than the word of the Lord, which
first disturbed the peace of Jonah's mind, is cast forth
upon the wind, and there is a mighty tempest upon the
sea. He sleeps while the elements of wrath and terror
are all awake around him, and he is already beset by
greater dangers than any he sought to escape by his
guilty flight.

There is nothing more awful than the indifference
or slumber of guilty men in the midst of the terrors
and afflictions which the Lord has sent upon them to
bring them to repentance. And here is the fugitive
Jonah, dreaming of a sure escape from an unwelcome
duty, and already hungry death is gaping upon him
with a thousand mouths, and he knows it not. No
ship can fly faster than God's ministers of vengeance
travel over land and sea in pursuit of the guilty. It
is all in vain that the affrighted mariners cast out the
rich cargo into the sea. The angry deep will not be
satisfied with such an offering. The clamorous waves
lift up their voices for a living prey. The disobedient

prophet is a heavier weight on the wings of the ship than all the wares in the hold.

The pagan seamen call upon their gods, but there is none to answer, or to deliver them from the wrath of Him who holds the sea in the hollow of his hand, who hath his way in the whirlwind and the storm, and who maketh the clouds the dust of his feet— before whose coming the mountains quake and the hills are melted, and whose voice alone can rebuke the sea and make it calm.

So the shipmaster comes at last, in terror and despair, to this strange passenger, whom he finds fast asleep down in the hold of the ship and all unconscious of the uproar around him. He alone is the cause of all the peril, and yet he knows it not till awakened by the cry of the captain: " What meanest thou, O sleeper? Arise! call upon thy God, if so be that God will think upon us, that we perish not." Desperate as was the condition of all, the pagan seamen seemed to think at last that it was better with Jonah than with them. For he had a threatening and a chastising God, who might perhaps show pity and save, but they had no God at all.

And now they begin to eye each other with dreadful suspicions that some one of their company may be a fugitive from justice, whom the angry elements will not suffer to escape. The restless eye and haggard face of the awakened prophet now remind the fearful mariners of what they already knew, but of which they thought nothing till the terrors of death encompassed them on every hand. For Jonah had frankly told them when he came on board that he fled from the presence of the Lord. While the sea was calm and soft winds blew them on their way, it was a trifling thing to those hardened men that their poor, troubled Hebrew passenger paid down the advance fare to Tarshish and in his agitation told them that he was trying to flee from the presence of the Lord. Then they counted it no concern of theirs who he was, or where he was going, or why he went, provided he paid in advance. He might settle his own controversy with his God in his own way, and they would pursue their own business in theirs, without any thought of the God of heaven, who made the sea and the dry land. But they soon found that it would not pay to help men in their disobedience to God. The terrors of the tempest soon made them throw their fair-weather philosophy and their indifference about Jonah's God overboard with the cargo, to lighten both the ship and their own consciences. And now they beseech this moody and melancholy man to pray unto his God, that they perish not.

Many a time have worldly and wicked men, on board a foundering vessel or in the dark hour of public or domestic affliction, gathered around a poor, imperfect, unfaithful servant of God and besought him to pray for them. They may cast off fear and restrain prayer themselves in the high day of prosperity. But when peril and sorrow and death come it is a relief, even to the worst of men, to hear prayer from the lips of any who can offer it. They will then say to the very man, whom at other times they ridiculed and despised, as said the shipmaster to Jonah in the midst of the storm, "Call upon thy God, if so be that he will look upon us in our trouble, and we perish not."

It was only necessary for the danger to become imminent and terrible for Jonah to show that he was not altogether a recreant or a coward. Good men not unfrequently shrink from trifling burdens or yield to petty temptations when the greater trial calls their faith into exercise and gives them the victory. And this fugitive prophet, fleeing from the presence of the Lord, is more ready to offer himself a sacrifice to appease the raging deep, now that the storm has overtaken him, than the seamen are to obey his word: "Take me up and cast me forth into the sea!" He can now look those hard-featured men in the face and say, "I fear and worship the God who stretched out the heavens and laid the foundations of the earth, and who rules the waves and the stormy winds with his word."

He now begins to feel the force of the lesson taught him from his mother's lips and breathed forth in his infant prayer, "All the terrors of the warring elements and the violence of numberless foes are less to be feared than disobedience to God." And now, strong in the recovery of that faith, the awakened prophet declares himself ready for the sacrifice for which the hungry waves yawn and the tempest clamors with a thousand voices. If he had begged to be spared, or if he had resisted those rough and 'reckless seamen, they would have flung him overboard as unhesitatingly as they had cast the merchandise into the sea. But the composure, the resignation of the offered victim, deprives them of all power to lay hands upon him. His entire freedom from fear makes those iron-hearted mariners afraid of him. And it was only after a more vigorous and vain effort to bring the ship to land, and not until they saw that the storm grew more and more violent, that they took up Jonah, with many prayers unto Jonah's God to be forgiven in what they were doing, and cast him forth "into the tumbling billows of the main," and then at last the sea ceased from its raging.

The astonished mariners are saved, and they offer sacrifices and thanksgivings in token of gratitude for their rescue. The clouds are dispersed from the face of the sky, the sun breaks forth with new glory and the deep smiles as joyously as if mariners had never found a grave beneath its billows.

But the recreant prophet, who had fled from the presence of the Lord to escape danger or to avoid a troublesome duty or to gratify his moody and passionate temper—where now is he? Down beneath the billowy mountains of the sea, the waters have compassed him about to the very soul. The floods have swallowed him up; the earth hath imprisoned him

with its stony bars beneath the bottoms of the moun-
tains and the monsters of the deep are the inmates of
his watery dungeon. But even there in the bowels of
leviathan, in the living belly of hell, the word of the
Lord finds him out. The call of duty is still louder
than all the voices of the sea. The waves cannot
drown him; the open jaws of destruction cannot devour
him till his duty is done. The abyss has no hiding-
place for the man who would conceal himself from the
Infinite Eye. The monster of the deep will vomit him
up on shore that he may learn henceforth to believe
that neither land nor sea will afford rest or even a
peaceful grave for the fugitive from duty and from
God.

We need not pause to ask how the life of a man
could be preserved for three days and nights in the
body of a sea-monster beneath the surface of the deep.
If we believe that the veritable word of the Lord came
to Jonah at his quiet home in Galilee, if we doubt not
that the same word sent forth a mighty tempest to
overtake the fugitive prophet on the sea, we shall not
find it any more irrational to believe that the same
Divine power could preserve him alive in his living
grave and cast him forth again by a mysterious and
miraculous resurrection upon the dry land. And we
must not busy ourselves so much with the mystery of
the story as to forget the one grand lesson which the
story teaches. And this is the lesson—all the elements
of terror and of power in the whole creation are less to

be feared than disobedience to Him whose word of love
and of law speaks in the secret place of every soul.

And now the Divine message comes again the second
time to this man who has been brought up from the
abyss of death that he may the better teach others
how dreadful a thing it is to disregard the word of the
Lord: "Arise, go unto Nineveh, that great city, and
preach unto it the preaching that I bid thee." Jonah
finds it easy to obey that word confirmed as it is now,
in its repetition to him, by all the terrors of the sea,
and by the remembrance of his three days' burial in
the belly of hell. The long journey of five hundred
miles and the hostile faces of the myriad multitude
in the streets of the great city are nothing to him com-
pared with the displeasure of God.

He girds his shaggy mantle close around him, slings
his leathern scrip upon his shoulders, takes his pro-
phet's staff in his hand and travels day after day with
the dreadful sound of the sea in his ears to urge him
on, and with the resolution of one who bears an urgent
and an awful message. At last the great city with its
lofty walls and its fifteen hundred towers appears upon
the distant plain. He approaches the open gate and
passes in among the throng unnoticed or only pitied
for his humble garb and haggard face. No one sus-
pects that he brings with him from his distant home a
word of woe that shall smite the heart of the great city
with terror and despair.

He begins in the early morning and he travels on a

whole day's journey within the circuit of the walls. On every hand he passes parks and pleasure gardens and palaces; magnificent temples, colossal images of winged bulls and lions with human faces, and all the most elaborate symbols of idolatrous worship. In every direction he sees warehouses stored with the merchandise of all nations; monuments and princely mansions, the master-pieces of invention and proficiency in every art; trophies and inscriptions commemorating victories gained in conflict with the mightiest foes; elephants, camels and dromedaries bearing burdens; chariots and horses running swiftly; soldiers marching and the multitude flowing, a living tide, through all the streets and squares.

And on, where the crowd gathers thickest and the uproar of business and toil and pleasure and lordly command is loudest, moves this one lonely man, uttering his one cry of woe, which is the more appalling for its melancholy and pitiless monotony: "*Od arbaim yom venineveh nehpâcheth;*" "yet forty days and Nineveh overthrown." Gradually the strange messenger arrests attention. The awful earnestness of his tone, the fire of God's inspiration in his eye stops the mouth of the reviler and divides the multitude before him wherever he chooses to go. His solitary cry is taken up and repeated by other voices till it has pierced every habitation and sounded in every ear. Gradually the loud laugh is hushed, the roar of business and pleasure dies away, the crowd in the streets, pale and panting with terror, glide silently to their homes. The cry of the prophet goes down into the lowest depths of the prison-house; it ascends through the marble gates of the palace, and the king on his throne hears it with as much consternation as the slave in the slime-pit and the criminal in his cell. This one man, who trembled at the bare name of Nineveh when five hundred miles away among the hills of Galilee, has conquered the great city by one day of prophecy. At the going down of the sun, the whole living population, from the monarch and nobles down to the very slaves and beasts in their stalls, are covered with sackcloth and ashes, and every human voice is crying mightily unto God, if peradventure he will turn from his fierce anger and the city perish not. So much can one man do with nothing but the word of the Lord in his mouth and courage to do God's will in his heart.

But, alas! how fickle and passionate is poor human nature, even when honored by the message of Jehovah and speaking by the spirit of Divine inspiration. The extraordinary success of this one day of preaching was too much for Jonah's intractable spirit to bear. Humble and obedient as he had been made by the terrors of the sea and the storm, all his old pride of heart was restored by safety and success. Forgetting that the very object of declaring the Divine threatening was that Nineveh might have opportunity to repent and be saved, he begins to fear that his word will not be fulfilled. In his angry desperation, he would rather die himself than outlive the forty days and see the threatened city still standing. He would rather see fire come down from heaven and consume or the earth open and swallow up a half million human beings alive, than that one should say to him in after time, "Thou camest all the way on that long and terrible journey to declare the doom of this city, and now, at the end of the appointed days, it is still standing!"

He has no word of hope for the fasting Ninevites, although he well knew that God is gracious and merciful, slow to anger, and of great kindness—forgiving iniquity and repenting of the evil threatened upon them that repent. He does not wish to have them repent lest they shall be saved. He was once afraid of them, and now that they tremble at his word he spurns and despises them in their misery. The sackcloth and ashes of their humiliation are an abomination unto him. Their cries unto the Lord madden him, for he is afraid that they will be heard, and if they are to live he would rather die himself.

At first he would flee from the presence of the Lord, and now he cannot bear the presence of those who repent and humble themselves at the word of the Lord. As the sun goes down and darkness comes on, he makes his way out of the city to a hill on the east, bends a few branches together as a covert from the dews of night and the sun by day, and there he sits alone, as miserable as a proud and angry man can be, waiting for the threatened vengeance to fall and im-

patient because it delays its coming. There he sits all
night long, hearing the wail of the great city, waiting
for the avenging thunders to crash from the skies or
the cataracts of fire to flame up from the abyss and
fulfil his prophecy. Having delivered his message he
might go home in peace. But no; he must stay and
see those proud towers leveled with the dust and
hear the last bitter cry of agony and death go up from
the overthrown city, and then he will be sure that no
one will ever taunt him with having uttered a vain
prophecy.

The night passes and the morning comes, and the
burning sun of noon pours its beams with maddening
fervor through the boughs of the hastily-constructed
booth, and there sits Jonah angry with himself and
with Providence, still waiting to see what would become
of the city. And now the Lord causes a new and
strange plant to spring up and spread its broad leaves
and thick branches over him to deliver him from his
grief. And the petulant prophet, who thought he
would rather die than not see the destruction of a city
with a half million inhabitants, is made exceeding
glad by the shade of a few green leaves. But the
friendly plant died the next day. And when the
parching wind of the East began to blow, and the sun
beat down upon the head of Jonah, he grew faint; and
again, out of all patience with himself and with every-
thing about him, he wished himself dead. He could
murmur and be angry for the gourd which grew in a

night and perished in a night, for that took away a little of his own personal comfort. But he could look with satisfaction upon the utter destruction of a half million human beings in the plain below him, for that would gratify his pride of character as a prophet and his natural prejudice as a Hebrew: "And God said to Jonah, Doest thou well to be angry for the gourd? And he said, I do well to be angry even unto death!"

The sacred record, with its sublime indifference to the gratification of mere curiosity when once the essential truth is told, says no more of Jonah. As we close the brief narrative, it seems as if this angry imprecation were his last words and he had his wicked wish in death. Nevertheless the book which bears his name could hardly have been written by any other hand than his, and that, too, after his restless spirit ceased from its anger and found peace in full acquiescence with God's better will.

The brief story of this strange prophet teaches, what all need to learn, that there is no escaping from the presence of the Lord. Every step upon the path which God forbids is a step toward destruction. Every advantage gained by disobedience to the word of the Lord is purchased only by exposure to infinite loss. Every moment of ease or self-indulgence secured by neglecting the Divine call to earnest and self-denying duty, sows the seed for harvests of sorrow and supplies fuel for the fires of endless remorse.

In the vision of the Apocalypse, four mighty angels

16

were seen holding back the four winds of the earth's perils and sorrows, and forbidding them to blow till God's servants were sealed and safe. And he who holds the powers and perils of the universe in his hand will ever make a safe path for his children through whatever watery deeps or burning deserts he commands them to pass. But he leaves the ministers of vengeance to pour all their tempests and thunders upon the dark way of transgression. Set it down, then, as a first article in your practical faith—*the servants of God are always safe.* The way of obedience to him, however hard and dark it may seem, is always the path of life.

The law of duty is supreme. It claims authority over reason and conscience, over talents and possessions, over everything that is greatest and noblest in man. It admits no rival, makes no abatement of its high demands, enters into no compromises with any opposing power. The voice of duty is the voice of God in our souls. Obedience to its claims brings us into living and personal agreement with the highest law in the universe. It lends greatness to the humblest occupation, crowns the lowliest position in life with glory and honor, brings man into alliance with God, associates him with plans and purposes that have existed in the infinite Mind from eternity, and which run on toward their appointed completion through all coming ages. In every act of duty we go out of ourselves, and beyond the narrow scope of present interest and selfish gratification. We become subjects of a kingdom that is universal and everlasting; we adopt principles of action which may be safely and wisely obeyed everywhere and for ever; we present the homage of our hearts to the supreme and eternal Sovereign; we do all in our power to fill his great empire with peace and blessedness.

A duty shunned or a duty delayed is a duty still. There is no Tarshish of business or pleasure or indolence where a man can hide himself from the infinite eye of Him whose word of command is the highest law for every soul. No man can cease to believe that he ought to do God's will. The excuses which men make for neglecting their duty cannot diminish their obligation. You may put off till to-morrow what conscience commands to-day. And when to-morrow comes with its cares and toils and temptations, it may be easier to defer again. But the obligation to serve God will not die or diminish its claims. As the Lord of hosts, in whose presence we all are, shall live, and as our souls shall live, so certainly will our obligation to serve him last as long as we have our being. We can no more flee from duty than we can flee from the presence of the infinite Jehovah. It is only by obedience to him that we can have peace.

You may not think so now. It may seem to you that much is to be gained and little to be lost by denying for the present God's claim upon your heart. But in that gentle whisper of duty, which you now so easily deny or suppress, is the very hiding of God's infinite power over you to make you happy or miserable for ever.

Duty done will make the voice of conscience sweet as the harps of heaven to your soul. It will make the cup of life run over with blessing. It will snatch the crown of victory from the hand of all-conquering death. Duty neglected will arm the voice of conscience with the terrors of the judgment to come. It will fill the secret chamber of the soul with reproaches and with the sentence of condemnation.

Think of this, O ye who have been neglecting duties till they are almost forgotten! They are duties still. And now in this gracious hour they all come back like God's angels of mercy, pleading for admission at the door of your hearts. If you continue to shut them out, they will be swift witnesses against you in the final day. Open the door and let them in. Give them a supreme command over your whole conduct. So shall every path of life be safe for your feet, and in the valley of the shadow of death you shall fear no evil.

The Night-Watch in Mount Seir.

He calleth to me out of Seir, Watchman, what of the night? Watchman, what of the night? The watchman said, The morning cometh, and also the night.—ISA. XX. LI, 12.

We turned aside through fantastic rocks, and encamped at last at the entrance of the pass, and waited for the morning: one isolated rock with an excavation inside indicated the regions we were approaching, apparently an outpost for a sentinel, perhaps the very one which the prophet had in his eye in that well-known text, " Watchman, what of the night ?"—STANLEY.

T. MORAN.   S. SARTAIN.

NIGHT WATCH IN MOUNT SEIR.

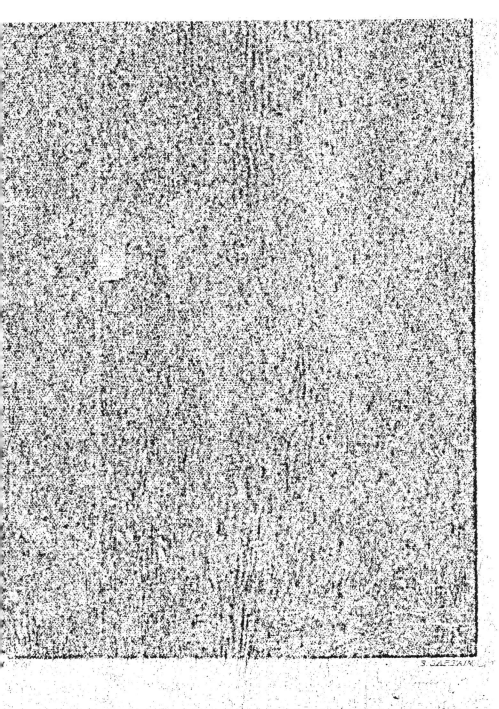

XI.

THE NIGHT-WATCH IN MOUNT SEIR.

THE voice that calleth out of Seir inquires for the signs of the waning night and the breaking dawn. The watchman that answers sees the promise both of continued darkness and of coming day. The double question and the doubting reply are well suited to the changing aspects of nature in a mountain land. To the inhabitants of such countries, inquiries for the winds and the clouds, the morning and the night, are as familiar as the words of daily salutation. And the variable condition of human society, the advance and decline of nations, the concealments and revelations of Providence, are well illustrated by the darkness and the day, the shadows and the sunshine among mountains.

Imagine a company of pilgrims encamped for the night in one of the narrow passes of those mountains of Seir out of which the voice of inquiry calls to the watchman of Israel. They are waiting impatiently for the coming dawn, that they may start upon their journey in the cool air of the morning, and reach their place of rest before the burning heat of noon comes on.

247

They turn with frequent and eager gaze to the quarter whence the light is to break. They wonder that the day is so long in coming, and the longer it delays, the more their imaginations are excited with the wildness and desolation around them. To them the jagged rock overhanging the narrow pathway looks like a grim giant ready to crush and trample upon the passing traveler. The solitary cedars crowning the rugged height seem like spectral sentinels set to guard the forbidden passes of the mountains. The roar of the distant torrent, breaking the awful silence with its prolonged echoes, sounds like the tramp of armed men or the thunder of horsemen rushing to battle. The night wind wails and moans as if foreboding deeds of rapine and blood.

At last the rosy hues of dawn appear in the "dappled east." The blue, star-spangled curtain of the night is slowly lifted from the dark ridge of the encompassing mountains, and the travelers can see the golden fringe upon the robe of the king of day. They rejoice that the reign of darkness is past, and that the whole surrounding landscape will soon gladden again in the smile of the all-beholding sun. They lift up their voices in loud thanksgiving to the great Father of light that the morn cometh. Higher and higher ascends the dawn, and in its growing light the wild landscape loses its threatening and awful aspect. The winds murmur with the music of gladness, and the torrents leap from the cliffs with silvery laughter.

Joyful for the coming day, the pilgrims forget the terror, the weariness and the watching of the night, and start upon their journey before the sun appears.

Meanwhile, the fresh mountain air, through which the feeblest stars shone with crystal clearness in the still midnight, becomes agitated by the approach of day and breaks up into conflicting currents of warm and cold, damp and dry. The morning wind sweeps down from the chilly heights and condenses the crystal vapor in the warm valleys into thick clouds. Soon the driving and darkening mist conceals every trace of the coming day upon the distant hills. It folds down its impenetrable curtain upon the far-reaching valley. It rolls its heavy burden upon the wind. It sweeps around every ridge and mountain peak and down through every gorge and defile. Soon every way-mark is hidden in the whole landscape, and the travelers find themselves enveloped in a darkness more bewildering and inextricable than that of midnight. It is neither day nor night. They have neither the light of the sun nor of the stars. They may return to the place from which they started, while they suppose themselves to be advancing upon their journey. Now, with more anxiety than before the day began to dawn, they lift up the cry, "Watchman, what of the night?"

And yet they know that the mist which has surrounded them has not put out the sun. The morning star has not been stayed in "his steep course," nor has the day-spring forgotten its place. The path of the pilgrims is indeed darker and more perplexing than before. But they know that guidance and deliverance are constantly approaching.from on high. To them the morning cometh and also the night.

They press forward darkling and fearful upon their journey, climbing the steep and slippery height, winding around the projecting crag, overhanging the fathomless abyss, yet all the while assured that the unconquerable light will struggle through the gathered clouds; the sun will ascend the heavens with meridian brightness; the everlasting mountains will appear upon their old foundations; the pilgrim-band will reach their noonday rest in safety and in peace. To them the morning surely comes, though for a time it seems veiled in a deeper night. The light shall disperse the darkness, and the world shall rejoice in the crowned and conquering day.

Such is the scene set before us by the voice of the night-watch crying out of Seir. And such are the interminglings and alternations of light and darkness, hope and fear, in the lot of individuals and in the history of nations. In every faithful picture of human life, the night must mingle with the morning; the shade of sorrow and calamity must darken the dawn of hope and gladness; the journey that begins with joy must be pursued with peril and uncertainty. The successful seeker after earthly happiness has only time to cry, "I have found it," when the possession glides from his grasp, and he is left to mourn with empty hand and sorrowing heart.

Sometimes, while pursuing our journey of life, we seem to have entered some quiet vale, where the healthful air revives the weary frame, the whole landscape delights with its beauty, and we promise ourselves long and secure repose. But soon the clouds gather darkness on the distant heights, the sun is hidden, and the tempest pours its angry flood through the whole valley, and our promised paradise becomes a scene of desolation. Our blooming hopes are withered in the blossom; our peaceful retreat is invaded by a thousand cares and sorrows. The morning comes with unwonted brightness and beauty, but it is night before noon.

If we stand aside from personal contact with the struggling and conflicting world, and observe the vast and ever-rolling torrent of human life sweeping by us while we listen to the voices and study the changing aspects of the tumultuous scene, we shall find our hearts constantly moved by the same conflicting and changing emotions of hope and fear, joy and sorrow. We see darkened nations rejoicing in the bright promise of the near-approaching day. We are confident that soon their whole land will be bathed with the full effulgence of Gospel light and liberty. And then all our hopes are blasted by the sudden coming on of deep, dreadful night. The morning of millennial glory is not indeed stayed from its appointed hour, but to our imperfect human vision the envious night keeps even pace with the dawn. The full day of truth and righteousness and liberty must be ushered in by a horror of great darkness, and a cup of trembling, and the earthquake throes of revolution. A nation finds peace in the same way that rest comes to the weary and burdened soul—through dark clouds of fear and doubt and sorrow, and through the agitations and conflicts of penitence and remorse.

In the history of nations light sometimes breaks forth from an unexpected source after long intervals of darkness. As we read the record we see the thronging millions of an emancipated people going out in joy and led forth in peace. The earth, which has long cried to heaven by the unavenged blood of its many martyrs, breaks forth with its mountains and its hills into singing and the trees of the field clap their hands. We seem to see already the fulfillment of the prophetic word that a nation shall be born in a day. Suddenly a cloud sweeps over the fair prospect, and its darkness is sevenfold more horrible by contrast with the recent light. The decree of Providence appointing the progress of nations is not reversed or forgotten, but the advance must be through cloud and conflict. The morning cometh and also the night.

We see great and mighty nations, in a single day, violently breaking asunder the chains of ignorance, superstition and oppression with which they have been bound for ages, lifting up their multitudinous voices, like the roar of the ocean in storms, and swearing by the awful name of the King of heaven that unto him alone will they henceforth bow the knee and acknowledge no other for their rightful Lord. The thunder of that mighty voice is the signal for the casting down of thrones. The tyrants of mankind fear that their hour of judgment has come. They are ready to call upon the rocks and the mountains to fall upon them and hide them from the wrath of their emancipated subjects, breaking loose from a thousand years of bondage in one awful hour.

But the first outbreak of jubilant voices has scarcely died upon the wind before the dethroned and terrified power of darkness and despotism begins to recover its self-possession and its authority. Under a different name it climbs back to the vacant throne, and casts its baleful shadow far as the breaking light has shone. And again we are compelled to say that if the morning of deliverance from dark and cruel bondage cometh to the nations, so also the night of ignorance and oppression keeps even pace with the coming day. Shocked by the excesses and discouraged by the ignorance and self-confidence of the uprising spirit of liberty and reformation, we are ready to exclaim:

> " The sensual and the dark rebel in vain,
> Slaves by their own compulsion; in mad game
> They burst their manacles and wear the name
> Of freedom graven on a heavier chain!"

Such was the history of the Hebrew nation under the

especial guidance of Divine Providence in ancient time. Such has been and still is the history of peoples and opinions in the European world. The good and the glorious days of Samuel and David and Solomon and Hezekiah were followed by the dark and evil days of Saul and Jeroboam and Ahab and Manasseh. Athanasius and Augustine, Luther and Calvin, Cranmer and Knox, Whitefield and Wesley, the great champions of truth and reformation, found their dark shadow and counterpart in Arius and Pelagius, Loyola and the Inquisition, Voltaire and the French Revolution. The bright dawn of a better day has always been overcast with dark and angry clouds.

And yet the providence of God is wiser and mightier than the policies of man. The night which comes with the morning is partial and temporary, although it seems for a time to devour the day and cut off the hopes of mankind. In the darkest periods of human history we need only the clear vision of faith to see the day approaching. If we take only human feelings or human philosophy for our guide, we shall be ready to admit that the "tide in the affairs of men" of which poets write is only a tide, sometimes advancing with crowned and crested billows, gleaming in the light and breaking upon the old bulwarks of the shore with resistless shock and thundering sound, and then retiring to its original bed to repose and recover strength for the repetition of the same aimless and ineffectual charge. But if we take the sure word of prophecy for our teacher, and with such a guide endeavor to forecast the destiny of nations, we shall see that the night of conflict and disaster which comes with the morning of hope and progress is only the temporary darkness of an unsubstantial mist, which must dissolve and disappear before the light and heat of the coming sun.

Our human prophecies may utterly fail. All our wisest counsels may come to naught. Men in their madness may shut their eyes to the light and set on fire the temple of their own liberties. Intoxicated with pride and success, they may overthrow the fairest structures that their own hands have built, and bury themselves beneath the ruin that their own madness has made. But these excesses and disasters to the cause of truth are only the brief night that comes with the morning. The perishable structures of man must be overturned and removed to give place to that living temple whose foundations are everlasting, and whose golden gates and sapphire wall shall be reared by God's own hand. He hath sworn by the immutability of his own word that the kingdom and the greatness of the power under the whole heaven shall be given unto Christ; and through whatever conflict and calamity the human family must pass to the fulfillment of that prophecy, the night shall not outlive the morn. The Sun of Righteousness shall fill the heavens with the full day. In every human dwelling there shall be light, in every nation there shall be peace.

It is ever God's way to bring light out of darkness, joy out of sorrow, rest out of weariness for the waiting and longing soul. The most exalted and blessed of the redeemed host before the throne of God and the Lamb have come to their heavenly seats and starry crowns out of great tribulation. And it would seem impossible for us to attain the highest experience of peace and rest in this life except through some great and terrible trial—some awful and costly sacrifice. If we would reign with Christ, we must be willing to drink of the cup and be baptized with the baptism of his sufferings. We shall never acquire any great capacity for joy, the blessed peace of God will never possess our mind and heart, so long as we can be frightened at shadows, so long as we shrink from self-denial. The darkness which rests upon our path in the time of trial is the pavilion of the Divine presence, the veil with which God covers his glory when he comes to bring us new blessings and to kindle the light of new hopes in our hearts. God comes in the thick cloud of mourning, in the deep night of sorrow, in the sharp conflicts of trial and temptation, in the sacred demands of hard and pressing duty, and yet it is a message of light and of love that he brings. He may have spoken a thousand times with the voice of peace and prosperity, and you heard him not. You took the gift and forgot the Giver. You walked in the light with no thought of Him whose sun shone upon your path. And now he comes, or at some future time he will come, to you in the greater mercy of chastisement and affliction, that you may not be given up to the dreadful doom of those who live without hope and without God in the world. And you must look in the direction of the cloud if you would see the coming day. You must learn to feel that God is nearest to you in the very hour when your mourning heart is ready to exclaim, "Why hast thou forsaken me?"

I have seen the sky the nour before sunrise, among mountains, clear, cold and beautiful; the stars shining from the blue firmament with a pure and silvery light; the constellations of the north circling around the pole in the silent order of their eternal march; the snowy heights without a cloud; the white torrents like bands of light leaping from the dark cliff. Then again, looking upon the same landscape the hour after the sun had risen, I could not see the blue dome of the sky. The stars were hidden. Clouds covered the mountain-tops. Darkening mists swept down from the cold heights and rolled in billowy torrents through the narrow valleys. The jagged cliffs assumed an aspect of terror. The wind moaned through the pines, and the voices of the streams sounded like a wail for the lost glories of the morning.

But I knew that the sudden darkness had been caused by the near approach of a greater light. If the night had continued, the sky would have been clear and the stars would still be seen. But I knew that the sun would soon scatter the mist which had been raised

17

by his coming, and that instead of the faint starlight we should have the full day. And I was happy for a while to walk beneath clouds and to face the driving mist that I might rejoice the more in the sunlight and rest on the mountain-top in the cloudless noon.

The highest reach of faith in this earthly life is only the starlight of a fair morning that foreruns the full and eternal day of heaven. And the near approach of the coming glory will sometimes raise thick clouds, and make the hour before the dawn seem the darkest of the night. The moment of the greatest discouragement and difficulty is the moment when the Divine Helper is nearest to those who are listening in the silence to hear his voice, and feeling in the dark to find his hand. Six times of failure and disappointment in a good work may be all necessary to prepare for the seventh of success and joy. When a great trial comes upon you in an unexpected way—when the course of duty is hedged up by many and great difficulties—when you are just ready to give over to utter discouragement and despair, you may be sure that Heaven's glory is hovering behind the cloud that darkens your path. You have only to press on in the way of duty, and the full day will shine around you, and you will look back with joy and gratitude upon all the trials and difficulties through which you have passed.

It is the glory of God to conceal himself and his ways not by withholding knowledge, but by surpassing our utmost capacity to know. So long as our minds are finite we shall know only in part. The infinite whole of God's nature and works will still continue to be the unexhausted science and the ever-lasting song of all eternity. It is by the unsearchableness of his being and his judgments that God commends himself to our faith. He gives us the most glorious and satisfying revelation of himself when he shows us that the mystery of his being is incomprehensible by finite minds, and that his ways are past finding out. All that he makes known of himself, all that he can communicate to the most exalted mind, only serves to show that there are loftier heights of power, greater depths of wisdom, greater immensities of love, a far more exceeding glory yet unrevealed. The love of Christ, the way of salvation through a Divine, incarnate, crucified Redeemer, impresses us more deeply by what we do not know and cannot comprehend of its infinite riches of grace, than by all that we can see and explain.

When traveling among the Alps, I came down from the Tête Noir Pass into the vale of Chamouny at the close of a summer's day. For years I had thought that it would be one of the great and rememberable events of life if for once, from the depth of that wild valley, I could gaze on the unclouded summit of Mont Blanc. But the day had been one of mingled light and shadows among the Alps, and when the sun went down the snowy diadem of the monarch of mountains was veiled in clouds. I could only sweep with my eye slowly upward from the green valley over the silent sea of pines, and along the track of the avalanches and across the "motionless torrents and the silent cataracts" of the glacier, till the clouds forbade all further ascent, and then leave imagination to measure the unrevealed height beyond.

The view was sublime and transporting beyond expression; but all that I could see only made me long the more intensely for the clouds to clear away and disclose the bald and awful form of the mountain in its full extent. The morning came, the sky was clear, and I rose before the sun to secure the loftier view which the clouds of the evening had denied. There stood Mont Blanc, rising in cold and silent majesty from earth to heaven, its snowy crown transmuted to gold in the morning light, every outline of its vast proportions clearly defined and embraced in one glance of the eye. But it did not seem to me as lofty, it did not impress me as deeply, as it did the evening before, when clouds veiled the summit, and all that I saw only helped me to imagine a greater reality which I could not see. I gained my loftiest vision of the monarch of mountains when its crowning glory was veiled in clouds. I was most profoundly impressed with the vastness and sublimity of Alpine scenery when I felt that there was a still more glorious vision which I had not beheld.

So the mystery which envelops the being and the

works of God gives us the most awful and impressive view of his greatness, and warrants us in offering him the most profound homage of our hearts. It is because we cannot measure his immensity, because we cannot by searching find out the limit of his works, that we believe in him as God. And the only veil with which God hides himself from us is the excess of light. The clouds and darkness round about his throne seem thickest to us when he shows us the most of his glory. We are bewildered and blinded by the vastness of the vision because so much is revealed.

Do not be afraid, then, of mystery. Do not clamor for the short and senseless creed of him who believes only what he can understand. There are mysteries in every pulsation of life and every perception of the mind which the deepest philosophy cannot fathom. Do not be troubled and cast down because you cannot always see your Father's face; you cannot know the reason of much that he requires you to do, much that he does himself, much that he permits to be done. You must have faith enough in your God and Father to believe that the night around you is day to him, and that in him there is no darkness at all. The true greatness and joy of life come from faith in things unseen. The heroes and conquerors of whom the world is not worthy are those who can march into the deep and face the king of terrors without fear, when God gives the word, " Go forward !"

Those who believe in God and live to do his will

should never despair for themselves or for the world. It is a heathenish and infidel philosophy which puts the better ages in the past, and predicts darkness and degeneracy for the future. Christianity is the religion of progress. Whatever light or blessing it may have given, it always has more and greater to bestow. To our feeble vision and fainting hearts it may sometimes seem as if the powers of darkness had put out the sun and hung the heavens with black. But God has made a covenant with the morning and it shall advance to the full day. Philosophy may set up reason as the antagonist of revelation. Science, falsely so called, may grope with blind eyes in the book of nature for a contradiction of the book of life. Ingenious criticism may set the inspired record to confute itself. Skepticism may treat the sacred claims of the Gospel with scoffing and denial. The base spirit of worldliness may corrupt the many and control the few. The cause of truth may seem to maintain its ground only by great exertions and costly sacrifices.

Still, the promised morning shall come, and the shades of darkness shall flee away. We have only to discharge our individual duty and leave the times and seasons in God's hand. Christ shall yet see the travail of his soul and be satisfied with the world's redemption. If we walk with him, we shall see his triumph and share his joy. We must expect conflict if we hope for the crown. Our greatest riches must come by sacrifice and self-denial. Like our Divine

Master, we must be made perfect by suffering. But we can walk safely in the darkest path if we have the Light of the world for our guide. We can have peace and joy in the most wretched home if Christ abide with us.

The Gospel is a revelation of light and of hope. But to make the light seen, it is thrown upon the dark background of mystery, and to persuade us to lay hold on the offered hope it is contrasted with the awful blackness of despair. Revelation leads the heavenly pilgrim by the double symbol of light and cloud. The light shows the way of safety and of peace, and the cloud shows in what direction the one infinite mystery lies. The Divine word pours light into the most darkened understanding and at the same time makes the most cultivated feel their ignorance and deplore their blindness. It makes a man most intensely dissatisfied with himself, that it may fill his mind and heart with a peace that passeth all understanding. It lays heavy burdens upon the conscience, and pierces the soul with the sharp arrows of conviction, and at the same time it offers rest to the weary and the heavy-laden, and it heals the wounded heart. The boldest flight of imagination would not dare to picture such an exalted and glorious destiny for man as is set before him in that very book which humbles him in the dust and puts all his pride and ambition to shame. To the poor, stricken soul, weary of his wandering, and longing to come back, no hour is so dark as the one when he is just about to see his Father coming forth to meet him, and to give him the kiss of reconciliation and peace. To the burdened and benighted pilgrim no part of the heavenly journey seems so hard and cheerless as the spot where the mountains and the hills are ready to break forth before him into singing and all the trees of the field to clap their hands.

The Night of Weeping.

Weeping may endure for a night, but joy cometh in the morning. . . . They that sow in tears shall reap in joy.—Ps. xx. 5 ; cxxvi. 5.

XII.

THE NIGHT OF WEEPING.

LIFE is a conflict of forces—the weak against the strong, the bad against the good, the earthly and the sensual against the heavenly and the divine. It is the joy of existence to attempt and succeed—to contend and conquer. This is the law of nature, of providence and of grace. The body must waste away or it cannot grow; the mind must be wearied or it cannot rest; the soul must fight against temptation or never win the prize of perfect peace. The new growth which gladdens the heart springs from the old decay which destroyed its hopes. The living generations have all come up from the dust of the dead, and the footsteps of life are everywhere followed by the hounding pursuit of death.

Every change gives signs of its coming; every substance betrays its hidden quality; every law is uniform in its conditions and consequences. The contradictions and paradoxes with which we seem to be surrounded are only parts of the Divine harmony, which displays infinite variety in nature and infinite wisdom in Providence. Let it not seem strange that peace comes by conflict, and that surrender should be the condition of conquest in the spiritual life. The appearance is as little like the reality in the matter-of-fact world which we see, and a part of which we are.

. The reddening clouds of the evening foretoken the fair weather of the morning. The fiery bolt that crashes through the sultry air of an autumn night is the harbinger of a clearer sky and a colder day. The mists that hide the sunrise among mountains give promise of a cloudless noon. The intense cold of the severest winter's day is the last effort of the cruel frost to lock the earth in fetters of eternal ice. To-morrow the crisping snow will soften in the breath of a more genial air, and the hazy skies will give signs of coming rain. In tropic climes the tornado that lashes the sea into madness, and the earthquake which drives its ploughshare through the solid globe, are announced by a breathless and awful calm.

The diamond is the most purely combustible substance in the whole kingdom of nature, and yet in a fire intense enough to inflame the earth the diamond would be the last to burn. The membranous coating on the convex surface of the eye is the only portion of the living frame which can *feel* the contact of light. And yet that fine network of nerves may be cut or rudely torn and feel no pain. It is insensible to any other force or substance save that which is so delicate that no balances can detect its weight and no other sense can discover its existence. The tones of the human voice, the outlines of the human face, the general movement of the human frame in walking, the personal characteristics of individuals, are so much alike that we cannot describe the difference in words, and yet we seldom confound them with each other. Everywhere around us we see infinite variety under an aspect of perfect uniformity. Conflicting forces neutralize each other—discordant elements unite in harmony.

The riddle propounded by the strong man in the time of Israel's judges is solved and verified in the history of each successive day: Out of the eater still cometh forth meat, and out of the strong still cometh forth sweetness. Out of the fetid and formless dunghill the delicate flower distills the sweetest perfume and builds up the perfection of beauty. The fallow field is enriched by years of neglect to bear a plentiful harvest. The volcano pours a fiery stream upon the fertile plain, and so relieves a wider district from the more wasteful destruction of the earthquake. The bow of promise spans the cloud which bears the thunder in its bosom.

All these are things of daily experience and personal observation in the common life of men in this world. And they prove conclusively that paradox and conflict and mystery do not belong exclusively to the realm of the spiritual life or the higher walks of Christian faith. The material and moral world both came from the same creative Mind, and are in harmony with each other. Things seen and temporal shadow forth the reality and surpassing glory of things unseen and eternal. The struggle and conflict of the spiritual life have their parallel in the travail of this groaning creation, and in the mystery which clothes the common things of daily experience and casts its shadow upon every path. The lessons of religious instruction, which make the highest demands upon faith and patience and submission, are confirmed and illustrated by a thousand analogies in things which we all see and trials that we all suffer.

The material and matter-of-fact mind has no right to put aside the high claims of spiritual truth on the plea that it stands too widely apart from the common walks of human experience and the common demands of human necessity. He who is most in earnest to lay hold on the crown of eternal life need not be surprised or disheartened because every step of advance toward the heavenly prize must cost effort and encounter opposition. The dumb earth which we tread, the voiceless seasons which visit us in perpetual round, the laws of growth and decay which govern all living things, the conditions of success and failure in all worldly schemes, illustrate the same truths which we are to believe, and the same principles which we are to obey, in setting our hopes and affections upon things unseen and eternal. The children of this world have only to become as wise in considering the wants and capacities of their immortal nature as experience compels them to be in providing for the necessities of the present, and they, too, will become children of light. The whole theory and practice of the Christian life are as rational, consistent and applicable to man's higher being and destiny as the lessons of prudence and foresight by observing which men succeed in this world.

It is constantly maintained in the work of Christian instruction that it is good for men to tread a hard and humble path, to encounter difficulties, to experience disappointment, to suffer affliction. Faith grows by conflict with doubt, virtue gathers strength by resistance to temptation. The toil and travail through which the children of God pass in their journey to the heavenly rest are the merciful chastisement of their peace. The life of the good soldier of Jesus Christ is but a battle and a march. For him there is no rest, no home till he gains the better country. His repose after conflict must be upon the field with his armor on. Success only increases the demand for effort and sacrifice. The spoils of victory supply new incentives to press on more vigorously in the ceaseless advance to meet the decisive struggle and the final foe. When at last presented faultless before the throne of glory with exceeding joy, he is clothed in robes which have been washed from the defilement of sin in the blood of the slain Lamb. Thus, all the way, pain is the price of pleasure, sacrifice is the condition of success, life eternal begins with the agony of death;

" And beauty immortal awakes from the tomb !"

Now, the man of the world who prides himself upon his ability to devise objections to spiritual truth, and who deems it a mark of intelligence to doubt, calls this a needless and an unnatural process. He sees nothing but contradiction in the statement that the peace which passeth all understanding must be the growth of continual conflict. He demands to know why the rest of heaven can be reached only through the toil and weariness of earth; why the harvest of joy can spring only from seed that has been watered with the sower's tears. In the last great day, when the circling seasons of time have completed their round, why shall the angel reapers shout their harvest-home over sheaves that have been saved as from the fire, and gathered from fields that have been sown in sorrow and ploughed in tears?

In answer to all such questions and complaints, we might say, The conditions of life and peace are ordained of God. He has full power and right to do as he will. We must comply with his conditions and live, or submit to the alternative ordinance of death. Men may say that the terms of salvation are arbitrary and irrational; they may think that self-denial and self-abasement and cross-bearing are poor preparations for the crown and glory of immortal life. Still, it is the part of a wise man to take the infinite gift of salvation upon such terms as the Infinite Giver chooses to impose.

But we can say something more than this. Whatever may be the reason for it, there is no doubt as to the fact that the deepest joy is attained through suffering, the highest exaltation rises from the depths of humility(hope in God springs to life when every other hope has been torn from the heart.) And this is the lesson taught most constantly by a thousand conditions and analogies in this earthly life. Everything which is best worth possessing even in this world is ordinarily secured by efforts that are most painful and costly. The daily experience of this present life teaches us to sacrifice everything to attain the infinite inheritance of the future. We give toil and study and patience and pain for possessions that perish. Shall we be less willing to give all earthly gains, and life itself, for possessions that will crown us with glory and honor, and fill the soul with joy and peace through everlasting ages? We do not think it strange that the good things of this world can be secured only by toil and sacrifice and conflict. Why, then, should we be surprised that the infinite treasures of the soul, the inheritance which passes all estimate in value and duration, should cost us our all? Why need any one say or think or feel that a religion of self-denial and spiritual conflict is a forced and an unnatural religion, or that the hope of an eternal and blessed life can ever cost too much?

It is to be feared that many entertain this thought, and that some even go so far as to ask why a Being of infinite beneficence *need* bestow his blessings at so severe a cost upon creatures that are utterly poor? Why should not the Supreme Giver take to himself

18

the greater glory of giving without conditions, and making his unhappy children blessed without effort or sacrifice on their part. "Why," says the proud and perverse spirit, "need I be cast down and crushed before I can be permitted to stand erect and unrebuked before my Maker? Why must I be pierced through with the sorrows of penitence and self-abasement before I am permitted to share the peace that passeth all understanding? Why should not the path to heaven be made easy, and all the walks of duty resound with music and gladness to allure unwilling feet?"

All such questionings and objections are not simply against the way of restoration and the theory of duty taught in the Gospel. They are against the whole constitution and order of nature, against the primary elements of our spiritual and responsible being, against the only way in which the sinning and unhappy can ever find peace. No experience or philosophy, reason or invention of man, has ever found rest for the sinning soul save that which comes through penitence and sorrow for sin. The deepest joy of the heart springs from the deepest humiliation. The most enduring strength and nobleness of character are built upon the foundations of patience and trust and submission to God. Tears are not always the evidence of weakness. Grief does not necessarily spring from despair. When one has sinned against a holy and merciful God, when he has committed a deep and dreadful wrong against the best Friend he has in the universe, there is nothing more just or noble for him to do than to confess and deplore his sin in bitterness of soul. He will never recover his lost self-respect, he will never feel entitled to the confidence of the wise and the good, until he does. The Christian mode of building up a strong and symmetrical character begins at the foundation by causing man to meet the demands of truth and duty as they are, and so giving him respect for himself, confidence toward God, preparation for all that the future may bring.

And so the Christian mode of cultivation combines great tenderness of feeling with great firmness of purpose, great susceptibility of heart with inflexible strength of will and unconquerable patience and endurance. A thoughtful man sees much in the world around him, and more in his own heart, to make him weep. A brave and strong man, who had faced torture and death to do his duty in ancient time, said, when contemplating the sin and misery around him, "Oh that mine head were waters, the mine eyes were fountains of tears, that I might weep day and night!"

And the man must be very insensible to his own condition, and the condition of the world around him, who never has any such feeling. The trials of life are many and great, and the sins which we have all committed against God are flagrant and awful; and it does no credit to the feelings or the conscience of any man to talk about such things as if they were trifles. Embittered and vain as are the joys of earth, the human heart must grieve for their loss or cease to be human. The earthly husbandman who would join the angel-reapers in shouting the harvest home, in the great reaping-time of the earth's ripeness, must sow precious seed beside all waters, mingling his tears with heaven's rain and the night's dew. In his sore pilgrimage of trial and of sorrow he must have prayed many a time, in unison with the prayer of the Hebrew exiles in the strange land, "Turn again our captivity, O Lord, as the streams in the south!"

"The streams in the south," of which the captives sung by the waters of Babel, were summer torrents, flowing only when rain had fallen on the distant hills. In anticipation of their coming, the husbandman sowed the parched ground, and then waited for the fertilizing flood to flow among all the fields. But while it delayed its coming, he watched every gathering cloud; he listened for the sound of the wind that might foretoken the needed rain; he rose early to observe the goings forth of the morning; he studied the reddening hues of the setting day; he noted all the signs of the earth and sky, if peradventure he might gather any promise of help from the distant hills, any hope of the returning streams among the valleys. He would carry every day a heavier load upon his heart while the clouds refused to form, and the whole air was hot and hazy with powder and dust, and the stony beds of the torrents were bare, and the fields were burnt with drought, and the food of the flocks dried up, and famine looked in at the peasant's door. And when at last the blessing of the skies came in a single night, there was music for the husbandman in the voice of the thunder, and there was beauty in the blackness of the storm. And when the morning shone upon the gladdening torrents bursting from the hills, and the reviving herbage rose with new life from the fresh baptism of the flooded streams and the falling rain, then the husbandman needed only a human heart to rejoice with tears of gratitude and to sing aloud for joy.

So, from natural and necessary reasons as well as from Divine appointment, must we all learn to toil and to wait. As faithful husbandmen in God's great field of the world, we must sow with tears and with patient expectation, if we would reap with joy unutterable when the pitying heavens are bowed and the gracious rain descends and ensures a plentiful harvest. The tears shed in the time of sowing give promise that the reaper shall bring home his full sheaves rejoicing. The troubles and sorrows, the temptations and burdens which try the spirit most severely, only give it wings to rise and help it on in the heavenly way.

There is a bird in Eastern lands possessing a form so graceful, and a plumage so brilliant with all the hues of heaven, that it has seemed to men too bright and beautiful a creature to be an inhabitant of a sinful world; and as if supposing it to belong to the glory lost in Eden, they have named it the " Bird of Paradise." We are told by intelligent travelers that that bird never, from its own choice, *flies before the wind.* When compelled by fright or danger to do so, its gorgeous train of delicate plumes is disordered and torn by the favoring breeze, and soon the bird, so beautiful with all the hues of heaven, is wearied, baffled, beaten down, and all its glorious plumage trailed in the dust. But then again, let it mount upon the wing and face the rushing wind, and soon the dust is swept from the soiled plumes by the opposing breeze, the bird recovers her seemly shape and graceful motion, and ascends with unwearied flight to the gate of heaven.

The most beautiful thing in all this earth is the soul of man when purged from sin and renewed in the image of Christ. In his new creation he is the child of immortality, whose robes are Divine and whose destination is paradise. Angels come down to attend and guide him all the way, until he reaches the better country and rests in everlasting habitations. And yet even such an one, with angels to guard and God to help him, and his name already written in the book of life, can secure his promised possession only by struggle and conflict. To rise from the earth he must lay aside every weight—to reach his heavenly home he must face the storm. The favoring breeze of worldly prosperity will disarray the garments of his glorious beauty. The wings of faith and love will be soiled and burdened by worldly success. The abundance of temporal blessing will impede his upward flight, or even make him content to dwell in the dust. He must be willing to sow in sorrow if he would reap in joy. He must be bowed down with penitence and humiliation for his sins, if he would stand unrebuked in the presence of the King of kings.

And this penitence, this sorrow for sin, which the Gospel requires, is the beginning of all strength, all self-mastery, all nobleness of character. Let me suppose the case of a careless worldling, by accident or by contempt, entering the room where a little company of God's children meet for evening worship. Their heads are bowed low in the act of devotion and the voice of one ascends in tremulous and fervent prayer. But he has not come there himself to pray. He looks around with indifference or with idle curiosity upon the supplicating throng. He cares little for that mercy which they are seeking with tearful earnestness. He takes no part in the confession of sin which they pour out with sighs and brokenness of heart before God. He has lived for this world alone, and his conscience does not rebuke him very sharply for what he has done. He only smiles while others weep around him. His heart is shit against all the appeals of the Divine word. He is insensible to the presence and power of the Divine Spirit, by which others are so deeply moved. He thinks it only a matter of course that he shall leave that room and say lightly that it was only from curiosity or to gratify a friend that he went there.

But no; while he is revolving such thoughts, a

shade of deep seriousness steals over his face. His lip quivers with rising emotion. He has caught the deep feeling which is struggling in the hearts around him. He bows his head and covers his face, and tears burst from fountains that had been sealed long ago. He begins to feel himself to be a sinner in the sight of God. He sees his whole life to have been a perpetual wronging of an infinite Friend. His whole soul is seized and shaken by the Divine sorrow which is the beginning of peace and joy.

And let no one call it weakness that he weeps. That rising emotion is evidence that his lost strength is coming back to him. The angel within him is getting the mastery over the demon, and he will be a man again. He is stronger, greater, superior in every excellence of character, now that he has shown himself capable of weeping for his sins. The penitence and humility with which he bows at the foot of the cross are infinitely nobler and better than the scorn that was upon his lip and the pride that was in his heart.

Let me suppose, again, a boy of noble and manly feelings to commit a flagrant wrong. It is done in a moment of thoughtlessness or passion, and regretted as soon as done. But his companions applaud the deed, and his pride is enlisted to deny or defend it. What shall he do? Confess and deplore the wrong, or shut it up in his heart to poison his peace and embitter his life? The tempter will tell him to disown his sin and hide the sense of guilt in his own bosom. But if he takes that weak and wicked counsel, he will submit to be led by blind passion; he will bring on himself the intolerable tyranny of an accusing conscience; he will make himself a grief to his best friends; he will wound and destroy his self-respect and his peace of mind. He may assert his proud superiority to the relenting of a contrite heart, and the tenderness that dissolves in flowing tears. But he will only avail so much as to become, "lord of himself, that heritage of woe."

But if, on the other hand, his feelings are deeply touched when he begins to reflect upon his misconduct, if the trembling lip and gathering tear indicate that penitence and sorrow for sin are getting the mastery of his heart, you may be sure that genuine strength and nobleness of character are still his. He will prove himself greater, purer, stronger by every tear that he sheds for the wrong he has done. Joy will again spring up like a living fountain in his soul. He will reap the blessed fruits of penitence in gladness and peace.

This, then, is the conclusion to which we come. Peace must be sought through conflict with the temptations of the world and the wandering desires of our own hearts. This earthly life will be well spent if we make its whole course a pilgrimage to the heavenly rest. Meekness and lowliness of heart are the qualifications for strength and victory. The kingdom of the blessed and the crown of glory are waiting for him who is willing to take his place in penitence and humiliation at the foot of the cross. Blessed are they that weep and mourn for their departures from the living God. Blessed are they that return from their wanderings with confession and brokenness of heart. They shall find their Father looking and waiting for their coming. Their names shall be written in his book of remembrance, and they shall be precious in his sight.

The Night Feast of Belshazzar.

Belshazzar the king made a great feast to a thousand of his lords, and drank wine before the thousand. . . . They drank wine, and praised the gods of gold and of silver, of brass, of iron, of wood and of stone . . . . In that night was Belshazzar the king of the Chaldeans slain.— DAN. V. 1, 4, 30.

XIII.

THE NIGHT FEAST OF BELSHAZZAR.

BELSHAZZAR was the last of the Babylonian kings. The great feast which he made for a thousand of his lords was on the last night of his reign. He belonged to the proud and profligate race of the Chaldeans, whom the Hebrew prophets describe as tender and delicate, given to pleasures, dwelling carelessly and trusting in wickedness. Their young men were showy, sensual and self-indulgent. They dressed themselves in dyed garments of brilliant colors. They curled their hair, used unguents and perfumes, wore jewelry, carried walking-sticks with the beak of a bird or the head of a serpent carved on the handle. They were fond of silver-plate and splendid carpets, costly furniture and great suppers. They frequented dramatic entertainments in which female singers and dancers appeared on the stage with little dress and less decency for the amusement of the audience. They drank wine and sang lewd songs, and were out late at night, and they did everything else that wild, half-intoxicated young men are most likely to do.

All this can be abundantly shown from the Hebrew prophets, Isaiah, Jeremiah and Ezekiel; from the Greek historians, Herodotus, Xenophon and Diodorus, and from inscriptions on monuments that remain to this day. And knowing all this concerning the young men of that great and mighty city of ancient time, we are not surprised that Babylon became a desolation. The day of doom is not far off from any great city when its young men have become " tender and delicate" and given to pleasure; when they have grown effeminate, self-indulgent, fond of amusement and afraid of work; when they are excited and passionate about trinkets and trifles—nerveless and spiritless about the nobler demands of effort and duty.

There is no more effectual way to destroy a great and mighty nation than to give its young men all the money they want, provide them with plays and festivities and amusements and dances and wine, and then leave them to sweat the life and manhood out of body and soul in the hot-bed of pleasure and self-indulgence. That is the way Babylon was ruined. That is the way imperial Rome became an easy prey to northern barbarians. That is the way Christian Constantinople came under the debasing and abominable sway of Mohammedans. That is the way Venice ended a thousand years of independent and glorious history with shame and servitude. And nothing worse could come upon the fairest and most Christian city in the world than to have a generation of tender and delicate young men, without energy, without principle, without conscience, but with money enough to support elegant pleasures and costly vices. Let such young men give tone to public opinion, and take the lead in the highest circles of society in any city of our land, and they would soon make it the Sodom of America.

Belshazzar had everything to flatter his pride and indulge his passions. He was an absolute monarch, holding the life and property of his thousand lords and his countless people entirely at his disposal. His servants were princes. His concubines were the daughters of kings. His capital was enriched with the spoils of nations—his provinces were cultivated by captive people. He was hasty and violent in temper, yet effeminate and luxurious in his habits of living. He was gracious and indulgent toward his favorites; and yet when their best efforts to please him did not happen to suit his caprice at the moment, he would be cruel as the grave. His anger kindled at the slightest provocation, like flax in the flame, and he yielded to the seductions of pleasure and flattery as the early frost melts in the morning sun. In his soft and passive mood he could be moulded like wax by those who studied his caprices and played upon his weakness; but let him be crossed in his will, let him receive a slight or a sudden provocation, and his effeminate face would darken with the ferocity of a demon.

The great hall of the palace, in which he feasted his thousand lords reclined upon couches, was large enough to accommodate four times as many guests arranged as we now seat ourselves at table. It was adorned with carvings and sculptures of colossal dimensions, and the lofty walls were emblazoned with the trophies of war and the symbols of idolatrous worship. The profane orgies of royal mirth were adorned with every artistic decoration that the genius of the age could supply. I believe that the fine arts are capable of ministering to the highest and purest civilization, but thus far they have done little to enlighten the ignorant, to lift up the degraded, or to help the world forward in the career of moral improvement. They have always flourished in the corrupt and reeking society of a dissolute and licentious age. Rome, the modern Babylon, was never more depraved and abominable than when it had Michel Angelo to build St. Peter's and Raphael to fresco the Vatican. The capital of France was never more like Rome than when the Grand Monarque, Louis the Fourteenth, dazzled the world with his splendid court, and the great masters of every land were decorating the palaces of Fontainebleau, Versailles and the Louvre with the loftiest achievements of art. And to-day, if we would look for some of the most ignorant, vicious and degraded of the whole European population, we shall find them under the shadow of architectural structures which are the wonder of the world for beauty and magnificence. They have grown up from youth with full opportunity every day of their lives to gaze upon statues and paintings which the greatest artists of the present age can only imitate, never excel. In three hundred years the highest art has done less to refine and improve the common people in Rome and Naples than would be done by the spelling-book and New Testament in one year.

We have several independent statements in regard to the dimensions of Babylon, and although they all seem like immense exaggerations, we shall venture to take them as they stand for the purpose of illustration, without attempting to improve upon them by our conjectures. Let Herodotus, the father of history, be our principal authority.

The front of the great palace of Belshazzar was six times as great as the front of St. Peter's Church at Rome, four times as great as the length of the Capitol at Washington. The whole structure was surrounded by three walls, so high that it would take thirteen tall men, standing erect one above the other, to reach the top. The outer wall of the palace enclosed more ground than Central Park in New York. The city, in which Belshazzar reigned, was a square fifteen miles on a side, surrounded by walls as wide on the top as a large church, and seventy-five feet higher than the highest tower or steeple in America. If Broad street, in Philadelphia, were graded and built up to the full extent of the city limits, it would be the longest, straightest, widest street in the world. Ancient Baby-

19

lon had fifty such streets, straight as an arrow, crossing each other at right angles, and wider by one-third than the widest street in Philadelphia. And this mighty city of old was furnished with towers and temples and palaces and pleasure-gardens correspondent to its greatness. Belshazzar's so-called father, Nebuchadnezzar, was the most magnificent builder the world ever saw. According to Herodotus, he put into the walls of his capital alone more than five thousand millions of solid feet of masonry. Babylonian bricks a foot square, inscribed with the name of Nebuchadnezzar, have been found by Sir Henry Rawlinson in more than a hundred different places in the country about the ruins of the great city, and there are millions of such brick to-day lying just where they were placed by the hand of the workmen twenty-four hundred years ago.

Belshazzar inherited the pride, the glory, the riches, the power, the palaces, the capital, the kingdom of his great father. He inherited enough to ruin any young man who was not fortified by great strength of character and a severe mastery of his own appetites and passions. He was admitted to a share in kingly power at fifteen, and the glory, which was too great for the mighty Nebuchadnezzar, easily turned the head of an effeminate and giddy youth, who had earned nothing of all he had by his own exertions. He lifted himself up against the Lord of heaven, and he despised the kings and armies of the earth.

At the time immediately preceding the great feast which Belshazzar made for his thousand lords, the province of Babylon had been overrun and the capital assailed by a great army from the north. But, for some strange and inexplicable reason, the besieging force had apparently withdrawn. No effort appears to have been made to discover what had become of the enemy or what had occasioned their disappearance. It was enough that they could no longer be seen from the towers and walls. It was taken for granted that the siege was abandoned and the war was over. The whole city was immediately given up to rejoicing and every form of riotous excess. Belshazzar set the example, and people and princes were only too ready to imitate their king. The retiring enemy were ridiculed. The guards deserted their post. The gates in the palace-walls and the river banks were left open. No attention was given to the strange and startling fact that the water in the river was beginning to fall, and that when the night of the great feast began the bed of the stream was in many places bare, and that the empty channel left an open pathway for an army to march beneath the walls. There was feasting and dancing everywhere, and the mad revelers thronged the streets and houses, the palaces and pleasure-gardens through all the city. The flames of idolatrous sacrifice rose high into heaven from the lofty tower of Belus. The hanging-gardens were hung with lanterns and torches, till they seemed like a mountain of fire at midnight. Torchlight processions flowed like rivers of flame through the broad streets. The light of lamps outshone the starlight, and the blue Chaldean heavens looked black above the blaze of the great illumination.

Meanwhile, Belshazzar has entered the hall of banquet—

> " And a thousand dark nobles all bend at his board;
> Fruits glisten, flowers blossom, meats steam, and a flood
> Of the wine that man loveth runs redder than blood;
> Wild dancers are there and a riot of mirth,
> And the beauty that maddens the passions of earth;
> And the crowd all shout, while the vast roofs ring,
> All praise to Belshazzar, Belshazzar the king!"

"The music and the banquet and the wine; the garlands, the rose-odors and the flowers; the sparkling eyes, the flashing ornaments, the jeweled arms, the raven hair, the braids, the bracelets, the thin robes floating like clouds; the fair forms, the delusion and the false enchantment of the dizzy scene," take away all reason and all reverence from the flushed and crowded revelers. There is now nothing too sacred for them to profane, and Belshazzar himself takes the lead in the riot and the blasphemy. Even the mighty and terrible Nebuchadnezzar, who desolated the sanctuary of Jehovah at Jerusalem, would not use his sacred trophies in the worship of his false gods. But this weak and wicked successor of the great conqueror, excited with wine and carried away with the delusion that no foe can ever capture his great city, is anxious

to make some grand display of defiant and blasphe-
mous desecration:

> " ' Bring forth,' cries the monarch, ' the vessels of gold
> Which my father tore down from the temples of old;
> Bring forth, and we'll drink while the trumpets are blown,
> To the gods of bright silver, of gold and of stone.
> Bring forth.'   And before him the vessels all shine,
> And he bows unto Baal, and he drinks the dark wine,
> While the trumpets bray and the cymbals ring,
> ' Praise, praise to Belshazzar, Belshazzar the king.'
> *Now* what cometh?   Look, look! without menace or call,
> Who writes with the lightning's bright hand on the wall?
> What pierceth the king like the point of a dart?
> What drives the bold blood from his cheek to his heart?
> Let the captive of Judah the letters expound.
> They are read; and Belshazzar is dead on the ground.
> Hark! the Persian has come on the conqueror's wing,
> And the Mede's on the throne of Belshazzar the king."

The graphic lines of the modern poet do not exag-
gerate the rapidity with which the ministers of ven-
geance came upon Belshazzar and his thousand lords
on the last night of his impious reign. At the very
moment when their sacrilegious revelry was at its
height, the bodiless hand came forth and wrote the
words of doom upon the wall of the banqueting-room,
the armies of Cyrus had turned the Euphrates out of
its channel and marched into the unguarded city along
the bed of the stream beneath the walls; they were
already in possession of the palace gates when Bel-
shazzar and his princes were drinking wine from the
vessels of Jehovah and praising the gods of gold and

silver and stone, and that great feast of boasting and of blasphemy was the last ceremonial of the Chaldean kings.

The reckless and the profane not unfrequently display the greatest gayety and thoughtlessness when they are on the very brink of destruction. The feeling and the appearance of safety are not always to be taken for reality. Death still enters the banquet and the ball-room as well as the bed-chamber. The last opportunity to prepare for a safe departure out of the world comes to many, and they employ it only in doing their utmost to stay here as long as they can. The last word of warning and instruction is spoken to many while they are so much absorbed in earthly things that they do not know that they have been addressed at all.

The last opportunity for any good work is apt to look just like all that came and went before it. We seldom know that it is the last until it is gone never to return. Our only safe way to improve the last opportunity is to use all that come as if any one might be the last. On any night of the year multitudes are spending the precious hours as they would not wish to do if they knew that to them it would be the last night of earth. Many go to places where they would not wish to be found when the messenger of death comes to change their face and send them away. Many are living in the indulgence of habits which they would be very unwilling to continue if they knew that they had already entered upon the last year of life. Many are in the habit of speaking as they would not be willing to do if they were conscious that what they say is to pass from their lips directly to the book of final account. The Bible gives us this one instance of a great king and his princely associates in ancient time suddenly arrested in the midst of their wildest revelry and blasphemy, to teach all readers of the sacred story never to utter words that might not be fitly spoken if they should prove the last; never to be found in a place where the feeling of God's presence is a source of disquietude; never to do anything which would cause regret if it should prove the last act of life.

The apparent thoughtlessness of the gay and worldly does not prove that they are at peace with themselves. A smiling face and a reckless manner are sometimes put on to hide an anxious and an aching heart. There are more troubled and weary souls in the halls of gayety and the saloons of riotous mirth than in the house of God. There are more unhappy ones in places where people go to be amused than in places where they go to be instructed and to do their duty. The young man who says, with the most prompt and passionate decision, he does not care anything about religion, may be the very one who feels most deeply that he is poor and miserable without it. The young lady who thinks she cannot give up the pleasures of the world for peace with God, may be the very one who finds least satisfaction in a worldly life

To find joy in everything we do, we must do everything for God. To have the light of heaven upon our faces in all the dark hours of trial and trouble, we must have heaven's peace in our hearts. There will be no need of pretending cheerfulness or of seeking pleasure in the frivolities and dissipations of the world when once the love of Christ has opened fountains of pure and endless joy in the soul. The message of the gospel is God's way of peace for man. Religion is given us to make us happy here and happy for ever hereafter. There is indeed much gloom and despondency among Christians. But their religion does not make them unhappy. There are some things hard to be understood in the Bible, but there are still greater and more awful mysteries in the world without the Bible. If all would enter God's way of peace and accept his offered rest, the happy change would shed light upon a troubled sea of sad faces, and lift the heaviest weight from a world of weary hearts.

Belshazzar and his thousand lords did not profane the golden vessels of Jehovah until they had drunk wine. Indulgence in the intoxicating cup prepares the way for every excess and profanation. No man can be sure that he will be saved from any degree of shame or crime when once he has "put an enemy in his mouth to steal away his reason." For most persons the only safeguard against drinking too much is not to drink at all. If none ever took a temperate glass for pleasure, none would ever drown themselves in full beakers with intoxication. Put away the wine-cup from the feast, and profanity and lewdness will go with it. Shut up the dram-shops, and the houses of licentiousness will be purified and the cells of the prisons will be empty. A heathen historian explains the fall of the mightiest city of ancient times, when he says: *"Babylonii maxime in vinum, et quœ ebrietatem sequuntur, effusi sunt."* (The Babylonians were greatly given to wine and to those things which follow intoxication.)

The eye of the Great Judge is upon every scene of profanity and dissipation. The handwriting appeared upon the wall of the banquet-room in Belshazzar's palace in the hour of their wildest mirth, to show that God was there. And God is in every scene of wickedness and dissipation not less really than in the Holy Place of his own sanctuary. The finger of God is ever writing the witness of his presence with us upon the living tablets of our hearts. So long as we have a conscience we must have a voice within us to tell us that God's eye is ever fixed upon us, and that we must give account to him for all we do and for all we are. That infinite and awful Witness is in every storehouse, workshop and place of business every day of the week and every hour of the day. His eye scrutinizes every transaction in trade, every quality in goods, every degree of fidelity or neglect in work. His ear catches every word that passes between the buyer and the seller, the employer and the workman, the master and the servant, the mistress and the maid. He balances the books of the broker, presides at the board of trade, searches the vaults of the bank, judges the solvency of every debtor and the justice with which every creditor enforces his claim. He stands as a silent witness to every statement of prices, of quality and of value in the dry-goods palace, behind the shaded windows of the pawnbroker and beside the shivering huckster in the street. The omniscient God is witness to every oath in the courts and custom-house, in the office of the attorney and the tax-gatherer, upon every report of income and every showing of assets and liabilities in failure and bankruptcy. There is nothing said or done or thought that can escape the Infinite Eye. In the deepest solitude we must all have one companion. To every act and word of our lives there must be one witness, and that witness is the holy and sin-hating God. The bodiless hand that wrote in flaming letters upon the walls of Belshazzar's palace is ever writing upon every heart: "God is here—God is everywhere!"

Surely, then, it must be our wisdom so to live that the sense of God's presence shall be peace and joy to the soul. We cannot hide anything from him. Why then do anything which we would not wish him to know? We cannot escape our accountability to him for all we do. Why then not live so that we can give him our account with joy?

Conscience is a mysterious and mighty power in us all. The great and terrible king Belshazzar was completely mastered and unmanned by its secret whisper.

His countenance changed and his thoughts troubled him, and he trembled like the aspen before he knew the meaning of the writing on the wall. He was afraid, because an accusing conscience always makes darkness and mystery terrible to the guilty. It is mightiest in the mighty. Milton's Satan, Byron's Manfred, Shakespeare's Macbeth and Richard the Third are truthful illustrations of the harrowing torture produced in the mightiest mind by the calm, solemn voice within, which only says, "You are wrong." The Supreme Creator has put us absolutely in the power of that mysterious judge which pronounces sentence upon all our conduct and motives in our own bosoms. And we cannot conceive anything worse for a man than to die and go into the eternal world with an unappeased and accusing conscience to keep him company and to torment him for ever. And the infinite mercy is manifest most of all in providing a way by which the high and awful demands of conscience can be answered and the guilty soul can find peace. Within the whole range of human thought and inquiry there is no greater mystery than this—the rescue of men from the misery which they suffer from their own consciences.

Belshazzar had riches and pleasure and glory. He was absolute master in the greatest palace and the greatest city the world had ever seen. But what is his life worth to the world now, except to warn men not to live as he did? With all his splendor and luxury he lived a wretched man, and he died as the fool dies

He lifted himself up against God, he trusted in wickedness, and so he became but as the chaff which the wind driveth away. While he was yet in the height of his power and glory, his days were numbered, his character was weighed and found wanting before the infinite Judge.

And the same sovereign God counts out the days of life to us all. He weighs our character, our conduct, our motives in the balances of infinite truth. And there is no deficit so damaging as that which is charged to one who is found wanting before God. A man may be weighed and found wanting at the bank, at the board of trade, at the commercial agency, in the circles of fashion and social respectability, and yet be able to lift up his head and walk the earth with the firm step of an honest and an honorable man. There are heirs of infinite and everlasting riches and honor whose names would not turn a feather's weight in the balances with which the world is most apt to weigh the worth of men. The doors of the best houses on earth are not always open to those who can "read their title clear to mansions in the skies."

But oh to be wanting when God weighs motive, character, life, soul; to be wanting when judged by the most compassionate, indulgent and generous Friend; to be wanting in love to Christ, when he died on the cross to draw all hearts to him; to be wanting in the fruits and joys of a holy life, when God bestowed ten thousand gifts and instructions to help us gain that great reward; to be wanting in a hope sure and steadfast when God takes away the soul; to be wanting when the book of life is opened and the eye of the final Judge turns to see whose name is written therein,—who would not see to it earnestly and always that no such fatal deficiency shall be found against him when the last account of his life is balanced before God?

It has been said that the thought of our responsibility to God is the greatest thought ever entertained by the greatest mind. Certainly the discoveries and demonstrations of science cannot carry our minds so far over the sweep of ages and over the expanse of the universe as the bare thought that our individual being is bound inseparably and for ever to the being of the infinite and eternal God. Whatever we do, wherever we are, we can never cease to be responsible to him. For he has appointed us to do his work. He has given us the means, the faculties and the opportunity, and he holds us answerable for using them well. So far as we are true to our high destiny, we are warranted in looking upon ourselves as co-laborers with the Builder of all worlds, ambassadors of the eternal King, executors of the supreme Will. Thus our accountability to God, fully accepted and faithfully met, will raise us above everything that is mean and selfish and impure. It will make us believe and feel that we always have something great and glorious and good to live for. It will make us earnest, cheerful and strong under all the burdens, discouragements and difficulties of life. What the world wants most is men in whose minds the great thought of responsibility to God is ever present—men who are made strong by the consciousness that they are doing God's work, and they mean to do it so as to receive his approbation.

A Night with Jesus at Jerusalem.

There was a man of the Pharisees, named Nicodemus, a ruler of the Jews. The same came to Jesus by night.—JOHN iii. 1, 2.

XIV.

A NIGHT WITH JESUS AT JERUSALEM.

ONE of the most memorable and important inter-
views which ever took place between two indi-
viduals in this world was held on a raft in the
middle of the river Niemen, at the little town
of Tilsit, in Prussia. At one o'clock precisely, on the
25th of June, 1807, boats put off from opposite sides
of the stream and rowed rapidly toward the raft. Out
of each boat stepped a single individual, and the two
met in a small wooden apartment in the middle of the
raft, while cannon thundered from either shore, and
the shouts of great armies drawn up upon both banks
drowned the roar of artillery. The two persons were
the Emperors Napoleon and Alexander, and the his-
tory of the time tells us that they met " to arrange the
destinies of mankind." And the hastily-constructed
raft, on which the interview took place, will be re-
membered as long as the story of great conquests and
mighty revolutions can interest the mind of man.
The conference lasted but two hours; it was entirely
private between the two emperors, and yet it was
fraught with momentous consequences to millions. It

was one of the great crises in human history when the currents of power that govern the nations take new directions and break over the bounds and barriers of ages.

Go back eighteen hundred years beyond the treaty of Tilsit, and we can find a private conference between two individuals of far more momentous and lasting importance than that between Napoleon and Alexander. This more ancient interview was not watched with eager expectancy by great armies; it was not hailed by the thunder of cannon and the shout of applauding thousands; it was not arranged beforehand by keen and watchful agents guarding the interest and safety of the two who were to meet. It was in a private house, at a late hour of the night, and it was brought about by the mingled curiosity and anxiety of an old man to know something more of a young teacher who had recently appeared in his native city. And yet from that humble night-conference of Jesus with Nicodemus there have gone forth beams of light and words of power to the ends of the earth. The plans formed by Napoleon and Alexander at Tilsit were reversed and defeated long ago, and it is impossible to trace their influence in the condition of European nations to-day. The words spoken by Jesus to his wondering and solitary listener that night have already changed and glorified the destiny of immortal millions, and they have more influence in the world now than in any previous age; and they are destined to go on increasing in power until they shall be received as the message of life and love by every nation under heaven.

We shall do well to observe the time, the place and the occasion when this aged inquirer came to Jesus and drew from him words of such momentous importance to himself and the world. The time was night. The place was Jerusalem. The occasion was the feast of the Passover.

Jesus had come up from Capernaum to keep the great national festival at the sacred city of the Jewish people. Multitudes had come on the same errand from every portion of the land and from the principal cities of far distant nations. The houses in Jerusalem were all full. The streets were thronged. The courts and squares were crowded with pilgrims. The valleys and hill-sides beyond the walls were covered with tents. Josephus says that by actual count, on one occasion, it was found that two hundred and fifty-six thousand lambs were slain between three and five o'clock in the afternoon, and that two millions seven hundred thousand persons—three times as many as the whole population of the largest city in America— partook of the feast. So great a multitude in so small a city as Jerusalem could make their way only by struggling and crowding through the narrow streets. And the overflow of pilgrims camping outside the city would make the neighboring hills and valleys black with tents and alive with people.

The temple was the chief attraction to the vast multitude during the day. The sacred associations of the spot where the daily sacrifice had been offered with little interruption for a thousand years; the choral service led by vast choirs of priests and Levites, and supported by thousands of voices in the great congregation; the dazzling assemblage of domes and columns and arches and aisles, which made the whole area of the holy hill a wilderness of architectural beauty; the greetings and gatherings of friends after long separation; the passionate enthusiasm with which the Jewish people entered into their great national festivities,—all made the occasion such an one as could not be repeated elsewhere on the face of the earth. The Olympic games in Greece, the triumph and public shows attendant upon the return of a conqueror at Rome, never stirred the hearts of the people so deeply, never had so much to do with the formation of national character, as did the festivities of the Jewish Passover. Considered simply as an anniversary, a national festival, the Passover was the most stirring and impressive ceremonial that has ever been observed by any people. It is now more than thirty-three hundred years since the Paschal feast was first kept by the Hebrews in Egypt with staff in hand and sandals on. And it is still kept in the same manner by "the tribes of the wandering foot and the weeping eye."

When the night of the great festivity came, the multitude in Jerusalem divided into little companies to eat the Paschal lamb and to sing the songs of the Passover. In the early morning preceding the festive night, Jesus mingled with the crowd that filled the courts and colonnades of the temple. He was indignant to find the enclosure of the holy place changed to a cattle-market, and the loud cries and contentions of trade drowning the voices of praise and prayer. He sternly bade the bargaining crew to leave the holy place and take their merchandise with them. With an appearance of severity unusual with him, he overthrew the tables and scattered the changers' money on the marble floor. Alone and a stranger as he was in Jerusalem, there was something in his look and tone which made the most hardened men feel his power and obey his word.

All day he had been instructing the rude and excited people, reasoning with the contentious and caviling Scribes, and attesting his Divine authority by healing the sick, the blind and the lame that were brought to him in great numbers as he spoke. When night came on and the crowded city was calm, he must needs seek a place of rest, and in doing so he probably went out to some quiet retreat on the slope of the Mount of Olives.

Among all who had heard his words and seen his mighty works that day, one aged and venerable man It that he could not sleep another night until he had known something more of this wonderful Teacher that had come out of Galilee. This old man was a great master in Israel, a member of the national council, known to all in Jerusalem for his wealth, his learning and his liberality. The Jewish Talmud speaks of a Nicodemus so rich that he could support a whole city ten years on his own resources, and could give his daughter a dowry of five millions of dollars. Afterward he became so poor that his daughter had to live by begging. This is supposed to be the man of the Pharisees who came to Jesus by night. Making all needed allowance for the wonted exaggeration of the Talmud, we may safely infer that he was a man of high distinction in Jerusalem at the time.

Jesus was so completely surrounded and beset by the multitude all day that he could not be approached and talked with by so remarkable a person without exciting public curiosity and subjecting him to that kind of remark and exposure which such a man would be most likely to shun. The noise and interruption of the crowd would prevent anything like calm and continued conversation. Unwilling as men in his position are apt to be to draw the attention either of the rulers or of the rabble, Nicodemus chose to wait till the crowd had dispersed and then make his way through the quiet streets alone, to the house where Jesus had gone to rest for the night.

Imagine this old man, at a late hour leaving his house without letting it be known where he was going, making his way cautiously through the unlighted lanes and alleys of the city, avoiding the more public streets lest he should meet some one that might know him, stumbling over beasts of burden and houseless pilgrims lying upon the pavement, passing out at the eastern gate, which was kept open all night during the week of the Passover, stepping slowly down the zig-zag path into the valley and across the bed of the Kidron, and then up the western side of Olivet, among tents and gardens and stone houses, to find some humble cottage where he had learned by special inquiry during the day that the young Galilean Teacher would be most likely to lodge for the night. He reaches the door, but his heart hesitates and his hand refuses to knock. Whom will he find within? If Jesus should be there, how can he excuse himself for coming to talk with him at such an hour of the night? In what way can he begin the conversation so as not to commit himself too far? What will be said in the city when it comes to be known that he had shown so much anxiety to see Jesus? Rich, learned, honored as he is, how will he dare to show himself again in the great and venerable Sanhedrim after it comes to be known that he has been out at night alone to talk confidentially with this young, unlearned, unhonored Galilean?

So men doubt and question and hesitate to this day when they are just beginning to cherish a feeble and half formed purpose to learn something more positive and definite about Jesus and his salvation. Christianity has been in the world eighteen hundred years. It has proved itself mightier than all the powers of the earth. It is the source of life and permanency to the most advanced and progressive nations. It has brought light into thousands of dark homes and peace into millions of wretched hearts. And yet there is hardly anything about which men are so slow, so unwilling to be seen and heard inquiring as about Jesus and his salvation. They have no hesitation in showing themselves anxious about trade and prices and work and health and the means of living. They will read books and hear lectures and write letters and inquire of friends and strangers and travel far and near to get information about houses and lands and goods and worldly occupations—all of which are valuable in their place, but are as nothing compared with what Jesus can tell us about ourselves, about God and heaven and eternal salvation. And yet men are so reserved, so cautious, so sensitive, so timid, even when they begin to be in earnest to know what they shall do to be saved. Men who can talk fast and well on everything else will be silent and shy as soon as the grand question is raised— What is to become of us all when we leave this world? Surely it ought not so to be. If there be one thing about which a wise, considerate, conscientious man should have no hesitancy, no reserve, no fear of man or of anything else, it should be the grand infinite concern of his own eternal salvation. It is better to fear and hesitate and delay about everything else rather than that, the one subject which most deeply concerns our relationship to God and eternity.

Nicodemus, rich, learned, powerful—a member of the proudest and strictest sect of the Jews as he was—feared and hesitated when in the very act of seeking Jesus. It is much to his credit, however, that he overcame his fears and hesitancy, entered the humble abode where Jesus was, and acknowledged himself an inquirer for the truth—a trembling, doubting, unsatisfied seeker after light. The most becoming, the most honorable place for any man, however rich or learned, is that of an humble, earnest inquirer at the feet of Jesus.

Imagine, then, the scene in the quiet house on the slope of Olivet, on that memorable night. The old man anxious, agitated, wondering, trying in vain to put on an air of composure and dignity and to make it appear a great act of condescension in him to come there at all, and Jesus calm, kind, inspiring his venerable guest with awe and searching his very soul with a look—Nicodemus endeavoring to smooth the way for his inquiries by courteous and complimentary expressions, and Jesus, with solemn, direct and tender precision, laying bare at one word the great burden and necessity of the old man's heart—Nicodemus surprised, and affecting more ignorance than he felt, and Jesus declaring again, with a still more solemn and awful emphasis, that even such an one as he—kind, generous, learned, a master in Israel—must be born again, must have a new heart, a new life, or not see the kingdom of God. Nicodemus sitting in silent amazement at the thought of a kingdom so pure that even he could not enter it without becoming a new man, and Jesus going on to declare the wondrous love of God in giving his own Son, not only to the learned, the rich and the noble, but that the ignorant, the poor and the vile might have eternal life.

This is the one great truth which must lie at the foundation of all plans, efforts and instructions to make the world better and happier. This is the one ruling and distinctive idea which stands first and foremost in that peculiar system of truth called the Gospel of Jesus Christ—man depraved and lost in his natural condition, and man renewed and saved by the gracious help of God in the Gospel. A full and practical acceptance of this truth is the way of entrance into the blessed and eternal kingdom of life. The spring and fountain of all good to man in this world, and the beginning of an endless and blessed life in the world to come, is a new heart—a pure, lowly, loving, obedient heart—a heart that shuns evil and seeks good of its own free and happy choice. The master in Israel came to Jesus by night to talk about things of the first and greatest concern to man. And Jesus told him that this one principle lies at the foundation of all true wisdom; it is the beginning of all better hopes, the source of all right conduct, the bright dawn of heaven on earth: all must spring from a new spiritual life in the individual heart. In that obscure house, on that memorable night, speaking to one solitary man, Jesus the Divine Teacher set forth truths of greater importance to man and the world than are ever discussed in the cabinets of kings or the councils of nations. He laid down the principle that should govern us in all our efforts at self-improvement and in all our labors for the good of others. With nothing but the words of Jesus to Nicodemus for our guide and commission, we can enter upon a successful crusade against all the wrongs and miseries of the earth—we can promise a perpetual millennium of peace and prosperity to all who accept and obey these words.

Man's life, as the Gospel of Jesus finds him, is a waste and a perversion, and he needs to begin all anew. He must have a life from above, that he may be in harmony with God and at peace with himself. He is a wanderer, and he must be called home. He is in bondage to his worst enemy, and he must be made the freeman of the Lord. He is in subjection to the old man of sin and misery, and he must be made a new man in Christ Jesus. He is an alien and a stranger from the holy and blessed kingdom of God, and he must be made an heir of God by faith and a son by gracious adoption. Let this mighty spiritual change be carried on and accomplished among men, and all other blessings will follow in its train, and the kingdom of heaven will come on earth.

We do not know with what thoughts Nicodemus went back to his home that night; but the solemn words which Jesus addressed to him should lead every one who reads them to put to his own heart the question: "Have I myself experienced this great change which is needed by all in order to see the kingdom of God? Have I been born again? Has the old life of sin and worldliness and alienation from God been given up, and have I begun the new life of love and trust and obedience to God? Have I turned my steps back from the dark way on which the shadow of death rests, and am I now walking in the heavenly path upon which the favor of God shines with everlasting light?"

If any doubt the need of this great and radical change to fit men for the service of God and for heaven, they need only consider what the Bible says about it. It everywhere describes man without a Saviour as a lost creature. He is provided with a gracious and complete salvation just because he is lost. Christ comes to seek and to save the lost, and no others. If one does not feel himself to be lost, then he is not prepared to turn to Christ for hope; for Christ's great salvation is prepared for, and is adapted only to those who are utterly without hope in themselves. The Bible describes the ruling natural disposition of men as one that cannot be used at all in the service of God. It would not let a man feel at home and at ease in heaven itself. It must be overruled and given up, and a Christ-like disposition put in its place, before the man can be content with the society of the holy and the occupations of the blessed. The moment the man renounces the sway of what the Bible calls the carnal, the earthly, the worldly principle, he enters the kingdom of God. He takes the place that was made for him and that will fit him for ever.

There is no denying that the Bible gives very hard names to all who have not put on the new man which after God is created in righteousness and true holiness. It says that they are dead in trespasses and in sins, and they must be quickened and raised up to a new and holy life. They are sold under sin and they must be bought with an infinite price. They are in bondage and a mighty Deliverer must set them free. They are blind both to their interests and their obligations, and their eyes must be opened that they may see. All this is said in sad and solemn earnest many times over by the Holy Scriptures when describing man's need of a Saviour. And when men come to be as much in earnest as the Bible is in providing the best possible relief for the world, they say as much against themselves as the Bible says. The best men that have ever lived on earth have poured out their souls in the most sorrowful and agonizing confession of their subjection to a dark and evil power, and of their need of help from a Divine source.

The Bible says that man in his unrenewed state is without love, without peace, without hope, without pardon. He is at war with himself and with the only possible conditions of attaining peace. He carries a heavy burden upon his heart, and he cannot shake it off. He remembers the past with regret, and a dark cloud rests upon his prospects for the future. Whosoever studies history, society, individual character or his own heart with earnest and impartial scrutiny, will not be surprised that Jesus should say man must be born again or he cannot enter .the pure and blessed kingdom of God. Even in describing the lives of good men, the Bible only says that they have some excellences mingled with many imperfections, and they differ from the rest of men only in the fact that they are sorrowful for their sins and they are earnestly striving to lead a better life.

And if we shut up the Bible and throw away all our theories and theologies, and only read the book of human nature as its dark and appalling pages are open before us every day, we shall find reason enough to say, Human character will have to be made over anew and utterly changed, or there can be no hope for the world. The great and terrible mystery is not that men must be born again to see the kingdom of God, but that they should be unwilling to accept the help that is offered—they should persist in declaring themselves better off without it.

But only let the heart be changed, let the Divine love come in and drive the worldly spirit out, and what a wonderful and glorious creature poor, unhappy, fallen man becomes! Renewed, righted, he starts upon his heavenward journey with joy in his heart from the exhaustless river of God's pleasures, and with light upon his path from the fountain of eternal day. He is like the blind man from whose eyes the scales of darkness fell at the word of Jesus, and he found himself in a new creation of surpassing splendor and beauty. He is like the bird that has just escaped from the net, and that springs exultant on the wing, and bounds away over forest and field with a cry of joy and with the speed of the wind. The man with his changed heart, with his life begun all anew, is free, wearing no chain save the sweet and welcome bond that binds him to Christ. The world is overcome and put under his feet. The forces of the tempter are routed and scattered, and good angels encamp around him for his protection.

There is no greatness, power, glory, joy, attainable by man on earth to be compared for a moment with that which becomes the possession and birth-right of the new-born child of God. The great military commander scatters the armies of nations, and shakes the thrones and empires of half the world, and then dies of disappointment and in exile. The great poet pours the devastating flood of his fiery passion upon the hearts of millions, and revels in proud misery over the ruin which he has made, and then dies with curses upon his lips. The great philosopher ranges through all the harmonies and glories of the universe, everywhere tracing the manifestations of creative power and infinite wisdom in the formation of worlds, yet finding no God. Such examples of human greatness startle the world and attract the admiring gaze of millions. But they pass away like the pestilence and the storm, and are remembered chiefly by the desolations they have made. A more exalted greatness, a more benefi- cent career, a more enduring glory belong to the renewed and redeemed child of God who is made heir of all things in Christ. He is made sure of an inherit- ance that will better satisfy the soul than all the riches of the earth. He shall be crowned with a glory that shall brighten with the progress of ages. The change wrought upon his heart has brought him into harmony with the will, the power, the law that governs all things. His name is enrolled as a citizen in the record-book of heaven. He is expected to arrive there at no very distant time. Preparations have been made for his reception. An apartment in the house of many mansions is waiting for him. Messengers from that world come all the way, flying swiftly, to guard and to guide him in his journey thither. In all the universe no higher work can be found for God's mighty angels than to minister unto the heir of salva- tion. A single angel could blast the conqueror and all his legions with death in a single night. And yet that mighty minister of Jehovah is happy to wait upon the least of the disciples of Jesus. He can explore the sun and stars and all the infinite host of heaven. He can range the universe with unwearied flight, tracing everywhere the great and marvelous works of the Lord Almighty. He can lead the worship of the adoring host in the presence of God, and amid the splendors of the eternal throne. And yet that honored and mighty one, so exalted among the hierarchies of heaven, is happy to leave his shining seat among the many thrones of the blest, and to come down to this darkened and suffering world upon an errand of love and mercy to the man who is struggling to shake off the grasp of the low, sensual, earthly spirit, and lift himself up to a higher, purer, better life. No depth of darkness or affliction can hide the suffering child of God from his angel-comforter, who comes all the way from the service and the song of heaven to cheer his heart and strengthen his faith in the hour of need.

Go to the meanest couch that can be found in all the damp cellars or stifling garrets of the great city where a servant of Christ lies down in poverty and neglect to die. Look on the wretchedness of that vile abode, and weep, as you may, to learn that no human friend has been there before you with the offer of help and consolation. You may be sure that God's mighty angels have found out that dark abode. If your eyes could be opened to behold their glory, that wretched apartment would seem to you the vestibule of heaven—the miserable pallet would become a throne of triumph. You would be ready to fall down and worship at the feet of the mighty messenger who stands waiting to bear the emancipated spirit of the dying disciple to the throne of Jesus, to the mansions of the blest.

And the greatness conferred on the new-born child of God rises to a far more exceeding and ineffable glory. The everlasting Father bows the heavens and

21

comes down to dwell with him.   He makes his abode in the renewed and contrite heart.   The Son of the Highest calls him a brother, and receives him to his confidence as a bosom friend.   He is preferred before all temples for the indwelling of the Spirit of the Holy One.   He is permitted to ask what he will of Him who has everything to give.   He is a peculiar treasure unto him to whom the riches of the universe belong.   All that the eye has seen, the ear has heard, or the heart has felt, fails to give us terms for the description when we speak of the birth-right inheritance of the new-born child of God.   We can only go to the utmost of our capacities in describing the possession, and then say it is greater, richer, more enduring, more satisfying than anything we can describe, anything we can conceive.

Would you have the whole creation appointed to be your tributary and to fill your heart with the abundance of peace?   Would you receive the ministrations of mighty angels and rejoice in their protection wherever you go ?   Would you have faith to believe that the infinite God dwells with you, and that you are an accepted and beloved child of the everlasting Father?   You have only to desire this great inheritance more than anything else, and it shall be yours.   You have only to open your heart to receive it, and the new life will come in and dwell with you for ever.

Jesus' Night on the Mountain.

And it came to pass in those days that he went out into a mountain to pray, and continued all night in prayer to God.—LUKE vi. 12.

JESUS' NIGHT ON THE MOUNTAIN

XV.

JESUS' NIGHT ON THE MOUNTAIN.

MOUNTAINS hold a sacred and sublime pre-eminence in the glorious imagery with which the inspired writers invest the word of revelation. Both the science and the poetry of modern times make them the grandest feature on the face of the globe. They stand up in silent and awful testimony to the greatness of the Power which of old stretched out the heavens like a curtain and laid the foundations of the earth. Whether rising in solitary magnificence from the bosom of the wide-extended plain, or piled up as a separating wall through the length of a whole continent; whether belching angry flames from their blasted summits, and groaning with the intolerable fervor of inward fires till the solid earth shakes with the throes of their great agony, or standing for ever in rapt and voiceless communion with the silent skies of noon and the solemn stars of night; whether soaring aloft snow-clad to the untrodden heights where eternal winter dwells in "icy halls of cold sublimity," or displaying the wide reach of genial slopes to the life-giving sun, blue with the mantle of cloudy pines and

musical with the voices of streams that entice the deli-
cate-footed Spring to plant her flowers on the edge of
the glacier;—in every aspect and in every form, in every
age and in every land mountains are the fit representa-
tives of everything greatest and mightiest in the mate-
rial world. They may be traversed with sacred awe—
they may be studied with devout emotion as exhibit-
ing upon their scarred summits and rocky sides the foot-
steps of the "dreadful God." On their ancient walls
and cloven battlements we may read the record of the
goings forth of creative power in the building of
worlds.

The sacred language of the Hebrews does not con-
tain the technical terms of modern science, but it often
speaks of the mountains as if they had a living soul,
and could sympathize with one who had retired to the
sanctuary of their solitudes for prayer and worship.
One who had been from early youth a devout reader
of the most sublime passages in the Psalms and Pro-
phets would have the most sacred images and lofty
thoughts thronging upon his mind when alone among
mountains. When God came from Teman, and the
Holy One shined forth from Mount Paran with the
retinue of the ten thousands of his saints, and his glory
covered the heavens, and the earth was full of his
praise, it is declared by the prophet that the everlast-
ing mountains were scattered and the perpetual hills
did bow. When the richest blessing is promised to
the people that faithfully keep the commandments of

the Lord, it is declared that theirs shall be the chief
things of the ancient mountains and the precious
things of the lasting hills. When God would give the
strongest assurance of the immutability of his promise
to them that trust him, he declares that the mountains
shall depart and the hills shall be removed, but his
kindness shall not depart nor the covenant of his
peace be removed. When the servant of God is ready
to sink under the waves of affliction that sweep over
his soul, he looks for help to the everlasting hills—he
lifts up his eyes to the high places of the mountains
and waits for the dawn. In the day of deliverance the
mountains bring peace to his soul, the mountains and
the hills break forth before him into singing. The
herald of glad tidings comes with beautiful feet upon
the mountains. In the last days, when righteousness
shall fill the earth, the mountain of the Lord's house
shall be exalted above the hills and all nations shall
flow unto it.

If we turn from the figurative to the historic lan-
guage of the Scriptures, we shall find still more to im-
press the mind of a devout Hebrew with the feeling
that the mountains afford a fit sanctuary for prayer
and communion with God. He made them the scene
of the most awful and glorious manifestations of him-
self on earth. He set them up as witnesses and monu-
ments of his own mighty acts in the government of the
nations and in the redemption of man. They are ap-
pointed to bear the impress of his finger and to tell of

his greatness, until the conflagration of the final day shall sink them again in the same fires by which they were upheaved of old from the molten sea of a chaotic world.

The primitive Eden was adorned and made glorious in the eyes of its blest inhabitants by mountains. From their snowy tops and secret springs sources were supplied for the great river whose fourfold branches encompassed and watered the whole land of Paradise. When all the families of the earth, with a single exception, were buried in one universal grave, it was the mountains that first rose above the avenging waters in token of reconciliation with the surviving representatives of a disobedient race. It was the mountains that extended their rocky arms to receive back the weary fugitives of the waves to the forfeited inheritance of sunny hills and fertile plains and revolving seasons. The trial of faith which made Abraham the father of the faithful for all time was appointed for him upon a distant mountain. He went a weary journey of days with his beloved son, carrying the dread secret of the commanded sacrifice like a barbed arrow in his aged heart, and the sacred height which the Lord showed him afar off was destined to be the scene of the great and final sacrifice for the world's redemption. When the Ancient of Days bowed the heavens and came down to proclaim his fiery law to the gathered tribes of Israel, it was upon a desolate and hoary mountain that he made his seat. For twice forty days the mighty

God set up his throne upon the rocky heights of Sinai. His descent was proclaimed by the trumpetings of archangels; he was attended by the myriads of the heavenly hosts, and the place of his glory was veiled with clouds and thick darkness on the holy mount. And the same heights were swept by the strong wind and scorched by the devouring fire and rent by the earthquake when the mightier power of Jehovah spoke to Elijah in the still small voice. When Aaron, the first high-priest, and Moses, the great lawgiver of Israel, had completed their course, and the time had come for them to be gathered unto their fathers, by command of God they went up into a mountain to die alone. When the pillar of the cloud and the fire had led the wandering tribes into the possession of the promised land, the awful symbol of the Divine presence settled down upon a mountain and made it the place of Jehovah's name and the Holy Hill for the gathering of the people. When Israel revolted and cast down the altars of the Lord, and the whole land was blasted with drought and famine in the days of Ahab, it was upon a mountain that the lost fire came down from heaven to rekindle the sacrifice at the word of Elijah.

All these and many similar facts in sacred history were familiar to the devout in Israel at the time when Christ appeared. As it was his purpose to confirm and complete the whole course of Divine instruction carried on in previous ages, we are not surprised to find him giving an additional consecration to mountains by his life and instructions. It was upon the top of an exceeding high mountain that he rejected the offered kingdoms and glory of all the earth, and in so doing triumphed for ever over the tempter's power. It was upon a mountain that he appeared in the majesty of meekness and love to begin his ministry by promising infinite blessing to the poor in spirit, the pure in heart, the mourning and the merciful. It was upon a holy mount that he was seen by the chosen three of his disciples transfigured and clothed with Divine majesty, and declared to be the Son of God by voices from the excellent Glory. It was upon a mountain that he completed in his own person the expiatory sacrifice which will be remembered in eternity as the greatest event of time. And when his earthly mission was accomplished, it was from a mountain that the Conqueror of sin and death reascended triumphant to his heavenly throne.

All this is in accordance with the sacred prominence which had been given to mountains in all the previous revelations of God to man. It all agrees with the Divine greatness which belonged to Christ as the eternal Son of God. But there is one thing more which draws our hearts to Jesus with the deepest wonder and sympathy. He was accustomed to steal away alone to the silent sanctuary of the mountains, and spend the whole night in prayer to God. All day long, in the crowded and stifling synagogue, in the narrow and equally crowded streets, and finally on the bright and burning sand of the sea-shore, he teaches the multitude and heals the sick. All are eager to approach him and weary him with questions—some from idle curiosity, some from vanity, some in the spirit of caviling and with the desire to catch him in his words, some to draw his attention to subjects of petty and personal interest, and some from an earnest and humble desire to learn the truth from his lips. The multitude around him is in constant commotion, swaying to and fro with the efforts of some to get nearer and of others to escape. His voice is sometimes drowned by the cries of the suffering and the insane, whom friends are endeavoring to press through the crowd and set down before him; and then again by the shouts and exultations of those who have been suddenly healed of long and hopeless disease. He speaks kindly, patiently with all, and is always clear, calm, earnest, amid all the tumult and excitement of the people. They give him no time to eat or to rest. Every applicant for help thinks his own case the most urgent, and no sooner is one relieved than another comes in his place. The immediate friends of Jesus think he is beside himself, and they try to withdraw him from the crowd, but without success. At last he goes down to the sea-shore, and as the people press upon him, still eager even to touch his garments, he enters a fishing-boat, and, thrusting out a little from the land, finishes the long and weary day by speaking from the boat to the crowd on the shore.

And now, when the sun has set and the night comes on and the people are scattered to their homes, the disciples think that the Master will rest, and that they shall see him a little while in 'some quiet home by themselves. But no; weary, hungry, exhausted as he is, he refuses to go with them to the town and seek refreshment and repose. He sets his face toward the dark and solitary mountains and moves off alone, forbidding his disciples to follow. He tells them where they will find him in the morning, but all night he must be alone in the lofty and desolate sanctuary of the mountains with God. They watch him as long as they can see his solitary form crossing the narrow plain and climbing the steep heights, and then they go to their homes to sleep, and he to some dark and shelterless spot to spend the whole night in prayer to God. He has no sins to confess, no pardon to seek, no griefs of his own to bewail, and yet there he pours out his soul, with strong crying and many tears, while the slow hours of the night wear away. The wicked world sleeps while the sinless One wakes in weariness and pain to pray all night that the world may be saved.

And this retiring alone to spend the night in prayer amid the solitudes of the mountains was a common practice with the holy Jesus. Before entering upon his public ministry he spent forty days and nights in solitary spiritual conflicts and mighty wrestlings of soul amid the most dreary mountain solitudes in all the land. The whole night before the delivery of the

sermon on the Mount he spent in prayer on some soli-
tary height above the elevated plain, whence he came
down to meet the people in the morning. When the
multitude would seize him by force to make him their
king, he stole away from them under the covert of
darkness, and went up into the solitary and unin-
habited table-land to pray. When he called and com-
missioned his twelve apostles, he had prepared himself
for that most important and critical selection by spend-
ing the whole previous night in prayer alone among
the mountains. In all the gospel history there is no
scene which appeals more deeply, tenderly to a devout
mind and susceptible heart than this—the Son of God,
alone in the solitude of the mountains, pouring out his
soul all night in prayer.

Jesus felt that he must pray, and that he must be
alone. The modes of living in the land of Palestine
and in the time of his ministry were such as to make
it impossible for him to have a private apartment for
retirement in the houses of the class of people with
whom he lived. He was surrounded by an excited
and eager crowd all day long, and when the work of
the day was done he must spend the night in the com-
mon sleeping-room of the house with many others.
Rather then forego the opportunity to pour out his
voice and his soul with the utmost freedom in long and
loud supplication, he chose to retire to the solitude of
the mountains and spend the whole night alone in
prayer to God. And his retirement at such times

gives no countenance to the practice of ascetic and monastic seclusion from the world. He withdrew from active intercourse with men for a brief season only that he might come back to labor more efficiently for their good. He came forth from the solitude of the mountains and from the night of prayer with a heart full of sympathy for the poor, the ignorant, the afflicted and the fallen, and with a mind ready to work all day for their relief and instruction. The mountain monasteries of Sinai and Saint Saba and Carmel and Athos have been in existence for centuries, but they have sent forth no streams of light and blessing to revive the waste places of ignorance and superstition around them. The saints who shut out the world with stone walls, and wake at night to pray in stony cells, and hide themselves away among mountains for the best years of their life, have little sympathy with the Saviour of sinners in his solitude. He sought for men wherever he could find them—in the public street, in the private house, in the synagogue or by the sea-side. He toiled all day in the work of healing and instruction, and then spent the night in solitary prayer, only to come forth again and renew his labor amid all the noise and conflict of the world. Moses and Elijah went up to mountain-tops to pray, and they spent long seasons in solitary devotion. But it was only to prepare themselves for active toil and for personal contact with the stirring interests of real life.

All great reformers, all good and wise leaders of

public opinion, all true philanthropists who lift the human race up to a higher and better life, have prepared themselves for their public work and acquired strength for great sacrifices by solitary communion with God and prayer. All men who are called of heaven to introduce a new order of things and to put the world forward in the course of improvement have learned to sympathize with Jesus in his retirement from the world to spend the whole night in prayer. They see what the world needs better than other men, because they look down upon the conflicts of opinion and the war of opposing interests from the serene and commanding heights to which they have been lifted by prayer. When they get discouraged because the work moves slow, and the obstacles are many and strong, and the darkness is thick around them, they know how to take to themselves the wings of prayer and ascend to the mount of God, and gain a new and clear view of the glorious and triumphant issue to which all present conflicts and uncertainties shall come. In the calm hour of renewed and exalted faith they hear the voices in heaven saying with one accord —The Lord God omnipotent reigneth. And then they come back to the field with faces full of heavenly light, making many strong by the strength of their mighty hopes, and cheering the fearful and despondent with the song of salvation.

So can we all go up the mount of God and survey the obscure and complicated course of this earthly journey from the heights and watch-towers of heaven. We can all repeat the observation when clouds drift across our path and the storm gathers its darkness around us. Every prayer offered in faith lifts the suppliant above the clouds of ignorance and the conflicts of passion. Prayer brings new light into the mind, because it scatters the clouds that keep the light from entering; it brings new peace into the heart, because it calms the agitations with which the heart is torn and weary. Every aspiration for a pure and a holy life opens the secret chambers of the soul for that life to come in. Every trial patiently borne, every blessing gratefully received, every temptation faithfully resisted, carries us higher on the shining way that leads to glory and to God. And all these steps of advance in the pure and blessed life can be best quickened and corrected by prayer.

The clearest and loftiest outlook upon the complicated affairs of this world is gained by prayer. When we keep near the throne, dwelling in the secret place of the Most High, we shall see the path of duty plainly and all things working together for our good. The highest and safest place of observation, from which to study the condition of the world and foresee its future history, is the place nearest to the seat of infinite power; and that is the place of prayer. While we take counsel with our doubts and fears, or try to solve the problem of the universe in the cabinets and laboratories of science, or to explore the depths of eternity with the feeble taper of human reason, we shall only increase our perplexity and deepen our disappointment.

The traveler in a mountainous region, while threading his way along the narrow valley, up the course of the winding stream and under the brow of wooded hills, has very imperfect views of the real features of the country and of the relation of its several portions to each other. He sees before him an apparent opening between mountain ranges, but when he approaches the supposed depression, he finds it walled up to heaven by precipices which the wild goats could not climb. He turns in another direction to ascend a commanding height from which to survey the whole region. But when he reaches the proposed elevation, he finds that still beyond mountains soar above mountains, " Alps on Alps arise." He endeavors to follow the dry bed of a torrent as the surest path in his descent to the plain. But that which seemed an easy and an open track in the distance becomes precipitous at his approach, and leads far away from the course which he wishes to pursue. He hears the roar of a waterfall echoing from some hidden glen, and he thinks he has only to turn aside a few steps to behold its beauty. But he toils on for hours in the vain endeavor to reach the sound which seemed so near. He proposes to ascend some lofty peak which rises clear and cold above all the lesser heights. He starts in the early morning and hurries on through the deep

22

valley and around the bold headland and up the steep
declivity, and when the day begins to wane and his
strength is exhausted, the same solitary peak hangs
over him, seemingly no nearer, no farther off, than it
was hours ago.

Such are the illusions and disappointments of a
traveler among mountains so long as he keeps him-
self down in the low valleys or only climbs the heights
of subordinate hills.   But let him toil his way up to
the loftiest peak, and from thence embrace the whole
landscape in one commanding view, and his former
perplexity will disappear at once.   What was before
an inextricable labyrinth of hills and valleys and
forests and streams, becomes as easy to trace as the
lines upon his hand.

So it is with men while pursuing the low and intri-
cate paths of a prayerless, faithless, worldly life.
They have no clear, connected, harmonious view of the
purpose of their own being, or of the order and tend-
ency of events in the world's history.   They have
no one object in view, so high and sacred that they can
afford to sacrifice all others to gain that alone.   They
struggle hard to make their way along the dark and
crooked paths of present interest, expediency or plea-
sure.   They lift themselves up for a wider view upon
the molehills of human pride.   They rise early and
outwatch the stars to study the uncertain standards and
landmarks which human wisdom has set up.   They
toil hard and make no progress.   They advance only-

to return to the point of departure. They make many calculations, only to leave the great questions of life and duty darker than before.

But let them go up to the mount of God where man meets his Maker in humble, trusting prayer. Let them accept the great truth that the supreme power governing the universe is a Being whom they can address as a personal Friend. Let them leave all the false guides which they have been following, and look only to Him who sees everything at one view and governs everything with a word. Let them believe that they can speak to that most mighty and Holy One at any time, and he will hear their voice and attend to their wants. And then the darkness and perplexity will vanish from their minds. They will see man and the world and life and death and time and eternity in their true relations. They will see that all life, power and blessing are centred in God, and the greatest possible privilege for man is to come to God and ask all things of him in prayer. Take away the privilege of prayer, and nothing would be left to man but a pilgrimage of darkness and a heritage of woe.

Prayer is the most rational and appropriate outgoing of the spiritual nature of man in the effort to grasp something higher and better than earth and time can give. In every act of sincere prayer the soul comes into living contact with the infinite Mind. We see no face bending over us with looks of compassion. No voice answers to our humble cry. No hand is let down for us to grasp. And yet in all prayer the heart pours itself forth to One whose awful presence is deeply felt, whose benignant answer is waited for with longing desire, whose safe guidance is sought with such confidence as the child seeks the parent's supporting hand. Prayer is a representative act, standing for all the duties and dispositions peculiar to a true, well-ordered life. Whoever prays aright looks away from man to God; from earth to heaven; from things seen and temporal to things unseen and eternal. All that is feared and shunned in hours of the most earnest watchfulness, all that is sought and hoped for as the result of the highest spiritual cultivation, all that rises to view in the glorious vision of faith, is present to the mind and impressed upon the heart in the solemn hour of prayer. We must say, therefore, that the true greatness and exaltation of life are utterly wanting to him who does not pray. The joy unspeakable, the peace that passeth all understanding, can never come into the mind and heart of him who holds himself aloof from the Giver of all good, and refuses to speak, with reverent and sacred familiarity, to the greatest Friend he has in the universe.

A Night Storm on the Sea.

The ship was now in the midst of the sea, tossed with waves: for the wind was contrary. And in the fourth watch of the night Jesus went unto them, walking on the sea.—MATT. xiv. 24, 25.

XVI.

A NIGHT STORM ON THE SEA.

THE Sea of Galilee is sacred in the annals and memories of Christian faith and affection for all time. The devout student of the Gospel history from distant lands counts it a memorable moment in his life when, with throbbing heart and tearful eyes, he first looks down from the neighboring hills upon its glassy waves and silent shore. "Here," he thinks, faster than words can utter his thoughts—"here was the earthly home and the heavenly work of the incarnate Son of God. Along this shining beach he walked in the light of the early morning. These lowly sands bore the impress of his feet, and these high banks echoed to the sound of his voice. The shadows of evening closed around him as he taught the multitude upon this once busy and populous shore. His sacred form was imaged in these bright waters. He was many times borne across from shore to shore in the fisherman's bark. The hot and quivering air comes up from this deep cleft between the hills now as it did when he toiled all day in the fierce heat and gave himself no rest from his work of instruction and mercy.

343

The wild winds that come down from these high banks heard his voice and were still. He walked upon the crystal face of this sea as if it had been solid ground beneath his feet. Yonder, on the desolate plain, was the little city which enjoyed the exalted privilege of being called his own. In its narrow streets he healed multitudes of the sick. In the white synagogue which the centurion built he spoke on the Sabbath day. In the mansion of the rich he raised the dead. Among the huts and homes of fishermen he made his abode. Up these steep hill-sides he climbed to seek the solitude of the mountain for midnight prayer. On one of these heights overlooking the lake he opened his ministry with an address which is destined to carry the words of blessing to every language of the earth and to every age of the world's history. On yonder grassy slope, upon the other side, he fed five thousand men with miraculous food. From thence he departed alone into the desolate mountains beyond, to escape the importunity of the excited multitude, who would take him by force to make him their king. On the shore of this lake he appeared again to his disciples after he had passed through the awful mystery of death."

Thus the sacred memories of the Son of God throng upon the mind of the Christian traveler when, for the first time, he looks down upon the Sea of Galilee. The cities that lined the shore and the boats that darted across the sea when Jesus walked on the beach are gone. The pensive pilgrim who reads the Gospel story amid the ruins of Capernaum may lift his eye from the page and take in the whole compass of sea and shore, and not discover a single human being in sight, unless it be a wandering Arab stealing along under the high banks so cautiously that his appearance increases the aspect of loneliness that marks the whole scene. Silence and desolation reign where once Jesus had only to lift up his voice and thousands would gather to hear. The basin of clear, bright water is girt with bare, steep walls of limestone, two thousand feet high, and the whole surrounding landscape is indescribably drear and melancholy. The doom which Jesus pronounced upon Chorazin· and Bethsaida and Capernaum, because they repented not, seems to rest upon the naked hills and silent shore. And the awful desolation that now rests upon the doomed cities of Gennesaret and the whole scene around the Sea of Galilee is a sign and shadow of the deeper and darker desolation that must come upon the soul when once the love of Christ has been utterly grieved away and his offered salvation finally rejected.

With all the changes that have taken place in two thousand years, there is one aspect of this sacred sea which brings back our Saviour's days with vivid and awful reality. It is a night storm, such as the disciples encountered when their ship was tossed with the waves. The word used by the Evangelist, in describing the agitation of the little bark, literally means "tormented," and it refers to the writhings and convulsions of prisoners when subjected to the torment of the rack or the bastinado. And the Sea of Galilee is wrought into such convulsions by the peculiar manner in which the sudden and violent stroke of the wind comes down upon its waves.

The lofty mountain wall on the northeastern side of the lake is tunneled down to the water's edge by deep, narrow ravines. These wild gorges have been formed by the winter rains falling on the distant highlands, gathering into torrents and rushing down to the sea with a fury that sweeps everything before it but the solid rock. In midsummer, the air in the deep basin of the lake becomes heated like the air of an oven, and rises rapidly into the upper regions, while the heavy, cold air flows down through the deep channels in the surrounding walls to fill the vacancy. Sometimes, when the sun has set, the icy winds from the snowy heights of Hermon and the lofty tablelands of Bashan come howling down the narrow gorges, and shoot out upon the lake with such violence as to lash and torture its whole surface into writhing and convulsive waves. And these terrible storm-winds often come down suddenly as the avalanche when there is not a cloud in the sky.

Such must have been the case on that memorable night when the disciples wearied themselves with rowing and were not able to reach the shore. The day must have been fair and peaceful in the balmy Syrian spring when Jesus taught the great multitude in the open air on the smooth grassy headland that pushes out into the northeast corner of the lake. The evening must have been as calm when he blessed the barley loaves and fed the five thousand seated in ranks by hundreds and by fifties on the green sward. And all was still calm on the sea and in the air when he constrained his disciples to enter the ship and start for the other side, leaving him to dismiss the excited people alone.

But no sooner were they out a little from the shore than the wild wind came down through the mountain gorges with sudden and resistless fury, and swept them far away from their course toward the southern extremity of the lake. They were strong men, accustomed to the oar and not easily frightened by the waves. And so all night long, for full nine hours, they pulled with tireless sinews against the wind, toiling hard to recover their course and reach the point where they hoped to take their Master on board. But all in vain. The wind was too strong for them. The waves beat upon the boat as the blows of the bastinado fall upon the writhing and tortured victim in the prison-house. The strength of the rowers was exhausted, while the merciless storm was still at its height and the sea was raging under the lash of the winds.

Just then Jesus was seen coming to their relief, walking upon the waves. His watchful eye had seen them through the darkness from the distant shore, and

he was ready to appear the moment when they needed
him most.   They were laboring hard to obey his com-
mand and reach the point where they hoped to receive
him on board.   And the Master does not assign a hard
service to his disciples and then leave them to struggle
unsupported and alone.   At the very time when they
think themselves .utterly deserted and in darkness,
they are watched by the eye of infinite compassion, as
the mother watches the first attempts of the child to
walk, withdrawing the supporting hand, yet always
near enough to arrest a fall.

At first the disciples were afraid when they saw
Jesus walking on the waves.   They thought it some
bodiless messenger from the spirit-world—some awful
shadow from eternity appearing to warn them that
they would soon be with the departed.   Nothing fills
the strong heart of manhood with such indefinable and
overmastering fear as anything which is taken to be a
voice or form or living messenger from the state of
the dead.   Men who deny that there is any conscious
existence beyond the grave tremble and turn pale
when any sudden event brings them face to face with
what they claim is nothingness, but which they fear is
a dread and awful reality.

When the disciples heard the voice of their beloved
Master saying, " It is I, be not afraid," their fear was
changed to confidence, and the foremost of their num-
ber was ready to step over the side of the ship and go
to Jesus walking on the water.   And the wonder is,

not that his faith failed him and he began to sink, but that he dared to go at all upon such a sea in such a storm. The hand of Jesus was near and strong to save. With a gentle rebuke for his doubt, he rescued the bold and impulsive disciple from sinking. The two came on board, and immediately the wind ceased and the ship was at the land whither they went.

The human heart is a great deep, troubled and tormented by the strong wind of passion, and finding no rest until Jesus walks upon the stormy waves with his blessed feet and brings a great calm to the weary soul. The great sea of human life is ever agitated with fear and conflict and change until Jesus comes with the message of peace. The whole history of the world, from age to age, has been a history of trouble and battle and storm, and the groaning earth will never have rest until the nations receive the Divine Messenger of peace.

Jesus always comes to the sorrowing world and the weary heart with the blessing of peace. And yet somehow the unhappy world is afraid that he comes to take away its joy, and the weary heart is troubled and terrified at his approach. When we speak of Jesus to worldly and wicked men, dark thoughts of death and eternity come over them, and they look as if they feared some avenging angel had come to call their sins to remembrance and to torment them before the time. A man will sooner be persuaded to accept every article of the most profound and difficult theology than to

believe that Jesus comes to him in the dark night of
spiritual depression to take the burden from his heart
and make him a contented and happy man.   To him
the offered sympathy of Christ 'is something to be
suffered and submitted to, rather than eagerly sought
and enjoyed.

When I say to the sorrowing, the disheartened and
disappointed, " Jesus is longing to come to you and
take all your griefs upon himself and give you rest," I
see a shade of deeper sadness stealing over them.
They are sorely troubled with their worldly cares and
disappointments.   But they seem still more troubled
when told that a Divine Comforter, with infinite
strength and sympathy, is ready to come to their re-
lief.   I go to the house of mourning, I stand up in
the solemn presence of the dead, and I try to speak
words of comfort to afflicted and bleeding hearts.   I
tell them that Jesus comes in the storm that has beaten
upon their household.   They have only to look and
they will see his radiant form in the night of sorrow.
They have only to listen and they will hear his voice
saying, " It is I, be not afraid."   And yet, when I
so speak of Jesus to the mourning and the afflicted,
they often seem afraid to believe me.   They see no
light in the cloud which surrounds them.   They hear
no voice calling to them in accents of love.   Jesus
comes to them in the night and in the storm, and they
are afraid.

I speak of Jesus to the young, the thoughtless and

the gay. I tell them that a life of worldliness is only a voyage upon a restless and treacherous sea, exposed to the tempests of passion and temptation, and ending in the wreck of the soul. Jesus only can give the peace, the joy, the hope for which they long. In saying so, I am warranted by the experience of millions who have found in one blessed moment of penitence and faith in Christ more joy than in years of devotion to the world. And yet the young and ardent and hopeful are afraid to receive Jesus to their hearts. They are afraid he will make them unhappy—afraid they will lose the dearest joys of life if he is to be with them always. When they become old and sorrow-stricken and disappointed, and are no longer able to enjoy the world, then they think they will be glad to have Jesus come to them. When they are tossed upon the sea of trouble, when the storm of affliction beats upon their heads, when the night of death is round them, then they think they will be glad to hear the voice of Jesus say unto them, "Be not afraid." But now, so young, so full of life, with so much in the world to enjoy, they cannot think of receiving Jesus to their hearts. It only makes them sad to think that he is near.

Under the dark cloud that comes over the mind in some forms of insanity the unhappy sufferer is sometimes most afraid of his best friends. He is most anxious to flee from those who have done most for his relief, and whose hearts are breaking with grief for the affliction that is upon him. And such is the strange and sad mistake of those who are afraid to receive Jesus to their hearts when he comes to make them happy. They may toil like the galley slave all their life long, rowing hard against the wind, and all the while they may be driven farther and farther from the rest, the repose of soul which they are seeking. They have only to receive Christ's offered peace, and all the elements of change and trouble will become ministries of good to their souls, and every wind will waft them toward the haven of rest. Christ is Lord of all the tempests that shake the world, as well as of the fiercer storms that rage in the human soul. He walks abroad in the bright sunshine of youth and prosperity, as well as in the dark night of affliction and sorrow. Wherever wanderers are astray, he is near to show the right way. Wherever the weary and heavy-laden are sinking under their load, he is near to take on himself their burden. Wherever the young and thoughtless are in danger of mistaking the whole aim and purpose of their existence, he is near to offer the crown of life. He comes in the voice of his word. He comes in the lessons of his providence. He comes in the strivings of his Spirit. He comes early and often, and continues to come when many times rejected. He comes only to bring the blessing of peace to hearts that will never find rest without him.

And shall any be afraid of such a Friend? No not of him, but there is something of which even a brave man should be afraid. He should be afraid to sail upon the treacherous and stormy sea of life without Christ to calm the waves, to hush the winds and to bring him safe to the land of rest. He should be afraid to rush into the thick of the world's cares and pleasures and temptations without Christ in his heart to keep him in the hour of danger, and to show him the safe path through all the changes and perils with which he is surrounded. He should be afraid to give himself up to the vanities and ambitions and frivolities of the world, with the expectation that when he has become weary of such a life, Christ will come and drive them all out of his heart and make him a better and happier Christian, just because he has tried the world and found it wanting. He should be afraid to live in constant exposure to death, and yet without any settled and satisfactory preparation to enter upon the untried state of being beyond the grave.

It is the strangest and saddest thing in the world that men should be afraid of such a friend as Jesus has proved himself to be in the blessed experience of all who have received him to their hearts—Afraid to be known as the followers of him who wore the crown of thorns for their sake, and who now wears the crown of heaven—Afraid of him who bore our sorrows in the bitter agony of the garden and the cross, and suffered unutterable things in conflict with darkness and death, that he might give us the inheritance of eternal life—Afraid to have their names written with

23

the holy and the blessed of all ages of whom the world was not worthy, and who now stand before the throne of heaven with the palms of victory in their hands. They receive pride and envy and doubt and complaint and frivolity; they receive avarice and ambition and hate and selfishness to their hearts, and they are troubled all their life long with such unhappy and contentious guests within. But when the meek and gentle, the holy and the pitying Jesus comes and asks to be received by them, they are afraid of him, they reject him. And they keep doing this, although it is impossible to find a single individual on the face of the earth who will say, " I have received Jesus to my heart and he has made me unhappy."

When the disciples saw Jesus walking upon the waves, they thought they saw a spirit, an unreal and ghostly shadow, appearing to terrify rather than to comfort and deliver them. And yet he was the most true and real man that ever walked the earth. Men are still prone to think Jesus something unreal, spectral, ghostly. They think that the religion which bears his name is something hard to be weighed and measured like substantial things; they think it depresses or excites or bewilders people, and makes them act unlike themselves. And yet Christ is the highest realization of truth. In him the troubled, longing, weary soul finds the only reality which satisfies its great want. He is more real, true and satisfying to the earnest, thinking, aspiring mind than wealth or learning or pleasure or power. His grand purpose in all his instructions is to make us true men—not angels, not beings destitute of any of the passions, appetites, affections that are essential to our humanity: he would make us true men. He stands before us in his human nature, complete, perfect, wanting nothing. And he would make us like himself, true in every purpose, feeling and thought—true in our whole heart and soul and being. This it is to be a Christian; this it is to be a follower of Christ, this it is to receive Christ to the heart. It is to be a true man. It is to have our whole human nature purified, ennobled, consecrated by the truth. Christian faith, Christian duty, Christian character are at mortal and everlasting enmity with all pretence, falsehood, unreality. The man who has the most of the life of Christ in his soul is the most true, genuine and complete man on the face of the earth. If any man hears Christ always and follows him perfectly, he is just what he seems to be, just what he pretends to be, just what he ought to be. To be a Christian it is only necessary to be a true man—to love, believe and obey the truth. Whatever it is which keeps one from being a Christian, it is something false; something as unreal as the spectre which the terrified disciples thought they saw walking on the sea; something that has no right to control the mind; something that perverts the judgment, misleads the heart and makes the whole plan and purpose of life a mistake. It is only when hearing the voice of

Christ and following him that man finds himself in his true place, all the feelings and faculties of his mind rightly and happily employed, all his dearest hopes resting upon everlasting foundations. All appropriate preaching of the gospel of Christ is an attempt to call men off from the pursuit of shadows and falsities, and engage them in work worthy of their immortal powers and their endless responsibilities. Conversion is turning back from a false way and beginning a life of obedience to the deepest sense of right, to the most solemn convictions of truth and duty in the soul. And however much men may fear and hesitate to begin a true, earnest life of obedience to Christ, nobody is ever afraid that he shall die a Christian. Nobody is afraid that death will find him too much absorbed in the service of Christ. No man can think of a more desirable close of life for himself than that he may be found faithful to his convictions, true to his own deepest sense of obligation.

When Peter stepped over the side of the ship to go to Jesus upon the water, he walked well enough while he kept his eye upon his Divine Master. But when he saw that the wind was boisterous, and he looked at the wild waves and he thought of the peril, then he began to sink. And if he had not had faith enough left to cry, " Lord, save me !" he would have sunk to rise no more.

Many try to walk on the treacherous waves of a worldly life at the bidding of the " prince of the power of the air." They step forth cautiously at first, not meaning to go far if there should be danger. But they give themselves gradually more and more to pleasure and to pride and to mirth, or to money-get ting and care and ambition, or to appetite and self-indulgence. They go farther and farther from the old safeguards of prayer and watchfulness, the Bible and the Sabbath and the sanctuary, Christian company and Christian influence. And all the while they are sinking deeper and deeper in the treacherous waves of a sea that they are trying to walk upon. They are becoming more worldly, more forgetful of eternal truth, more absorbed in things that can never satisfy the soul. By and by they begin to be alarmed. Trouble and fear come upon them, for they find they are sinking into an abyss which has no bottom. They are exposing themselves to a storm that no mortal can face. They are in danger of being overtaken by a night that is the blackness of darkness. Yet even then, if they will only cry as Peter did, "Lord, save me!" they will find the hand of Jesus near and strong. He will lift them out of the stormy sea and set their feet on the solid shore.

But, alas! too many will not look to Jesus in the hour of their greatest peril and sorrow. They look to the world for comfort, and they keep sinking deeper and deeper in trouble. They look to the world for pleasure, and they grow more unhappy. They look to the world for light, and they are all the while becoming involved in deeper darkness. They look to the world for hope, and they are answered with the groan of despair.

On a bitter cold night in mid-winter I was called from my bed to go ten miles away over a bleak and drifted road, and see a young man who was sinking in the deep waters of death. He was but twenty years of age. He had been a Sabbath-school scholar. He had been an attendant upon the sanctuary. He knew all about the way of salvation. But he had broken away from all these hallowed influences of earlier years —he had yielded to the enticements of evil companions, and now he was dying without hope. The messenger who came for me in haste was one of those who had helped him on in the way of darkness, but he could not lead him back to the light. I bade the dying youth look to Jesus, but his wild and wandering eye could see no Saviour in the darkness that was gathering around him. I besought him only to whisper the prayer, "Lord, save me!" I offered myself the petition which I desired to draw from his heart. His despairing look and heavy groan only answered, "Too late, too late!" He kept sinking, sinking till the billows of death passed over him, and no word or sign of hope came from his dying lips. And as I went back to my home in the cold starlight of that winter morning, it seemed to me as if the icy north wind that swept the frozen earth and swayed the naked branches of the trees by the road-side, took up the refrain of those sad and despairing words, "Too late, too late!" And I thought how many there are who have great need to offer every day the prayer once offered by the sinking disciple in the storm, " Lord, save me from sinking in this sea of worldliness and temptation with which I am surrounded ; save me from disowning Christ and denying the rock of my salvation; save me from giving up my heart, my life, my soul to the unsatisfying and perishable things of earth ; save me from living a stranger to peace and pardon, and from sinking at last in the deep waters of death, without a hope that shall be as an anchor to the soul."

Again, in the same city, on a summer's afternoon, I was called to visit a dying man. I walked hastily down by the river's side, where his humble dwelling stood in the midst of noisy workshops, and surrounded with all the sounds and activities of busy life. I entered his lowly room and approached his bedside with awe as well as compassion, for I felt myself to be in the company of heavenly messengers, who were waiting to conduct an emancipated soul from the bed of death to the throne of glory. I felt that I must speak fit words for a redeemed and immortal spirit to remember as the last accents of human lips in this world. And I spoke of Him who is the light of heaven and the hope of earth. The man was dying in great agony, but he could still signify, by the pressure of his hand and the glance of his eye, that in Christ was all his hope, and that beneath him was the everlasting arm.

He had lost the power of speech, but he wrote upon a slate with a wavering hand words that he wished to have read. I looked earnestly at the irregular lines, but could see no meaning. One word in the middle of the sentence was larger than the rest, and he pointed to that as if it contained the meaning of the whole. Still I could not spell it out. With dying energy he seized the pencil once more and slowly printed, "V I C- T O R Y." It was his last effort and it was enough. I could now read the whole sentence: "Thanks be to God who giveth us the *victory* through our Lord Jesus Christ." And as I went from that bedside to my home, it seemed to me as if the roar of the waterfall in the river, and all the sounds of busy life around me took up the word and echoed—*victory*. And for many a year, in the dark hours of spiritual conflict and discouraging toil, my waning faith has kindled into new life and my fainting heart has acquired new strength at the remembrance of that word written with dying hand in the chamber of death—*victory*.

The Last Night of the Feast.

Now the Jews' feast of tabernacles was at hand. . . . Then went up Jesus also unto the feast. . . . In the last day, that great day of the feast, Jesus stood and cried, saying, If any man thirst, let him come unto me, and drink.—JOHN vii. 2, 10, 37.

XVII.

THE LAST NIGHT OF THE FEAST.

EXT to the Passover, the Feast of Tabernacles was the most memorable and impressive of all the great national solemnities kept by the Hebrew people. For seven successive days Jerusalem was crowded by thousands of the faithful in Israel, gathered from all parts of Judea and from distant provinces of the Roman empire. The multitude seemed more immense because the resident population of the city, as well as the strangers, turned out of their dwellings and spent the week in the open air. They lived in booths or tabernacles of green boughs built upon the housetops, in the streets and public squares, in the courts of the temple and of private houses, and all up and down the valleys and hill-sides beyond the walls of the city. The whole of Mount Zion, with its compact array of flat roofs and stone battlements, was so thickly shaded with green boughs as to seem in the distance like a forest of palm and of pine, of olive and of myrtle. Seven days were consecrated with offerings and libations, with feast and song, with the grand choral symphonies of the temple music, and the even-

363

ings were given to illuminations and torchlight dances. The whole week was one long pastime of exhilarating and, in the end, of exhausting joy. The time was autumn. The fruits of the earth' had ripened and the harvests had been gathered in from all the fields. The whole nation was represented in the thanksgiving and festivities with which the capital celebrated the close of the year.

The night following the seventh day of the feast was the time when the interest of the great festival attained a pitch of the most wild and excited enthusiasm. Through the whole of that night four huge, golden candelabras, each sustaining four vast basins of oil, were kept burning in the principal court of the temple. The flame of these sixteen golden lamps illuminated the whole city. In the midst of the crowded court devout men danced with lighted torches in their hands, tossing them high in the air and catching them as they came down, at the same time shouting in unison with each other and singing psalms of praise. A vast orchestra of Levites was ranged up and down the fifteen stone steps of the temple, and they accompanied the dancing and the songs with harps, cymbals, psalteries, and all sorts of musical instruments. The vast mass of the people in front of the temple took up the chorus, at the same time waving branches of palm and of myrtle, and the swell of song rolled over all the housetops, and through all the streets, and overpast the walls of the city, and it was taken up in the tents on the hill-sides, until thousands upon thousands of voices joined in the strain, which was called the Great Hosanna: "Oh give thanks unto the Lord, for he is good, for his mercy endureth for ever." The singing and the dancing and the instrumental music were kept up all night.

When the first streak of dawn appeared, shooting up the eastern sky over the ridge of Olivet, the priests sounded with silver trumpets three times, long and loud, and the answering shouts of the people welcomed the Great Hosanna day. A procession of priests started immediately to bring water from the fountain of Siloam, which flowed at the foot of Mount Moriah outside of the city walls. When the procession returned, the brief twilight had grown to the full day. Their appearance was greeted with a blast of silver trumpets. They ascended the steps of the temple, bearing the golden beaker full of water in their hands, chanting the Song of Degrees as they went slowly up, keeping time with their steps: "Our feet shall stand within thy gates, O Jerusalem!" Then, in the presence of all the people they poured out the consecrated water in commemoration of the fountain that flowed from the rock for the tribes in the wilderness, and again they sung and the people took up the chorus with thundering voices: "The Lord Jehovah is my strength and song; therefore with joy shall ye draw water out of the wells of salvation."

On this occasion the music and the shouting, the glare of lamps and torches, the waving of palms and the blast of trumpets, the festive garlands and the excitement of the multitude produced so deep an impression upon all present that the Jewish people were accustomed to say, " He who has never seen the rejoicing at the pouring out of the water of Siloam has never seen rejoicing in his life."

Now, we have strong reason for believing that it was at this joyous climax in the great national festivity, when the people had exhausted themselves with singing and shouting all night, and the morning found them weary, hungry and thirsty, that Jesus stood forth and cried, " If any man thirst, let him come unto me and drink !" The long holiday was just closing. The supply of water had been greatly reduced by the unusual multitude gathered in the city. Joy itself had at last become wearisome. There was nothing more to excite or to interest the multitude that had been standing and walking and shouting and singing all night. The reaction of faintness and of exhaustion was beginning to overpower the people. Just then, the clear, calm voice of Jesus is heard in all the crowded court of the temple, speaking as never man spake, ringing out upon the fresh air of the morning like the blast of the silver trumpets, and saying, " If any man thirst, let him come unto me and drink. Whosoever shall drink of the water that I shall give him shall never thirst, but the water which I shall give him shall be in him a well of water springing up into everlasting life."

Never did the Divine Teacher himself preach his

own Gospel in more vivid and expressive terms. Never did he make a more touching appeal to the sense of need, to the deep feeling of want in the human soul. The time, the place, all the attendant circumstances conspired to give meaning and power to the words spoken. The people knew the voice, and they understood the figurative dress in which Jesus expressed the offer of salvation. To them the water of Siloam was the sign of the rock smitten by Moses in the wilderness, and the rock of Moses was the sign of their own Messiah. They felt the strange power, the sacred fascination of the voice which rung out clear and loud on that memorable morning in the crowded court of the temple. And some were ready to say, with the woman of Samaria, " Give me of this water, that I thirst not."

Eighteen hundred years have passed away since this cry went forth from the lips of Jesus in the hearing of weary, thirsty, exhausted men, but his words are more full of meaning and power to us to-day than they were to those who heard him speak. This is still the cry that goes forth from the Fountain of life to a lost world, " Come unto me and drink." This one invitation contains the ruling thought, the substance and meaning of the whole Gospel—the weary, the thirsty, the perishing invited to One who can relieve all their wants, now and for ever. If " *any*" man thirst—the poorest, the lowest, the worst ; the richest, the highest, the best—let him come to Christ. If any man "*thirst*"—

if he finds in his soul necessities that the world has
never answered; if he bears on his heart burdens
which no human hand can remove; if he has sought
for years and the earth over for peace and satisfaction,
and found it not; if he has passed through all the
extremes of poverty and riches, excitement and repose,
and never found anything worth living for—let him
come to Christ. The fact that one feels himself in
need is sufficient evidence that Christ calls him, and
that in obeying that call he shall find eternal life. If
the Divine Redeemer should leave the throne of
heaven and come back to earth to preach his own
Gospel in such a way as to satisfy some poor, doubt-
ing, troubled soul, he could say no more than he has
said: "If any man thirst—if any man be in want or
fear or trouble or sorrow; if any man desires peace
and pardon, the highest good of life while living and
the hope of heaven in death—let him come unto me."
So does the Saviour of the world commit himself by a
solemn engagement to save all who come to him with
an everlasting salvation. So does he send forth the
continual cry to the needy, the guilty and the unhappy:
"Come unto me, for I know that you are lost and
undone, and my heart is poured out with the desire to
help you."

There is nothing which men need so much as that
water of life which Christ offers to give when he says,
"Come unto me." The world has greatly changed in
many respects, and in most for the better in two thou-

sand years. In lands where the Gospel has been preached bodily comforts have been greatly multiplied; the means of instruction made common to the mass of the people; the oppressions of power have been abated; the spectres of fear and superstition have been driven away; intelligence flies with lightning speed; the ships of commerce encompass the globe; the poor can command comforts and conveniences now which princes could not buy when the incarnate Son of God dwelt among men. But still the essential nature of man remains unchanged. The great want of the human soul is the same now that it was when Jesus stood and cried to the thirsty, "Come unto me." No language can describe, no imagination can conceive, the destitution of man without a Saviour—man without forgiveness of sin, man without peace with God, man without the hope of eternal life. The awful sense of responsibility to the infinite God hangs heavy upon his soul, and he has no way to answer its demands, no way to silence its dreaded voice. In the most solemn and thoughtful moments of life he sees most reason to be dissatisfied with himself. At such times he hears most distinctly the bitter cry of want, of danger, of guilt in the depths of his soul. He may not be disposed to confess his sense of need. He may never be heard to ask with becoming earnestness, "What shall I do to be saved?" But if he should speak out the thoughts that haunt him in his most serious and tender moments, he would say, "Oh for some way to end this

24

wearisome conflict with my own heart! Oh what would I give to hear some voice from heaven saying to me, Thy sins are forgiven thee! How easy would it be for me to bear all the troubles and afflictions of earth, could I know assuredly that my name is written in God's book of life."

That cry of weariness and of woe is stifled in many a heart, while the voice speaks in a tone of thoughtlessness and gayety and the countenance wears a cheerful look. And that deep and dreadful want of the soul is the one fact which demands most serious attention on the part of all who would do anything to bring peace and contentment into the hearts and homes of men. All false religions, all efforts to seek satisfaction in a worldly life, all devices for pleasure, excitement and dissipation, all longings and struggles of weary hearts for rest, prove that there is some one great want in the very depths of man's soul, and that want must be answered first by Him who would be the world's Saviour. The burdens of life can be borne with patience, the sorrows of life can be sweetened and changed to joy, the pleasures of life can be made foretastes of heaven, when we have found a Saviour who can give us rest in our souls.

The thirst of the body is a fit and fearful sign of the great want of the soul without a Saviour. When extreme, thirst aggravates every other cause of suffering and it is itself most intolerable. The cry of soldiers dying upon the battle-field is not so much for relief from the pain of their wounds as for *water, water.* The exposures of wretched mariners on the deep, the tortures of martyrs on the rack, the consuming fire of fever burning in every vein and nerve, can bring forth no cry more agonizing than the cry for water. The only expression of bodily suffering which the cross extorted from the lips of Jesus was this, "I thirst." The cry of the lost soul when he lifted up his eyes in torments was for a drop of water to cool his parched tongue.

And if we fully appreciated the necessity of man in his sinful and hopeless state without a Saviour, we should feel that the terrible suffering of bodily thirst could only imperfectly indicate the greater necessity of the soul. Jesus uses that word to show that our desire for the water of life should be an intense and an irrepressible longing. It were a thousand times better to suffer the horrors of exposure day and night upon a single plank in the open ocean than to suffer the wreck of the soul, to live and die without a hope of entering into God's blessed and endless rest. It were a thousand times better to be left alone in the midst of the pathless desert, weary and fainting, afar from friends and fountains of water, than not obey that blessed voice of Jesus which sounds through all the waste places of sin and sorrow, saying, "Come unto me, come unto me."

Imagine yourself left to perish in the midst of the great African Sahara. The rays of the sun burn with pitiless fervor into your throbbing brain. The hot air seems like a blast from the furnace's mouth. The immeasurable waste of sand glows and quivers around you as if it rested upon an ocean of flame. There is no living thing in sight, no way of escape from that fiery sea of desolation. You have given up all hope. Maddened with thirst and paiu, you are ready to choose death rather than life, and you are impatient that death is so slow in coming. Suddenly there appears before you a being of radiant and celestial beauty. He looks upon you with such tenderness and compassion as a mother feels for her dying child. He touches the desert with his finger, and a living fountain breaks forth at his feet. With a voice that thrills through the depths of your soul, he says, " Come and drink." You think it a dream at first—you wonder, if it be a reality, why he does not himself press the cooling draught to your lips, without requiring effort on your part. At last you bow to taste the gushing spring, and in a moment your strength is revived, your waning reason is restored. Your lost hope returns. Again you hear the voice of your Deliverer saying, "Rise up and follow me, and I will give you to drink of the river of the water of life; I will lead you forth from this burning and cheerless waste; I will bring you to a home where you shall neither hunger nor thirst any more, where all pain and sorrow and death shall cease, and God shall wipe away all tears from your eyes." Revived, strengthened, you stand on your feet. You look the way your Deliverer points. Through the quivering haze and the illusive mirage of the desert you see the faint outlines of a glorious city afar. The shining domes and sapphire walls are built of light. The golden gates are open. Pilgrims from earth, in long and bright procession, are going up and entering in, while a wave of song floats down the ranks and angel heralds stand by the open gates, continually proclaiming with silvery voices, "Whosoever will, let him come." Would you hesitate to follow the Guide that had found you in the desert, revived your strength, shown you the way of escape and offered to lead you all the way from that wilderness of death to the gates of Paradise?

The picture is something more than fancy. The world is all a waste to him who feels the need of salvation, and has found no Saviour. The pleasures and occupations of the world have little charm for him whose soul is athirst, and he knows not where to find the Fountain of life. He feels that no language can be too strong in describing his need. The first and only ray of light that can break upon the darkness of the soul in its alienation from God must shine from the face of Jesus Christ. That light is a beacon to guide all wanderers to the port of peace. It is a star of hope that can never be covered with clouds. It is a sun of righteousness whose glory fills the earth and heavens. This is the message which Christ is sending forth through all this darkened and sin-stricken world. He searches out the poor, the guilty, the sorrowing in all the waste places of sin and misery, and he offers them infinite riches and eternal blessing. By the ministration of his own gospel he stands and cries as he did on the last great day of the feast at Jerusalem: " Come unto me and I will give thee of the fountain of life. Come unto me and I will take away all thy sins, I will bear all thy burdens, I will heal all thy sorrows, I will take from thee the fear of death, I will be thine advocate in the day of judgment, I will open for thee the doors of the hea- venly kingdom, and thou shalt live and reign with me for ever." Let the world receive this one word of Christ, " Come unto me," and thanksgiving will be- come the song of nations, and every land will rejoice in the promised reign of peace on earth.

The Night of Temptation.

Jesus said unto him, Verily I say unto thee, That this night before the cock crow, thou shalt deny me thrice.—MATT. xxvi. 34.

JOHN SARTAIN

THE NIGHT OF TEMPTATION

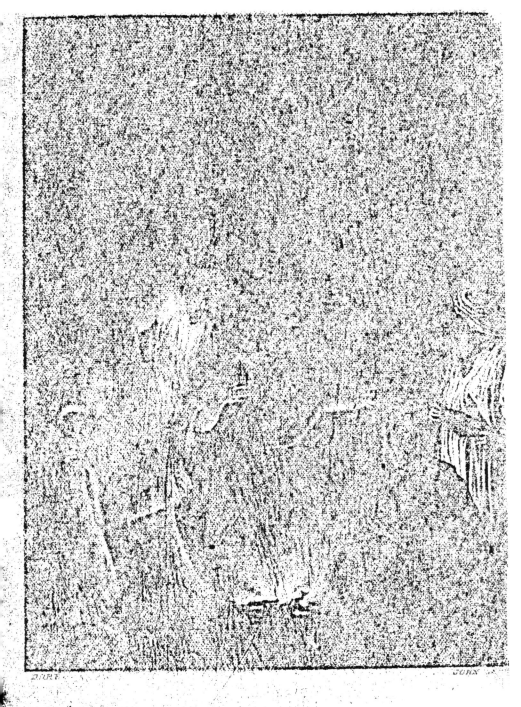

THE   TE

XVIII.

THE NIGHT OF TEMPTATION.

IT must have been a very hard thing for Jesus to say to his honored and beloved disciple Peter, in the presence of all the rest, and in the last tender and sorrowful meeting before his crucifixion, "This night thou shalt deny me thrice." That disciple was so ardent, so honest, so unsuspecting and outspoken in his attachment to his Lord, that the words must have pierced his heart as with a sword. We seem to hear him answer with mingled grief and surprise, "Oh no, beloved Master; how canst thou say that? Have I not forsaken all to follow thee? Have I not been with thee in all thy temptations? Have I not openly declared thee to be the Son of God? Have I not seen thy glory on the Mount and thy steps on the sea and thy power over death? Hast thou not given me the name of the Rock, and chosen me to be with thee in the most private and sacred scenes of thine own life? And after all this shall I say three times over that I know thee not? Dost thou think me capable of such falsity, such fickleness, such cowardice? Is this all the confidence that my Lord can repose in my sincerity, in my firmness, after I have been with him so long?"

And then again the occasion on which Jesus spoke these words must have added to the sorrowful weight with which they fell upon the disciple's heart. It was night in the upper chamber at Jerusalem where they were assembled. The Passover feast was done. The crowded city was calm. The song of thanksgiving that sounded in every Jewish home that night had ceased to be heard. The silence was no longer broken by the tramp of feet or the sound of voices in the street. The lights had gone out in the gardens and tents on the slopes of Olivet. The Roman sentinels on the walls paced to and fro as silently as if they had been set to guard a city of the dead.

In that still hour, just before midnight, the voice of Jesus is heard in the upper chamber, speaking to his disciples the blessed words which have comforted millions of mourners, and which will bring peace to troubled hearts to the end of time. They are all moved with tenderness and grief as they hang upon his lips and 'see the look of sadness upon his face. They are still more deeply touched when he pours forth his burdened soul in prayer that they may be kept from the evil of the world—that they may be with him and behold his glory when he shall be seated upon his throne with the crown of heaven upon his head. As they listen in wondering and weeping silence to that prayer, their hearts are all bound anew

in tender love to their Lord. Every one of them is ready
to go to prison and to death with him. And when they
all together break out in new and fervid expressions
of love to him, he says, with unutterable sorrow in
his look and tone, "All ye shall be offended because
of me this night." And when Peter, ever first and
foremost of the band, declares with renewed vehe-
mence his readiness to die for his Lord, Jesus makes
the still more startling and sorrowful declaration,
"This night thou shalt deny me thrice." It must have
been a sore surprise to the disciples to hear their Mas-
ter speaking thus at such a time, when their hearts
were so deeply touched, and all their affections were
drawn forth in renewed and fervent devotion to him.
And we do not wonder at the impulsive earnestness
with which Peter again and again declared his devo-
tion to his Lord. How could a man of his strong and
impetuous feelings hear such words from the Lord
whom he loved, and not feel called upon to express his
love in the strongest terms. He was not blamed for
making that declaration. Whatever else may be inferred
from his subsequent denial, his strong professions of
attachment to Jesus do not warn us not to make such
professions ourselves. They should not, indeed, be
made in a self-confident or presumptuous spirit. But
we are urged by the highest sentiments of duty, grati-
tude and affection to declare our readiness to go with
Christ wherever he may lead the way, and to suffer
cheerfully whatever it may cost us to be faithful to

him. Sometimes those who promise most perform least. But their failure to keep their good words is no reason for not promising. Those who promise nothing are still more apt to do nothing. A good and true man should never be afraid to say he means to do his duty. A faithful and loving heart will find some way of making its attachment known. And when the purpose to serve Christ is meekly and frankly declared, that very declaration will do much to make the life correspond to the profession.

While we do not blame Peter for the earnestness with which he declared his devotion to his Master, we have something to learn from his failure to keep his good and commendable promise. We know how literally the sad words of Jesus were fulfilled in the conduct of his best friends that very night. An hour passed on, and the blessed Redeemer was bowed down to the earth in great agony, pouring out his mighty sorrows with groans and tears and bitter crying and bloody sweat. And his favorite disciples were so little affected with his distress that they fell asleep within hearing of his cries. Another hour passed, and this brave and devoted band were all scattered. Jesus, left alone, was bound and led away by a midnight mob. The stout-hearted Peter followed afar off, hiding himself under the shadow of the city walls and behind the street corners, that he might not be suspected of being a disciple. Another hour passed, and the finger of a mischievous maid was pointed at him, and it made him a coward. By and by he saw suspicious eyes turned upon him, he heard it whispered that he was with Jesus, and he denied it with excited and angry vehemence. And then soon came the third denial, confirmed, as men are wont to confirm falsehood, by cursing and swearing. Then followed the startling knell of the hour and the pitying look of Jesus that broke Peter's heart and sent him out into the darkness of night to weep bitterly.

This is a sad story to be told of a brave, generous, warm-hearted man, and yet it was written in the spirit of kindness to him and of warning to us. Of the four forms in which the story is told, the one which bears hardest upon Peter is the one which in all probability was dictated by himself. And he desired to make the record plain and full, because what he did, many others may do, and all are in danger of doing. The story was written that it might inspire in every heart the daily prayer, "Lead us not into temptation, but deliver us from evil." Alas! how often do men go out from scenes of the most hallowed interest and the most holy aspirations and deny their Lord! How many fall asleep when they should wake and watch and pray! How many are misled by the demons of darkness when they rashly venture to walk in the night of temptation!

The young man goes forth from the home of his youth to enter into the great conflict of life alone. His heart is strong, his intentions good, his aspirations high. He goes from the quietude and the sanctity of a Christian home. He goes with the blessing of Christian parents upon his head. He goes with the solemn lessons of the sanctuary in his mind and the daily supplications of the family altar in his heart. A father's honor and a mother's love and a sister's affection and his own generous impulses concur in starting him well upon a pure and noble life. He sees the right path and he means to pursue it. His convictions and judgments and purposes are right, and everything promises a high and an honorable career.

He goes to the great city and plunges into the mighty stream where hundreds of thousands are struggling for life and it takes a strong swimmer to keep his head above the wave. He meets with some that are good and true, and with many that are bad and false. For a while he holds his own with a brave heart and strong hand. But he does not openly commit himself on the side of God and righteousness And there he makes his first great mistake. He does not quite dare to say that he means to live by prayer and watching and Christian duty. When he is enticed to countenance or to pursue some evil course, he does not refuse without doubt or hesitancy, simply because it is something a Christian should not do—it will lead him where a Christian would not go. And it is a very dangerous discovery for him, when evil men and seducers find that he can be tempted. He can be made to cringe and blush by the taunt that he is *green* and does not know the world. He can be shamed and put down by the impudent swagger of those who make a boast of sin.

And by and by, when it is found that that once noble, earnest, well-meaning young man is lost to virtue, to character, to peace of mind, and to the hope of heaven, the sad story of his fall is quickly told. He fell in the way of temptation, and he was not armed by watchfulness and a full committal of himself to God. He was jeered at by some hard and heartless man of the world; he heard his name spoken in derision by some mocking creature of frivolity and falsehood; he heard it said that it was manly to go certain steps in wickedness, and that it was mean and slavish to be always trembling and fearing to do something wrong. And before such false and despicable boasters of evil things he let down his high standard of character. He consented to be led by those whom he distrusted and despised, and who mocked him in their hearts for yielding. He went where he could not expect to meet the pure and the good. He learned ways of life and habits of speech and modes of thought, every one of which he knew was a step toward darkness and perdition. He degraded himself in his own estimate just to catch the vile applause of the worthless, the heartless and the vulgar. He gave up the freedom, the nobleness of his manhood to be a slave to things that he despised. He became a useless, disappointed, unhappy man, not from any settled plan or purpose to be bad, but from the want of fixed resolution to be good. He hesitated when he was first tempted. He feared and blushed to own himself a servant of God, a believer in truth and duty, when he came in the way of scorners and triflers. When he met the sneer of the skeptic, he did not dare to say, "I believe." When asked to join in some evil practice, he had not courage to say, "No, never!"

Oh it is the saddest, the most lamentable and dreadful defeat, when a frank, generous, open-hearted young man permits his high standard of duty to be pulled down and trampled upon by those who trifle with conscience, and sneer at religion and talk of immorality as if it were only a harmless pleasantry. Dear young man, keep your conscience if you lose everything else. Keep your heart pure, and God will keep you in the dark night of temptation which casts its shadow upon your path, and under the cover of which millions wander and fall to rise no more. Let it be seen and known that you can face the frowns and sneers and seductions of temptation with a look that silences the caviler and puts the worldling to shame. When asked to go where you cannot go, to do what you cannot do with a good conscience and a pure heart, do not hesitate to look the tempter firmly in the face and say, "I love and fear the great God in heaven, and I am not going to dishonor and disobey him for the fear or favor of any man on earth. I love truth and purity, and I am not going to soil my conscience and poison my heart by touching things that defile. I am not going to give myself to indulgences that embitter the best hours of life and make death-beds terrible!"

If every young man could have the faith and the fortitude to say thus, and act upon his words in the face of the hardened and practiced misleaders of the young, it would save many from premature and dishonored graves ; it would save some from a wretched and hopeless old age. A single word of decision, a calm, silent look of refusal, an unfaltering self-possession in the presence of temptation, is sometimes enough to rout all the forces of the evil one and set the soul free from further solicitation. And the earlier the young man can shake off the touch of the tempter the better.

In the dim light of memory, I see before me an old man with feeble step, tottering to his seat in the house of God on the Sabbath day. It is one of the genial days of opening spring. The fields are clothed with new beauty and the forests are musical with the voices of new life. And yet that old man is wrapped in the thick folds of his winter garments. He sits all through the service of the sanctuary with his head covered, for fear that the soft breath of June may breathe on his frame too roughly and send the cold chill of death to freeze the fountain of life. It is a strange and pitiable sight to see that aged invalid shivering beneath his thick robes on a summer's day, listening to that Word

25

which invites the wanderer to return and offers rest
to the weary in the heavenly Father's house.

What is the secret source of the great sorrow which
has laid heavy burdens upon that old man's shoulders
and made life a sad and weary pilgrimage to him?
In his young manhood he was tempted, and he had
not the courage or the conscience to say, *No, never!*
The seduction to sin came to him, as it comes to many,
in brilliant and fascinating forms.   He was surrounded
with the young, the gay and the thoughtless, who would
make life a holiday of pleasure and death a dreaded
thing to be thought of as little as possible.   In such
company, away from the restraints and safeguards of
the parental home and the family altar, the young
man thought he would enjoy life and never be the
worse for having seen and shared what the world calls
pleasure.   He did not once think of becoming a bad
man.   He did nothing which the gay world would
call by any worse name than youthful indiscretion.
The temptation which came in his path met him with
music and beauty and song and mirth.   He was sur-
rounded with the refinements of taste, and the splendors
of art, and the most finished and delicate fascinations
of gay and giddy life.   And he thought that when the
brilliant season was past, and he returned to his home,
he should be able to resume his place by the parental
hearth, and the jealous eye of affection would see in
him nothing but the ease and innocence of former
years.

But no. There was poison in the delirious cup of pleasure. The laws of life and health had been broken, and the unhappy youth must carry the consequences of his sin and folly to his grave. He repented fifty years in suffering and sorrow. He learned to pity the poor, to uplift the cast down, to reclaim the wandering. He would gladly have surrendered all his wealth and worldly expectations to have received back again the fresh, untainted constitution of his youth. He trusted and believed that the sin of his soul was forgiven. But no repentance or forgiveness can change or annul the law of eternal providence which lays the physical consequences of transgression upon the head of the guilty. A terrible lesson was the life of that old man to warn the young against temptation, even though it should allure with the voice of angels and strew the path to the pit with the flowers of Paradise.

One grand reason why the young are so easily deceived and led astray, is the fact that temptation addresses them with all the graces of manner and all the fascinations of beauty. They forget that ten thousand arts and efforts have been employed for ages in making the way to destruction easy and inviting. It has been the labor and study of millions of the human race, for successive generations, to increase the attractions of the broad road and to allure multitudes to walk therein. The one great engineer, who, in the beginning, cast up the highway to destruction, has been employing countless laborers ever since in keep-

ing the road open. He has laid every human posses-
sion and every talent of the immortal mind under
contribution to aid him in making the way to his own
dark dominions more alluring to the deluded souls of
men than the steep ascent to the kingdom of light.
Poets of the loftiest genius have sung in bewitching
strains to cheer the gay and gladsome company that
throng the path to the pit. Romance has built its
palaces of air, and peopled its imaginary world with
beings created only to make wickedness beautiful ; and
the ardent and unsuspecting youth has been fascinated
with the fallen angels of fiction, and whirled onward to
the kingdom of darkness in chariots of light. The arts
of painting and sculpture have toiled for centuries to
make the way to perdition one long gallery of beauty,
where every scene shall be followed by another more
fascinating to entice the heedless gazer on, until the
inexorable gates of death close behind him and forbid
all return. Millions of inventive minds, millions of
cunning hands, are ever busy in increasing the facilities
of travel on the downward way. If the pavement
sinks and a pitfall yawns with destruction disclosed
beneath, it is immediately covered over with flowers.
If some pitying angel of light drops an obstruction in
the path of some heedless soul to intercept his course,
nimble hands will be tugging with fiendish zeal to take
it out of the way. If those who have themselves been
delivered from going down to the pit set up warnings
or lift up their voices and cry aloud to alarm the heed-

less and the headstrong, their solicitude will be turned into ridicule, and the warning against the dangers of the way will be covered over and concealed by the more glaring advertisements of its delights and attractions. On the most crowded street of the great city there is many a door over which might fitly be written, as a sign of what is done within, "Destruction made easy." Amid the haunts of trade and the clustered homes of domestic life there is many a threshold, in crossing which the heedless youth passes the boundary which marks his destiny to glory or despair. On the one side is hope and light and heaven; on the other, darkness and despair and death. And there are eyes of light, yet baleful as those of the serpent in Paradise; there are forms of beauty arrayed like spirits of darkness in the robes of heaven; there are voices of music that allure only to destroy; and all conspiring to lend attractions to the way of death. The wealth of Mammon paves the path with gold, and proud reason demonstrates its safety, and imagination pictures the journey onward through an avenue of glories and delights, and ambition holds up glittering crowns in the distance to allure with their dangerous and dazzling splendor, and the muse celebrates the fame of those who have trodden it before in the loftiest strains of harp and song. And thus riches and power and genius and invention and pride and reason and passion are enlisted in the bad work of making the broad way easy and attractive.

And with so much to allure in the wrong direction, let no young man wonder that he must watch and fight and pray if he would keep himself out of the way to darkness. Take heed how you carry yourself in the face of temptation. Have the courage to say no, however fascinating the form and winning the address with which you are enticed. Be sure the voice which persuades you to lower your standard of duty is not the voice of a friend. The breath that whispers a concession to the pleasant and profitable steps of sin is not blown to your ear from paradise, but from the pit. Let no one think a slight or a single deviation from the path of duty a thing of little consequence. It is the first step which fixes the long journey.

There is a small lake upon one of the high passes of the Alps, the waters of which find their way to the ocean by two different channels. One portion takes the course of the "wide and winding Rhine," and goes forth to mingle with the stormy waves and crashing icebergs of northern seas. Another joins the blue current of the "arrowy Rhone," and finds its way to the Mediterranean along the vine-clad hills and the sunny vales of France. One finds a home under the cold splendors of auroral light amid the freezing horrors of the Arctic zone. The other blushes in the glow of Italian skies, and lingers idly around the classic shores and storied isles of Greece. So small is that mountain lake that a single flake of snow falling upon its surface and dissolving in its waters may supply a portion for each of the two mighty rivers. Different parts of the same drop that shot out the rays of the same crystal star in the snowflake may have a subsequent history and a habitation separated from each other by ranges of the loftiest mountains and the utmost diversities of climate and the diameter of the globe.

So there may be influences which seem fitted to crystallize the members of the same family into one symmetrical crown of beauty, and to make them a joy unto each other for ever. And yet some divergent force of temptation, some single choice or failure to choose on the part of one or another, may set them upon different tracks, and they may go on from slight beginnings to great extremes, until no one can pass the great gulf of separation that lies between them. The first step in the downward course is easy, either to be taken or avoided. But whoever takes that, will be most likely to take another, and then another, until the way of return becomes as steep and difficult to climb as the icy precipice of an Alpine mountain.

The child, sporting upon the embankment which has been raised to keep the mighty river in its channel, may remove a pebble or a few handfuls of earth, and the trench which the thoughtless boy has made to secure a current for his toy-wheel may be worn by the water, while he has gone home to his night's repose, deepened and widened till at length the strength of the imprisoned river is turned through the opening. And then in one irresistible deluge it rolls over the broad savannas, and the morning sun shines upon a wide expanse of waters, where, the day before, luxuriant harvests waved in readiness for the reaper's hand.

So, in the moral as well as in the material world, the mere wanton sport of a child may bring on himself and others consequences so great and terrible as to defy all calculation. A child, in the spirit of frivolity or in a pet of evil temper, may start upon a course of conduct so utterly wrong in itself and so fatal in its consequences, that in the end no hand less than Almighty can break the chain of evil habit with which he is bound. In one brief moment of passion or temptation the unguarded youth may kindle a fire in his own bosom that shall burn to the lowest hell.

Doubtless, in the moment of temptation, it seemed a small matter to the first human transgressor to do only one act which God had forbidden—only to pluck from that tree the fruit of which was beautiful to the eye and pleasant to the taste and to be desired to make one wise. But it was not a small matter that he thus forfeited his allegiance to the great Lawgiver, and opened a fountain from which should spring a boundless ocean of guilt and woe, heaving its destructive waves over a whole race of immortal beings, and rolling the ever-accumulating flood of moral desolation down the track of ages. And never can any one know, in the moment of temptation, the full measure of evil consequences that will flow from one wrong step. His only safeguard is to consider, without argument or hesitation, that no promise of profit or pleasure can be a sufficient reason for sinning against God.

Let no one think it strange that it costs effort to be good and watchfulness to be pure in the great conflict of forces with which our life is beset. It is only by long and sore discipline and the most determined exercise of will that we become superior to temptation. The course of duty is like the path by which travelers climb the passes of Alpine mountains. It turns this way and that way. It clings to the face of the towering cliff. It hangs on the brink of the fathomless abyss. It pierces the projecting crag. It crosses the narrow ravine. It bridges the roaring torrent. It sweeps the track where the thundering avalanche rushes down. Yet all the while it climbs higher and higher. The traveler can go on only by lifting himself at every step above the sunny fields, above the dark green woods, above the storm-swept pines and firs into the clear light and the bracing mountain air. But the very process of climbing makes the youthful mountaineer joyous and strong. The torrents sing with a more gladsome voice, the hoary peaks are crowned with brighter snows, the sky is tinged with a deeper blue, the sun shines with a more glorious light, the landscape unfolds with greater magnificence, to him who has braced his nerves and quickened his pulse and expanded his bosom by weary hours of climbing to the lofty heights.

So it is with all who climb the ascending path of

duty and of faith. Let the young man take the Divine
" Excelsior" for his watchword as he goes up the toil-
some steep. As he passes through dangers and diffi-
culties, making every step of advance by effort, and
gaining every victory by conflict, let him sing all the
way, " Higher, higher, higher," and he will find that
the air grows purer as he ascends. By persevering
toil he lifts himself completely above the range of
temptations that once endangered his soul. The hea-
venly landscape opens with increased clearness and
beauty, and as he passes from height to height he
catches occasional glimpses of the golden gates and the
sapphire wall of the city that hath everlasting founda-
dations, whose Builder and Maker is God.

With such a glorious career demanding his efforts
and encouraging his hopes, let no young man think
that he has nothing to do or time to waste. And if
any one has not yet begun to live for God and heaven
and eternity ; if he has not yet set his feet upon the
way that leads to glory and immortality, let him begin
the ascent without delay, and keep climbing till he
reaches the throne of the Lamb and the mansions of
the blest For the sake of God and heaven and
eternal salvation, for the sake of everything that is
highest and best in possession and in hope, do not
allow yourself, dear young man—do not allow yourself
to be carried away and lost in the dark night of temp-
tation.

The Night of Agony.

*Then cometh Jesus with them unto a place called Gethsemane, and saith unto the disciples, Sit ye here, while I go and pray yonder. . . And being in an agony, he prayed more earnestly; and his sweat was as it were great drops of blood falling down to the ground.—*MATT. xxvi. 36; LUKE xxii. 44.

XIX.

THE NIGHT OF AGONY.

THE approach to Jerusalem most frequented in modern times by pilgrims and travelers from the west lies across the fertile plain of Sharon and up the rugged pass of Beth-horon. The path, after leaving the plain, is a perpetual climb over rocks that are sometimes smooth and slippery, sometimes lying loose in huge angular blocks, and sometimes standing edgewise in successive strata, with deep furrows yawning between like crevasses in the glacier. Down this stony staircase the host of Joshua chased the Canaanites, while the heavens shot forth hail to help the spears of the pursuers, and the sun waited over Gibeon for the victors to complete the triumphs of the day. Up this rough mountain road the armies of the Philistines came many times to gather the harvests and garrison the towns and drive off the flocks of Ephraim and Benjamin.

Up this wild ravine the Christian traveler climbs, reading the book of the wars of the Lord all the way, till he emerges on the high place of Gibeon, and Jerusalem, with the Mount of Olives on the east, lies before him. Nowhere on earth have wilder shouts of enthusiasm burst from human lips than on that spot, where pilgrims from many lands for more than a thousand years have caught the first sight of the Holy City. Nowhere have so many hearts passed so suddenly from the memories of war and the inspirations of conflict to emotions of the deepest tenderness and to the silent expression of tears. There stood the mail-clad knights of the Crusade, their ranks thinned by battle and plague, their faces bronzed by long exposure to wind and storm, yet with mighty hearts throbbing beneath corslets of steel as they joined in the wild cry of their followers, *Jerusalem! Jerusalem!* And there still the more enlightened and less enthusiastic travelers of modern times from the cold North and the far West take up the shout that has come down without interruption from other ages, *Jerusalem! Jerusalem!* Every year peasant and prince, Christian and Moslem, Gentile and Jew, stand and gaze with unutterable thoughts from the heights of Gibeon, across the bare and broken waste of rocks and rounded hills upon the one city which is sacred for all time and the source of attraction to the whole earth.

There is little in the landscape itself to please the eye. No silvery streams winding between flowery banks, no green woods climbing gentle hills, no grassy plains cropped by herds of cattle, no lines or clusters of shadowy trees, no scattered houses embowered in foliage along roadsides, no smiling gardens in the valleys, but far as the eye can see a blank and life-less reach of rounded and desolate hills and naked rocks and bleached, sunburnt earth. But it is enough that in the midst of that desolation lies Jerusalem, the city of the Great King. Zion itself has indeed been ploughed as a field, according to the word of prophecy, and all her streets are piled with ruin. The paved courts and marble steps on which David stood in the new capital of his kingdom have been covered high as the house-tops with the ruins of ages. The engines of destruction have so many times been set against the towers of Zion, and the storm of war has so many times rolled over the sacred hill, that now we cannot trace the lines of the ancient city—we cannot tell the form of her bulwarks or find the polished stones of her palaces.

But the swelling ridge of Olivet is the same to-day that it was when trodden by the blessed feet of the Son of God. It is so near the eastern wall of Jerusalem that the little cluster of houses on the top seems in the distance to be a part of the city itself. The eye of the observer, dimmed with deep emotion from see-ing that great sight for the first time, wanders involun-tarily from the dark, ruinous aspect of naked walls and stone houses to the long green ridge with its central swelling summit and its slopes sprinkled with olive trees and lined with footpaths, on the east. After all the changes and devastations of ages, that sacred hill lifts the same outline to the sky, it casts the same morning shadows upon the city. It gathers around its summits and sides the most tender, the most hallowed associations that the human heart has ever cherished, or ever will cherish in all time.

The Jewish Targums say that Noah's dove plucked the olive leaf from this mount, and bore it to the imprisoned patriarch as a sign that the avenging waters had passed away and peace was restored to the smitten earth. The Rabbins affirm that when the Shechinah, the visible symbol of the Divine presence, forsook the Holy Place of the temple, it rested three years upon Olivet to see whether the Jewish people would repent, all the while proclaiming, " Return unto me, and I will return unto you ; seek ye the Lord while he may be found, call upon him while he is near," and then it went up to the holy place in the heavenly Zion. The Mohammedans declare that the immutable oath of the Almighty is sworn by the olive and the fig of this mountain. Both Jews and Mohammedans maintain that all nations will be gathered for the final judgment in the valley at the foot of Olivet, and that it is the greatest privilege the dying believer can ask to be buried on the slope of the sacred mount to be in readiness to meet the Judge at the resurrection of the just.

But Olivet has no need of fables or fanciful traditions to make it sacred and interesting to all believers in the inspired history of the Bible. Over this height the morning sun looked down upon the rocky platform of Moriah when Abraham had made it an altar, and stood ready to offer his beloved Isaac in sacrifice at the Divine command. To the top of this mount the devout David was wont to go forth from Jerusalem to worship. Up the steep ascent of its northern path the old king went weeping barefoot, and with his head covered, and the whole country wailing with a loud voice around him when Absalom rebelled. On the top of the mount he paused and took farewell of his beloved Zion with bitter weeping and a broken heart. From this consecrated ground the restored children of the captivity gathered myrtle and olive and palm branches for the celebration of the feast of tabernacles. These three bare mountain paths, which have been worn by human feet for near three thousand years, were trodden many times by the Son of God. In all Jerusalem as it now is, a city ten times captured and devastated since the days of Christ, there is no street, no house where we can stand and say, "Here we can be sure that Jesus of Nazareth passed by." But we can climb the sides of Olivet with the certainty that our feet are upon the footsteps of the incarnate Son of God. Up and down its bare and travel-worn paths he went and came, again and again. Just over the eastern side of the ridge he stood by the grave of Lazarus and called back the dead to life. Round the southern shoulder of the hill he rode in triumph, with the rejoicing multitude strewing garments and palm branches in the way, and thousands shouting with rapturous voices, "Hosanna! blessed is he that cometh

26

in the name of the Lord." On some green terrace or bare ledge of rock, over against the temple, he sat, as the setting sun gilded the towers and domes and colonnades beneath him, and told the doom that should come upon the proud city. In some humble dwelling among the olive trees, just like the stone houses that now cling to the face of the hill, he rested many a night. Somewhere along this central path to Bethany stood the fruitless fig-tree whose luxuriant leaves withered at the reproachful word of Jesus. The crimson flowers that fringe these paths every spring, and which are now called the blood-drops of Jesus, were here in all their bloom at his feet when he paused to weep over Jerusalem, and when the sweat of his agony fell like great drops of blood at the foot of the mount. Far more than Jerusalem, this sacred hill was the daily walk and the chosen home of the Son of God. It gave him the resting-place which he loved most of all on earth, and it was the scene of his most awful and mysterious sufferings and sorrows.

Upon this most hallowed scene, at the foot of the sacred mount, it becomes us to look with tender hearts and tearful eyes. The inspired record tells us that Jesus, at a late hour on the night of his betrayal, went out of the city, over the brook Kidron to the Mount of Olives. Somewhere just under the brow of the hill, in sight of the whole eastern wall, was a place where he was wont to go for retirement and midnight prayer. After spending the whole day in the excited and stifling crowd of the city, healing the sick, comforting the afflicted and reasoning with adversaries, he would go out to this quiet spot to pour out his soul in supplication and to commune with his Father alone. He mingled prayer with work, and he combined the most active public toil with the most complete retirement and devotion. His favorite spot at the foot of Olivet was a garden, and its name, Gethsemane, indicates that it contained a grove of olive trees.

The Passover moon shone from a sky which at that season seldom has a cloud. The lights in the city had gone out, the streets were silent, the voices were hushed in the tents of pilgrims on the hill-sides. The air was cold enough for soldiers and weather-beaten fishermen to seek the fire. The day and evening had been spent in excitement and sacred festivity, and all needed rest. The voice of Jesus had joined with his disciples in the upper chamber in singing the Passover psalm: " The Lord is my strength and song, and is become my salvation." He had spoken the last words of comfort and peace to the sorrowing band. He had told them of his Father's many-mansioned house, and of his future coming to bring them home to see and to share his glory. He had poured forth his soul in the great intercessory prayer for them and for the penitent and believing of all time.

And now at this late hour he comes out at the eastern gate with his disciples, descends the steep path to the dry bed of the Kidron, passes over in the still moonlight, and goes up the ascent of Olivet a little way to the gate of the garden. The disciples are amazed and deeply troubled at the unusual silence of their beloved Master. They have seen him wear the shade of sorrow many times, but never have they seen him look as he does to-night. And the strange sadness grows heavier and heavier upon him as he leads the way, and they dare not ask the cause. They think he is going, as he was wont, to find some place of rest for the night on the favorite mount, and that in the morning his sadness will have passed away.

But when he reaches the open gate of the garden alongside the familiar path, he says, "Sit ye here while I go and pray yonder." They are not surprised to hear him say so. For they knew that in the great struggles and conflicts of his work his constant resort was prayer. And now, silently selecting three from the rest to go a little farther with him into the thicker shade of the olive trees, he becomes more deeply agitated and bowed down under the weight of some mighty and mysterious sorrow. He feels that he must be still more alone, and he tears himself away from the favorite three disciples, and goes a stone's throw further into the recesses of the garden and casts himself upon the ground in an agony of weeping and prayer.

We cannot fully understand the cause or the depth of the grief and agitation that came upon the Man of sorrows in Gethsemane. But the sacred narrative, when carefully examined, discloses a very strange and startling

significance. The words of the evangelists imply that
Jesus was seized and possessed by a terrible and over-
powering fear—a shuddering and quaking horror—a
confused and distracting amazement. The sorrow that
came upon him was so overwhelming and crushing that
it pressed him down to the earth and penetrated soul
and body with insupportable anguish. Usually so calm,
so self-possessed, he now seemed utterly beside himself
with consternation and anxiety. At other times meet-
ing all his conflicts with an exalted and divine serenity
of deportment, now he is weighed down with some
strange and dark dejection, some restless and irresist-
ible disquietude of soul. In the utter loneliness and
desolation of this mysterious conflict he is ready to
utter the bitter cry of the cross itself: "My God, my
God, why hast thou forsaken me?"

This first paroxysm of agony, with its strong crying
and many tears, lasted, it would seem, a full hour.
Then he rose up and came to his disciples and found
them sleeping. And while he stood all tremulous and
exhausted, with the bloody sweat upon his brow and
his face changed and furrowed with pain, gently re-
buking them for their failure to watch, the mysterious
anguish came upon him even more mightily than
before, and he turned from them the second time to
hide himself in the deeper recesses of the garden.
Even the poor boon of their watching and sympathy
failed him, and he must meet his great conflict alone.
He could only pour out his soul again in the same

supplicating, submissive cry, "O my Father, if this cup may not pass away from me except I drink it, thy will be done!" Calmed and strengthened a little by that prayer, he hurries back a second time to get some word, some look of sympathy from his disciples to comfort him, and again he finds them sleeping. Before they could recover from their bewilderment enough to answer him when he sought to rouse them, the third and final onset of his great agony came upon him, and he turned away from his helpless human comforters to meet the conflict alone; and this time a heavenly messenger brought him the strength which man could not give. And now the battle is fought and the victory won. The Man of Sorrows has drained the cup of agony to the very dregs. He has conquered by submission, and he comes forth from the garden with his wonted serenity to enter upon the closing scene of mockery and death. It was meet that the Divine Sufferer should complete his great and mysterious conflict with the powers of darkness and gain the victory before his human foes began the cruel work of mockery and death. If the strange fears and the shuddering amazement of Gethsemane had come upon him when he stood before Pilate's bar, or when he was nailed to the cross, the world would have said that his soul was shaken with the fear of death. So much we may venture to say concerning the order of events in the mighty passion which extended through all the years of Christ's humiliation from Bethlehem to Calvary.

But I dare not attempt to explain this mysterious and awful night scene in Gethsemane. It seems to me as if it would be irreverent and unfeeling for me to enter this sacred garden, even in imagination, and calmly look on with a critic's eye while my Redeemer is bowed down to the earth with bloody sweat and bitter agony, and the anguish of his soul is expressed in strong crying and many tears. But one thing I know, and that will I say—Jesus suffered for you and me, dear friend—for you and me. It was not because he was afraid of death; it was not because he shrank from the shame of the cross; it was not from any fear or weakness or failure that he prayed in Gethsemane, " O my Father, if it be possible, let this cup pass from me !" This Holy One of God had no sins or sorrows of his own to bear. He was not one to shrink from bodily suffering. He could not be surprised by any sudden form of danger. It is impossible to explain his amazement and agony in Gethsemane except by admitting that he bore the sorrows of others, and that on him were laid the iniquities of a lost world.

This is the awful and most affecting lesson of Gethsemane. The holy and mighty and loving Son of God consents to have our sins laid upon him. He draws himself so near to us by his Divine sympathy and his desire to save that he consents to be taken as one of us and to be treated as a transgressor. He looks into the abyss of despair opened for us by our own sins, as if its darkness were destined to cover him for ever

In the dread conflict of Gethsemane the power of evil which he had undertaken to destroy appeared so malignant and mighty, the hell of sin so deep and black, the peril of man so imminent and awful, the work of redemption so difficult to accomplish, that his soul was troubled and amazed, his spirit fainted within him, and his anguish came forth in bloody sweat and in the cries of infinite sorrow. When his hour came and the burden of our sins was upon him, it seemed as if it were greater than he had thought it to be. He trembled in every limb. He was crushed to the earth by the weight. He cried out in an agony of tears and supplications.

Such a dreadful thing was it for the mighty Son of God to stand in the sinner's place for an hour! How much more dreadful a thing must it be for a feeble mortal to stand in the sinner's place for a whole life-time! How much more dreadful a thing must it be to stand in danger of going to the sinner's place for ever! We are not now amazed and agonized by our sins, as Christ was in the garden, just because we do not see and feel what a dreadful thing it is to sin against God. But if we were now perfectly holy, and all our present sins were laid upon us as if they were our own, we should feel ourselves crushed down by a mountain of agony as high as heaven and as deep as hell. It was because Jesus was holy that it made his mighty soul exceeding sorrowful, even unto death, only to be numbered with transgressors, while as yet he knew no sin. And if you and I, dear friend, were perfectly pure in heart as Jesus was, and the tempter should raise one impulse of rebellion against God in our souls in such a way as to make us think for the moment that it were our own, it would be like the agony of death to us until we could thrust it out.

Come, then, O man of the world—you who are careless about sinning against God, you who are content to live on year after year without any assurance in your own soul that your sins are forgiven—come and look reverently and thoughtfully upon this awful scene in Gethsemane. If I could take you to the bedside of one dying in great torture for his own sins, your feelings would be deeply touched. If I could show you one suffering indescribable pain from wounds incurred in saving your life, your heart would be melted with sympathetic anguish. Come, then, stand by this garden gate in the dread silence of midnight. See the holy and mighty Son of God prostrate upon the bare earth, writhing and trembling in great agony, bedewing the trampled ground with bloody sweat. Hear that voice from heaven which says, " He is smitten of God and afflicted for your sake. The Lord hath laid on him all your iniquities." Can you see that great sight and hear that heavenly voice and not be moved? Can you see how dreadfully your Divine Redeemer suffers in an agony, which is all of the soul and all for your sake, and not feel that the ransom of your soul is exceedingly precious? Can you believe the sacred story of Gethsemane and not be ready to say in an agony of earnestness, "Oh, what must I do to be saved from sins which are so terrible and crushing when laid upon the mighty Son of God?" '

And then again once more let me lead you to this garden gate, that you may see and hear the fullest expression of the Divine love to man. This suffering of Jesus in Gethsemane is not because he is already scourged or crowned with thorns or crucified. His soul is in agony with the desire to save sinners. He is agitated and anxious and amazed just because he finds men upon the brink of perdition, and he must save them or they will be lost. He must prevail on them to take his hand or they will sink to rise no more. He is troubled and agonized because it is so hard to make men willing to be saved. And shall not such unspeakable, such Divine sympathy draw the most reluctant heart to Jesus? Shall the bloody sweat and the exceeding great sorrow and the crushing agony and the thrice-repeated prayer of Jesus in Gethsemane plead with men in vain to accept so generous, so mighty, so compassionate a Saviour?

The First Night after the Resurrection.

Then the same day at evening, being the first day of the week, when the doors were shut where the disciples were assembled for fear of the Jews, came Jesus and stood in the midst, and said unto them, Peace be unto you.—JOHN xx. 19.

XX.

THE FIRST NIGHT AFTER THE RESURRECTION.

THE two great facts which complete and confirm everything else in the gospel history are the crucifixion and the resurrection. The appointed sacrifice of redemption itself was indeed finished when Jesus bowed his head in death on the cross. But the Divine seal was set to the sacrifice, and the full and final witness was given to the world when Jesus rose from the dead. We therefore truly say that the two greatest days in the world's history are the Friday when darkness veiled the awful scene upon Calvary, and the following Sunday when the white-robed angel, with a countenance like lightning, rolled away the stone from the door of the tomb where the body of Jesus was laid. The extraordinary events of those two days have exerted a controlling influence upon the history of the world ever since, and they are still doing more than great battles and mighty revolutions in forming the character and fixing the destiny of individuals and nations.

These events were all purposed and sure in the Infinite Mind. But to human judgment the most dis-

mal night that ever cast its shadows upon the hearts
and hopes of men was the last night that the body of
Jesus rested in the grave.   The brightest morning that
ever rose upon a darkened and 'death-stricken world
was the morning when the two Marys ran with won-
der and joy from the garden of Joseph to the gate of
Jerusalem, to tell the disciples that the tomb was empty
and the Lord was risen.   The disappointed and dis-
heartened disciples refused to believe the words of the
trembling and excited women.   And when the tidings
came again that Mary Magdalene had seen Jesus him-
self alive in the garden, and that a vision of angels had
appeared to others and had positively affirmed the fact
of the resurrection, still they believed it not.

The day which might most fitly have been spent in
rejoicing was one of confusion and perplexity of mind
to them, because the awful and glorious event of the
resurrection surpassed the utmost reach of their faith.
Friday had taken from them their living Master, and
now it seemed that Sunday would deprive them of the
last sad privilege of embalming his dead body in the
tomb.   Alas! how often do the sad thoughts of the
afflicted linger about the grave and cling to the perish-
able form of the beloved who sleep in Jesus, forgetful
of the angel-voice which speaks from the tomb, " He
is not here, he is risen !"   The great fact of an actual
rising from the dead, a continued and glorified life
after death has done its worst upon the suffering body,
is still what believers themselves find it hardest to be-

lieve. They still find it easier to talk of their lost friends and buried hopes and broken hearts than of the better life and blessed home to which the disciples of Jesus go through the gate of the tomb.

It will help us to correct our false impressions, and discipline our hearts to faith and patience, if we observe the fears and fluctuations of mind through which the disciples passed on the first day and evening after the resurrection. Late in the afternoon two of the number resolved to give up all further inquiry and suspense, and go home to quiet their excited and weary minds in a little village eight miles away from Jerusalem. As nearly as can be ascertained they went out of the city at its western gate, and pursued their evening walk with sad looks and heavy hearts. The path which they were to follow was one of the most dreary and desolate in all Palestine. First, they had to pass two miles over a bleak and barren level of loose stones and sun-dried earth and naked slabs of rock.

I think it must have been somewhere on this cheerless mountain ridge, at the beginning of their walk, that they saw a stranger coming up from behind with a quicker step and silently joining their company. They were so busy with their sad thoughts, and he was so gentle and courteous in his approach, that they kept on in their conversation as if they were still alone. He saw that their faces were sad and their words came forth from burdened and sorrowing hearts. He gently drew from them the cause of their grief, and in a few moments he entered into their feelings with so much earnestness, tenderness and sympathy that their hearts burned within them while he spoke. They wondered who he could be, and they expressed their wonder by silent glances at each other, while he went on with them and talked all the way. But they did not dare to ask him, or in any way to interrupt the flow of his gracious words, while he opened to them the Scriptures, and showed them how Christ must needs suffer and by suffering enter into his glory.

And so the three walked on together, the delighted and wondering disciples not knowing that they were listening to their lamented and risen Lord. They hear his step upon the stony road just like their own. He labors with panting breath in climbing the steep place, and he moves with cautious tread in descending the slippery path, just as they do. Nothing in his dress or manner or person leads them to suspect that he can be anything else than one of the pilgrims returning from the great feast to some distant home.

Having passed over the rocky platform immediately west of Jerusalem, on what is now the Ramleh road, they turn to take their last look of the city and brush away a silent tear at the fresh remembrance of all they had seen and suffered there within the last few days. Then they plunge down into a narrow glen and make their way cautiously over a dreary waste of bare ledges and confused drifts of gravel and rubble stone. They cross the dry bed of a torrent, and then climb slowly up a winding and zig-zag path cut in the limestone rock to the crest of another ridge. This height is no sooner gained than they begin another descent, again to climb a long, steep and winding track over loose stones and ledges that have been worn smooth by winter rains and spring torrents and the feet of travelers for centuries.

And all the way the Divine Saviour, the Son of God, who could say, " All power is given unto me in heaven and in earth," walks with these two men, taking as many steps as they, and talking all the while as they go up and down the steep places together. He spends more time in this long and laborious conversation with these two sad and despondent men than with all others on the first day of his resurrection life. This mighty Conqueror of death, who had unbarred the gates of the tomb for a lost world, would thus teach us his readiness to be with us and comfort our hearts in the hardest paths we have to tread. In his risen and glorified state he is still the Son of Man, having all the sympathies and affections of the human heart. He is still as near to those who desire his company as he was before he passed through the awful transformation of the cross and the tomb.

The sun has gone down behind the gray hill-tops, and the shadows of evening have begun to deepen in the narrow valleys, and the laborers have left the terraced orchards and vineyards on the hill-sides before the two travelers reach their home, and beg the kindly

27

stranger to go in and abide with them for the night. He would have gone farther, and they would not have recognized their Lord had they not yielded to the impulse which his words had kindled in their hearts and urged him to stay. He never forces himself upon any. He joins the company of many who are toiling along the hard journey of life, he interests himself in the sorrows that press them down, he warms their hearts with his words of love, but if they fail to ask him to abide with them, he passes on and they know him not. It is toward evening, and the day of life is far spent with some to whom Jesus has often drawn near in the way; the shadows of evening are gathering thick around them, and yet they have never said to him with earnest and longing desire, "Abide with us." The humblest home becomes a palace fit for a king when Jesus enters in to tarry there. And without him the most splendid mansion on earth can give no rest to the weary soul. Blessed is the home and sweet is the rest of those who let no evening pass without offering the prayer to him who walked from Jerusalem to Emmaus with the two disciples: "Abide with us."

It was only to draw forth the invitation to stay that Jesus made as if he would have gone farther. When asked he entered without delay. The three weary travelers sat down together in that lowly cottage home, and the mysterious stranger continued to speak his heart-burning words while waiting for the evening meal. When bread, the simple fare of the poor, was set before them, he put forth his hands to bless it. But what now so suddenly startles the wondering disciples? They see the print of the nails in the open palms, the sign and scar of the cross. And now that he breathes forth the blessing they recognize the tone, the manner, the look. It is he who hung upon the cross! It is he whose body was laid in the tomb! He lives, and they have been walking with him all the way! Now they are ready to cast themselves in wonder and in worship at his feet. But the object of his appearance and his long reasoning with them by the way is gained, and he vanishes out of their sight.

And now, that this great joy has filled their hearts, their weariness and their discouragement are all gone. They have no thought of hunger or of rest. They must hurry back to tell the tidings to their brethren in the city. In a moment they are out again upon the stony path with their faces toward Jerusalem. It is now night, and the moon which was full four days ago, has not yet risen. But it is all light in the glad hearts of the disciples who have seen their risen Lord. The sad looks and sorrowful words with which they went out in the bright afternoon are all exchanged for exultations of joy, now that they are coming back in the dark night. The world is all new to them, and the one dread horror of death is all gone, if Christ be risen from the dead. They cannot wait for the morning to carry such joyful tidings to the sorrowing band of their brethren

They hurry along the wild mountain road, plunging into dark glens, climbing over steep ridges, bending around shadowy hills, sometimes stepping from stone to stone, feeling the way in the dark with the pilgrim's staff, and sometimes slipping upon the smooth face of the steep ledges, and then losing the track in crossing the dry bed of a torrent. I have myself more than once traveled as wild and rugged a mountain-path alone by night, and I know that Cleopas and his companion must have had light hearts to have started out upon that night journey to Jerusalem, without waiting for the moon to rise or the morning to dawn.

But they carried in their hearts tidings of the greatest victory ever gained in this world—the victory over death, the unbarring of the gates of the grave for the whole human race. And well they might go, running when they could, climbing and descending with cautious step when they must, but rejoicing all the way. For they were bearers of the best tidings that human lips ever told. They could testify to a fact upon which all the hopes of man for eternity must depend.

Reaching the walls of the city at a late hour, they probably passed around to one of the eastern gates, which was kept open all night during the great festivities of the Jewish people. Having gained admission, they hurry along the narrow streets, guided now by the light of the risen moon. The doors are shut and the blank walls of the stone houses give no sign of life within. They make their way first of all, we may suppose, to that one memorable house with the upper chamber where Jesus spent the last evening with his disciples before he suffered. Late as is the hour, they feel confident that the band will still be together. The excitement of the day has been too great to let them think of sleep.

When they reach the door, they find it barred from within and they cannot enter. They knock, but none reply. They call aloud and announce their names, and then they hear steps and voices within, and the swift and cautious hands of their brethren unbolting the door. But they have not had time to enter or to unburden their hearts of the great joy which they bring, before the voices of all within break out in the exclamation, " The Lord is risen indeed, and hath appeared unto Simon !" And now, that all are within and the door is barred again, the excited and panting travelers take their turn and tell the wondrous story of the evening walk to Emmaus, the strange companion that joined them in the way, the burning words that he spoke as he climbed the hills and toiled along the steep stony path in their company, the blessing that he pronounced at the evening meal, the print of the nails that they plainly saw in his extended hands, the familiar looks of their beloved Lord shining out upon his face, and then his vanishing out of their sight.

They have scarcely finished their story, amid the wonder and joy of the listening throng, when, behold !

another stands in the midst of the room. They are startled and terrified at the sudden apparition, even as they were when they saw the bright form walking upon the Sea of Galilee. Every eye is fixed upon the stranger. There has been no knocking without. The door has not been unbarred. No sound of entering footsteps has been heard. And yet there he stands before the affrighted throng—a stranger, a spirit, a living man! What can it be? In the hush of silence which pervades the breathless group they hear a voice speaking as only their Lord could speak, and saying, " Peace be unto you." Then he shows them his hands and his feet, and they lean forward with fear and wonder to look upon the print of the nails, the signs of sacrificial suffering which he wears even now upon the throne of heaven. He lays bare his wounded side, and they shudder as they see the dreadful scar where the soldier thrust his spear. He bids them draw near and lay their hands upon him, and thus be sure that it is his real living body which they see. While they tremble and dare not approach, he calls for food and eats in their presence. And now at last are they glad and satisfied that they see their Lord. It is he that was nailed to the cross. It is Jesus himself, who died and was buried, and behold he lives and shall be alive for evermore.

And the first word which the risen Lord brings to the assembly of his disciples on this first night after his resurrection is " PEACE." He stands forth in the midst of the startled company with that blessing upon his lips. And when they have recovered from their fear and excitement sufficiently to heed his words, he says again, " Peace be unto you." His first appearance on earth was announced by angel voices with the same blessed word—peace. And after he has completed his work and passed away from the world, he comes back from the grasp of death and the grave to bring the weary and the sorrowing the blessing of peace. Peace to the troubled conscience, for the blood of the cross takes away the stain of sin from the penitent soul. Peace to the weary and heavy-laden, for all who believe in Jesus shall enter into rest. Peace to those who destroy their own happiness, for the love of Jesus reconciles the believing to God, to duty and to themselves. Peace to all troubled and restless and doubting and dissatisfied souls, for Jesus came to seek and to save the lost. Peace to all to whom the message of his Gospel is given, for the risen Christ lives in his truth and he comes to breathe the blessing of his own Divine and abiding peace upon all who hear his word. Jesus can enter the closed doors of the sanctuary and of the secret chamber. But he stands at the door of the heart and knocks and waits to be invited in. He knocks and knocks again. He waits and waits long. And many never invite him in. And yet the blessing of peace, for which every bosom longs, is never ours until we unbar our stony hearts and ask the waiting Saviour in.

Our life on earth is a continual conflict. We must fight against forces that never tire, and keep ourselves upon the watch against foes that never sleep. We are beset by countless temptations, and we must resist and put them down, or be overcome and destroyed ourselves. We are beset with cares and fears and anxieties, and we need something to keep us calm and collected amid the changes and agitations with which we are surrounded. We have a great work to do, and it will be a dreadful failure if we come to the close of life with our work undone. We are liable at any moment to be called out of time into eternity and to have our destiny fixed for ever.

To real men, living in a condition just like ours, Jesus showed himself on the first night after his resurrection. He stepped from behind the curtain which hides the unseen world, and stood before them as real and true a man as they had ever seen him in life. And his first word to them was peace. He had passed through the awful mystery of death, and he came back with no sign of trouble or agitation upon his face, with no word of fear or alarm upon his lips. They were excited and terrified, but he said, "Peace be unto you." It was as if he had said, "I have suffered all the agony and seen all the mystery of death, I have been to that unseen world which you look upon with trembling and horror, and I have come back to calm your troubled hearts and quiet your excited fears. I have traveled all the way which you will have to go through the valley of the shadow of death, and I have returned to tell you that it is safe to those who follow me."

And this blessed word of the risen Christ is for us as well as for the first disciples. He comes to us in Spirit as really as he came to them in the body, to give us a peace which shall abide in our hearts amid all the changes and agitations of this present life. He comes to us to say that to those who trust in him there is absolutely nothing to fear behind the impenetrable veil which hides the unseen world. To all who believe in him he says, " Fear not death, because I live, ye shall live also."

When the peace of Christ comes into the soul, it brings the calmness and the serenity of heaven. It enables the suffering and afflicted to sing for joy, as Paul and Silas sung in the dungeon at midnight. It enables the poor and outcast to rejoice more in their poverty than in all riches. It gives hope and triumph to those who are just about to meet all that is most awful and unchangeable in death and eternity. The early Christians took this word from the lips of the risen Christ, and they carried it with them wherever they went. When exiled to mountains and deserts, when treated as outcasts and the offscouring of all things, when left to die of hunger and cold and torture in dungeons, when surrounded by the fires of martyr- dom, when cast into the arena to be torn in pieces by wild beasts, they meekly folded their hands upon their breasts and waited for the worst in peace. When loving hands were permitted to bury the mutilated bod.es of those who had sealed their faith by the most awful death, they wrote upon the resting-place of the blessed martyr of Jesus, "He rests in peace."

The early Christians made everything of the resurrection of Jesus. To them it made their beloved Master Lord of the dead and of the living. It made his cross a throne, his death a triumph, his open tomb the gate of heaven. It is our privilege to make as much of it as they did. If we believe in Jesus, we too shall rise and share with him in his victory over death. His resurrection is the pattern of our own. He came forth from the tomb exhibiting the fullness of perfect manhood in his glorified form. His voice and look and manner of speech were all such as his friends and followers had known them to be in his former life. Though it seemed to some of them too much to believe that he should be alive, yet their hearts burned within them when they heard him speak. The tone of his voice, the glance of his eye, the sacred signs upon his hands, were to them better than all arguments to prove the reality of his resurrection.

And in like manner shall our beloved who sleep in Jesus rise again. They shall remember the past as Jesus remembered and reminded his disciples of his own words while he was yet with them. They shall speak so that when we meet them and they call our names, as Jesus called the name of Mary in the garden of the sepulchre, it shall be all we need to know them. In the shining hosts that throng the streets of the New Jerusalem and gather in numbers without number round the throne of Jesus and follow his steps wherever he goes, there shall be voices that we loved to hear in our earthly homes, there shall be faces that need no introduction to tell us who they are. However plain they looked in this earthly life, they shall still be themselves and yet their faces shall be radiant with the soul's immortal beauty in the resurrection.

The great artist has the skill to make a homely face beautiful in a picture, and yet everybody who knows the original will say it is a perfect likeness. And so the faces that we last saw on earth wrinkled with age or wasted with suffering, and void of all grace and comeliness, shall be the same when seen in the light of heaven, yet clothed with immortal beauty and fit for the companionship of angels. The infant of days, whose smiles of joy and cry of pain lingered in the mother's memory for years after the grave had closed over the beloved form, shall come to the parents amid the glory of heaven with such a look that they shall no more say they once *lost* a child. The aged mother, who died in faith, with children and grandchildren round her to receive her parting blessing, shall appear the same in the resurrection, and yet the glorified form made surpassingly beautiful by the expression of the sainted spirit dwelling within, just as the skillful artist makes the beautiful soul shine forth from the silent canvas when otherwise the picture would have no charm. Parents who prayed for beloved children, teachers who labored for the conversion of scholars, pastors who wore out health and life for the salvation of their flocks and died without seeing the result of their labors on earth, shall find many faces to know and hear many voices to recognize in the garden of Paradise, even as Mary knew the risen Jesus when she heard him call her in the garden of the sepulchre.

This is the lesson taught us by the familiar mode in which Jesus met his disciples after his resurrection. He spoke with the same voice. He wore the same look. He showed them the wounds in his hands and his side. He walked with them in their journeys. He met with them in their assemblies. He appeared on the shore of the lake where he first called them to follow him. He led them out as far as Bethany, talking with them all the way along the old path up the steep and over the brow of Olivet. And that loving and sacred familiarity with them was manifested by him after he had passed through the great horror and mystery of death.

How could he better teach us the human and home-like reality of the blessed life which shall be ours if by any means we shall attain unto his resurrection? Think of heaven as a home—a home for human and loving and grateful hearts. Think of its society as having all that is purest and best on earth perfected and glorified. Think of Jesus your Saviour there calling you by name, and showing you that he still wore that name nearest his heart, even when you wronged and denied him. Think of waking up beyond the grave and finding yourself in full possession of such a life, with all the horror and agony of death behind, and nothing but blessedness and glory before you to possess and enjoy for ever. Think of all that is ensured to every believing soul by the resurrection of Christ from the dead, and then say how much reason we all have to share the joy with which the disciples rejoiced when they saw their risen Lord.

The first word which Jesus spoke after his resurrection was one for a sorrowing world to hear, "Why weepest thou? Whom seekest thou?" Many spend their lives in seeking what they never find. All have bitter cause for weeping. The journey of life begins and ends with tears. Its whole course is a search for something that can take away grief—something that can call forth fountains of gladness and consolation in the waste places of the soul. And Jesus comes forth from the grave, the conqueror of sin and death, that he may lead our search for the lost fountains of joy and make it successful. He comes back from the tomb to tell us that the object of our lifelong search can be found only on the other side of that dark and mysterious change which we so much dread. He puts the question to all the sons and daughters of affliction, "Why weepest thou?" that he may draw their hearts and hopes to that land where there shall be no more tears. He says to the burdened and disappointed, " Whom seek ye ?" that he may show himself to be the desire of nations and the giver of rest to the weary soul. In the darkest and most desolate hour of life, this voice of Jesus comes ringing like the trumpet of victory through all the depths of the soul : " Weep not ; I have the keys of death. To him that overcometh I will give the crown of life."

Thus faith in the resurrection of Jesus dissipates the the dark and dreadful horror that overhangs every man's path in this world. By that mighty and crowning miracle, Jesus is proved to be the Son of God, with power to conquer man's last enemy, and to set up for all believing souls a highway of joy and salvation between earth and heaven.

The Night of Fruitless Toil.

They went forth, and entered into a ship immediately; and that night they caught nothing.   But when the morning was now come, Jesus stood on the shore.—JOHN xxi. 3, 4.

XXI.

THE NIGHT OF FRUITLESS TOIL.

HE last chapter in the Gospel of John is a second ending of the sacred story, as told by the beloved disciple, concerning all things that Jesus did and said. It seems to have been added in the old age of the last surviving apostle, for the express purpose of telling what Jesus said to Peter on the shore of the Sea of Galilee after his resurrection, and what he did *not* say to John. The narrative takes us back to the scene and circumstances of the early ministry of Christ, and it shows us that the Divine Saviour, in passing through the gates of death and completing the great work of redemption, had lost none of his interest in the homely and common things of daily life. The place of his appearance on this occasion is invested with peculiar sacredness in the Gospel history, and the words which he spoke are embalmed with the most tender and hallowed associations in millions of Christian hearts. We shall do well to make both the words and the place as familiar as possible to our minds, and to invest them with the utmost degree of clearness and reality.

In the vivid and artless style of the old man, who could talk of little but love, two pictures rise to view. The first is night on the Sea of Galilee. It is in the balmy and beautiful bloom of the Syrian spring. The peculiar quietude and peace which breathe through the inspired narrative of the beloved disciple persuade us to think of it as a night of deep calm. There is no breeze in motion. Not a ripple breaks on the white sand of the silent shore. The lake lies as clear and calm within its lofty banks as the crystal sea of heaven. The stars and the mountains are mirrored in its glassy face. The dark wall of frowning rock that frames the picture seems to rise from foundations deep beneath the wave. The lights in the watch-towers on the distant hills, reflected from beneath the surface of the sea, look as if they were set in the same under-firmament with the stars. From the solitary heights and pasture lands, where the flock sleeps in the fold, the occasional call of the shepherd and the answering howl of the watch-dog break upon the stillness of the night. A pleasure-boat darts out from the Roman town of Tiberias, and a wild heathen song, softened and chastened by the still air, floats over the waters, and seems in the distance as if it were a sacred melody to which the stars and the sea listen in silent rapture. Once an hour is heard the clank of steel scabbards and the clatter of iron-shod hoofs when the Roman horsemen pass on their solitary patrol along the paved road under the cliffs close by the water's edge. But all else is still.

The shore is silent as the sea, and the sea is silent as the stars.

In the midst of this deep calm, seven men come slowly and thoughtfully down to the narrow beach, enter a stranded boat and push out a little way from the land. They are clad in the coarse garb of fisher-men. Their faces have been bronzed with exposure to wind and sun. Their hands have been swollen with dragging the dripping net, and hardened with pulling the laboring oar. But they are men destined to hold the highest rank among the great masters and teachers of mankind. Their rude minds have already caught fire from the Fountain of light, and they are to spend their lives in carrying the torch of heavenly truth through the world. They have just begun to under-stand a little that there is a remedy for all our human woe, and it is to be their Divine commission to offer healing and salvation to the wretched and lost of every land.

Foremost of them all is the fiery-souled Simon Peter, ready to walk on the waters or to smite with the sword or to weep in sorrow at a look from his Lord. There is the gentle and loving John, who leaned upon Jesus' bosom in the blessed feast of the upper chamber. There is the slow, distrustful Thomas, so honest and obstinate in his doubts, and so quick to surpass all others in his faith when once he had seen the face and heard the voice of his risen Lord. There is the guile-less Nathaniel, from the hill-town of Cana, who was so startled when Jesus read the thought of his heart that he exclaimed, "Thou art the Son of God!" And there is James, at once impetuous in spirit and practical in judgment, and destined to be the first of the apostolic band to seal his faith with the blood of martyrdom.

These men begin to ply their hard and homely trade of fishing. Having pushed out a sufficient distance from the land, they cast the net into the deep sea, draw it up and find it empty. They change their ground, pass up and down the coast, row out into deeper water and come nearer to the shore, everywhere letting down the net, and always drawing it up and taking nothing. And so they spend the long hours of the weary night in fruitless toil, thinking and talking more of their absent and beloved Lord than of their toilsome occupation.

Twice have they seen him since his resurrection, but as yet their faith cannot fully grasp the great fact that he is actually risen from the dead. They are trying to live over the past, and they have no plan and little hope for the future. On this very lake they saw him walk in the wildest storm, as one would walk the solid earth. Here, he said "Peace" to the winds, and the winds were hushed. On yonder height he stilled a fiercer tempest in the human soul. In the dim star-light can be seen the grassy bank where he fed five thousand in the desert place. Nearer by is Capernaum, where he so often healed the sick and raised the dead and spoke the words of eternal life. Outlined on the western sky, under the evening star, are the twin heights of the Beatitudes and the oak-crowned dome of the Transfiguration. And a little way over the ridge where the sun went down is Cana, where "the conscious water saw its Lord and blushed to wine," and Nain hallowed for evermore by the raising of the widow's son, and Nazareth nestled among hills, where the Divine Child was sheltered in a human home and and nursed with a mother's love.

They think on all these things and are sad, while the long hours of the weary night are spent in fruitless toil. They keep letting down the net into the dark depths of the sea, and it always comes up empty. So in thought they plunge into the deeper and darker mystery of Christ's death and resurrection, and they can bring nothing to light. Sometimes it seems to them that they have only just waked up from a beautiful dream of their Master's reign on the earth, and found themselves nothing but peasants and fishermen, just as they were before he said to them, "Follow me." Weary, disappointed, deprived of the presence of their Lord, they toil all night and take nothing.

Alas! that there should be so many even now among us who spend whole years, even a whole life, as the disciples spent that sad night on the Sea of Galilee, toiling in darkness and perplexity and taking nothing! The world is full of toilers who never get any satisfactory return for their labor. Losing sight of Him who is the Light of the world, they work blindly and ineffectually, putting forth great effort and pouring out all their strength, and coming to the end of life without ever having found anything worth living for. The world is full of the disappointed and the unhappy, just because it is full of those who set their hearts upon securing that which, gained or not gained, can never satisfy the deepest want of the soul.

A young man launches his life-boat upon the troubled sea of toil and competition and temptation in the great city. He has firm health, a fair address, a quick mind and an eager heart. He has a high estimate of his abilities, and he means to make something out of life to be proud of and to enjoy. He puts a severe restraint upon appetite and passion. He has nothing to do with the idle and the vicious. He is intent upon turning every hour, every acquaintance, every opportunity to some account in advancing his own interest, enlarging his own possessions, securing a high position in the world. And he succeeds. In middle life he is rich, and in old age he is a millionaire, with everything that money can buy at his command. But, alas! money cannot buy that which man most needs. Money cannot buy happiness, it cannot buy faith, love, cheerfulness, buoyancy of heart. Money cannot buy pardon of sin, preparation for death and the hope of heaven. The capacity to make money is a great and sacred talent, which God gives men to be used in enriching their souls, enlarging their hearts and lifting up their hopes and desires to a better life. But when men use that talent only for self and the world, it only makes them poor in the priceless jewels of the heart, the more it gives them of the perishable treasures of earth. The harder they toil the less they get—the more they succeed, the worse they fail.

And now this poor-rich man feels that he has spent all his labor for naught. With all his success he has gained nothing that can satisfy the soul. He has lived only for the world, and the world is only waiting for him to die and get out of the way for others to fill his place and enjoy his possessions. Weary, disappointed, heart-broken old man, he has toiled all night and taken nothing. If he had given himself to Christ in early youth, and made it the great business of life to follow him who become poor that he might make many rich, if he had determined to use the peculiar talent which God had given him in making the world wiser and better, he would have been happier all the way while engaged in the severest toil, he would have had many to call him blessed in his old age, and in dying he would have entered upon the possession of infinite and eternal riches. There is not a sadder place on earth than the death-chamber of a successful man of the world, who has secured all that the world can ever give, and in dying must leave all his good things behind him and go into eternity to be poor for ever.

Another starts with the purpose to enjoy life as he goes along. He means to take it easy. He never strains himself up to meet the demands of any high and exacting principle. He never sets up any standard of success which it will cost him great effort to gain. Self-indulgence is his first law, and self-denial his greatest horror. Conscience speaks with too solemn and awful a voice for him to heed. He has little patience to listen when duty asserts its sacred claims upon his life and his heart. But he runs with eager haste at the call of pleasure. He is ready for anything that will divert a vacant mind or lend wings to a weary hour. He means to enjoy himself while young, and make a merry life while it lasts.

And yet the poor, frivolous creature is never happy. He has no solid peace in himself. His life is a pretence and an imposture. He lives to enjoy himself, and yet it is himself that he is least able to enjoy. He wearies himself to be happy and he wonders that he cannot succeed. He toils all night and takes nothing. If he lives to old age without changing his course, it is only to be a poor, heartless, disappointed man of the world, who has never found anything worth living for, and who in dying has less to hope for in the life to come.

O ye ardent, warm-hearted young men, who would enjoy life while it lasts! look for something higher, nobler, purer than a life of worldly pleasure. Do not consider it success to shun responsibility and leave the heavy burdens for other shoulders to bear. Bind yourselves in willing and holy alliance to Him who is infinite, unchanging, everlasting love, and you will find, even in suffering for him, a higher happiness than can ever be known by those who live only to gratify taste and indulge the senses. Let duty to God be bound as a law of affection and obedience to the heart, and you can find joy in anything. Let loving, grateful, enthusiastic devotion to truth, to purity, to everything that is good and lovely in Christ, become the animating, soul-stirring principle of your life, and you will not need to study the best ways of enjoying yourself. The brave, the self-denying, the dutiful are always happy. Everything in the world is made tributary to their happiness. It is impossible for anything to take from them the success, the joy of living. They have in their own souls exhaustless sources of peace and satisfaction. They come to the close of this earthly life with the assurance that the higher joy and the endless glory are just about to begin.

Here again is a young lady, whose susceptible heart is fascinated with the glitter and gayety of fashionable life. She turns away from her Saviour with graceful excuses, and she dismisses the claims of duty with a smile. She estimates the joy of life by the music and mirth, the gay diversion and the giddy dance. She learns to talk of trifles with glowing animation, and give delighted attention to those who make serious things a jest. She chooses the society of those who are never in earnest, who never speak truthfully of the great and awful things which concern us all infinitely and for ever. She loves light literature, light conversation, light company, light amusements, and so flatters herself that she can make life all a holiday, drinking only the froth and foam of its full cup, and pushing aside from her lips the bitter contents of toil and trial and sorrow.

Alas, mistaken creature! she wearies herself all night in the whirl of gayety and the giddy dance of pleasure, only to bring darkness and disappointment upon her soul when the great struggle of life comes, and she needs to be fresh as the morning and full of light as the day. She makes the great mistake of supposing that worldly gayety is happiness, and that there is a portion of life too cheerful, too hopeful, too light-hearted to be given to God. That mistake has made multitudes of the young throw away their best years and then find that their hearts are empty and unsatisfied. It has made them waste their young affections and buoyant susceptibilities upon trifles, and then left them to recover the lost capacity for happiness, if at all, only through the stern discipline of trial and sorrow.

Let every young woman put forth her purest and noblest capacities for trust and devotion by giving herself to that Divine Saviour who, when he rose from the dead, showed himself first of all to Mary in the garden of the sepulchre. Let her prolong and glorify the bright and beautiful vision of youth by lifting her hopes to that better land where the beautiful bloom in immortal youth. Let her keep her heart fresh and cheerful by setting her strongest and holiest affections upon that one Friend who changes not. Let goodness lend its nameless charm, and devotion to duty give its Divine strength to womanly character, and the woman, so endowed and disciplined, will find a joy and a satisfaction, a beauty and a grace in living, such as the most caressed and flattered creature of fashion and frivolity never knows.

Time would fail to tell of the many who make the great mistake of seeking happiness in the world first, hoping to turn to Christ when the world fails to satisfy and the soul longs for rest. The Sabbath-school scholar, just passing from youth to adult age, becomes ashamed to be seen studying the heavenly oracles, and goes away to toil for long and dark years to find something more interesting than the blessed book which pours light upon the grave and opens the glorious prospect of endless life beyond the river of death. The sons and daughters of parents who have entered into rest, and whose dying prayer was that their children might meet them in heaven, live on in the hard and unsatisfactory service of the world, seeking their rest here and finding it not. The Divine Comforter strives with many who shut their hearts against his gracious pleadings, and who only desire in their strange infatuation to be let alone, that they may go farther and farther in seeking what nobody ever found—peace without pardon, rest for the soul without coming to Christ. Could such mistakes be corrected, it would save a world of useless toil, it would bring peace to a world of heavy hearts. And I could wish for no loftier endowment or opportunity than to be able to set forth the better life of faith and obedience to God in such a light that the young would choose it in the bloom of youth, while the evil days come not, and those who have wandered far and long would return to the way of peace and salvation. With all the toil and weariness and disappointment inseparable from man's lot in this world, it surely is not necessary for the young to add the greater mortification of spending the best years of life in seeking happiness where none ever found it. It is not necessary for those who have tried for years in vain to satisfy their souls from worldly pursuits and pleasures to continue the experiment longer.

*   *   *   *   *

If we look again at the disciples who have spent the night in fruitless toil, we shall find the scene greatly changed. It is morning on the Sea of Galilee. Pale shafts of light are shooting up the eastern sky where the bright star of dawn hangs over the hills of Bashan. The wavy line of mountain-tops is beginning to redden with the fires of the coming day. Away northward, the white snows of the mighty Hermon are ablaze with the glory of an Eastern dawn. Southward the misty line marking the course of the Jordan brightens and looks as if the shining train of a cometary orb had fallen between the parted hills. A solitary lark springs from her nest and shoots upward with a gush of song, and soon the whole air becomes vocal with happy singers that vie with each other in carrying the morning hymn highest toward the gate of heaven. The dark gray wall of the distant hills draws nearer as the day approaches, and a flush of air shooting across the steel bright water makes a pathway of light, as if an angel's wing had swept the sea from shore to shore.

The weary disciples now cease from their fruitless toil, for the time of success has passed with the night, and still they have taken nothing. Suddenly they see a once familiar form standing on the white sand of the beach, and they hear a voice they have often heard. But they have been so wearied with toil and benumbed with the night that they know not at first who it is that speaks. He tells them to cast the net on the right side of the ship, and the success which follows their obedience to his word reveals the form and the voice of their risen Lord.

Immediately they forget the long night and the fruitless toil, in the joy of seeing Jesus manifest in the morning light on the shore. They have cheaply learned the great lesson that the highest skill and the hardest work are vain without the presence of Jesus, and that the success of life is obedience to him.

Simple, indeed, is the lesson, and yet how hard for the heart to learn! You may work ever so hard and long in the endeavor to draw up riches and pleasures and joys from the deep and dark sea of life. But it will all be a night of disappointment and failure until you see Jesus revealed in heavenly light on the shore. Pursue the most common and menial occupation in obedience to him,' and the result will be success and joy. His coming to the weary heart is like morning on the mountains to pilgrims who have spent the night in wandering and terror. The first act of free, genuine, heartfelt obedience to Christ will give more real joy than a whole life of bondage to the world.

O ye weary, toiling, unsuccessful seekers after rest, lift up your heads from your heavy tasks and listen. Jesus calls from the eternal shore. His voice comes sweeter than the harps of angels from the mansions of rest. He says to each of you by name, as he said to Peter on the shore of the Sea of Galilee, " Lovest thou me ? Lovest thou me ? Follow me." He does not say wait for others, but follow me thyself. He does not say to-morrow or by and by, but follow me now. The first step of obedience to that command will fill the troubled soul with a deeper peace than rested on the sea when Jesus hushed the storm. Every additional step in that course will be an advance toward the blessed shore where Jesus waits your coming and the ransomed host sing the song of the Lamb on the crystal sea of heaven.

The night wanes, the morning is breaking. Some who have long toiled in darkness can now see Jesus walking in heavenly light and calling to them from the blessed shore. Look, look in penitence and in hope, and you will see him clothed with such sweetness and majesty that you will forget all worldly attractions for the glory of that sight. Listen, listen with obedience and love, and you will hear him say what should bring a heaven of joy to every longing and weary heart: "Come unto me—come unto me."

Night wanes, the high places of the earth are bright with the coming of the full day. The night of superstition has been long and dark. The night of error has led millions astray. The night of sorrow has made every home a house of mourning. The night of wrong has laid heavy burdens on the poor and led the innocent into bondage and captivity. The night of conflict has darkened the heavens with the cloud of battle and deluged the earth with blood. The great human family has been toiling fruitlessly and in darkness for ages. But now the day approaches. The hours fly swifter as the morning advances. The light of the Sun of Righteousness is glancing from land to land and penetrating all the dark places of the earth. The fetters of the slave are broken. The wall of separation that divided nations is thrown down. Great conflicts turn to the advantage of truth and humanity. Reason and faith have met together. Science and revelation have kissed each other. Christianity is gathering honor and strength from all the arts and inventions, from all the learning and refinement, from all the riches and power of the world. The nations are looking to Jesus as he stands revealed in the glow of the morning on the eternal shore, and when they hear his voice and obey his word the night of fruitless toil will pass away and the full day will come.

Angel Visits in the Night.

29

*The same night Peter was sleeping between two soldiers, bound
with two chains: and the keepers before the door kept the prison
And, behold, the angel of the Lord came upon him, and a light shined
in the prison: and he smote Peter on the side and raised him up, say-
ing, Arise up quickly. And his chains fell off from his hands.*—ACTS
xii. 6, 7.

ANGEL VISITS IN THE NIGHT

XXII.

ANGEL VISITS IN THE NIGHT.

WHEN we climb to some mountain height and look forth upon the broad landscape of hill and valley and plain in the blaze of the bright noon, it seems as if our earth were the universe, and the sun were a single globe of fire hung in the blue vault to give it light. When we stand upon the deck of the ship in mid ocean at the same hour of the day, and survey the melancholy waste of waters stretching beyond the utmost reach of the eye in every direction, it seems impossible that there can be anything else in existence but the sun and the sea. When we look up to the silent sky at night, it seems as if the bright array of stars were only camp-fires kindled on the hills of heaven to guide some wanderer through the wastes and solitudes of earth, and that there can be no thought and feeling and sympathy beyond the reach of man.

These several observations make us think of one world and that our own, one race of beings and that ourselves only, and that bounded by what we can see. But it is only the inward and over-ruling impulse of the spiritual nature that can make

XXII.

ANGEL VISITS IN THE NIGHT.

WHEN we climb to some mountain height and look forth upon the broad landscape of hill and valley and plain in the blaze of the bright noon, it seems as if our earth were the universe, and the sun were a single globe of fire hung in the heavens to give it light. When we stand upon the deck of the ship in mid ocean at the same hour of the day, and survey the melancholy waste of waters stretching beyond the utmost reach of the eye in every direction, it seems impossible that there can be anything else in existence but the sun and the sea. When we look up to the silent sky at night, it seems as if the bright array of stars were only camp-fires kindled on the plains of heaven to guide some wanderer through the wastes and solitudes of earth, and that there can be no home of thought and feeling and sympathy beyond the habitations of man.

All these varied observations make us think of one world and that our own, one race of beings and that ourselves, one destiny and that bounded by what we now see around us. It is only the inward and over-ruling impulse of our spiritual nature that can make the visible world the shadow and representative of the invisible and unknown. When we go down into the depths of the cavern or the dungeon, and shut ourselves up in silence that never breaks into sound, and in darkness that never changes to day, it seems as if we were alone in the universe, with nothing but the sense of responsibility and the yearning for society to tell us that there are other beings beside ourselves. When we mingle with the multitude on the crowded street, and hear the roar of business and toil and pleasure that surges through all the channels of the great city from morning to evening, it seems as if man and earth were everything, and that there can be no real life or intelligence or power outside of this visible, material world, in which we all now live and move and have our being.

All these natural and uninstructed impressions conspire to narrow the range of our thought, and shut us up to the society and home and occupations of man alone. It is, therefore, a startling and a salutary disclosure of Divine revelation that we are not the only intelligent actors in the busy scenes of daily life which surround us. There are more living persons in the crowd than any human observer can count. There are more listeners in the public assembly than can be seen by the speaker's eye. There is no solitude of earth where we may not have the unseen companionship of beings that think and feel and work more mightily and constantly than ourselves.

And these invisible, unembodied partners of our toil and sharers of our spiritual life have sometimes stepped forth from behind the curtain that hides the unseen world, to show us that we may have witnesses of our conduct when we think ourselves most alone. We have only to turn to the sacred record to learn that these high and mighty ones, whose home is in some far distant world, have borne an active part both in the common and in the great events of this world which we call ours. They have taken the form of men, and shown themselves to human eyes, and spoken aloud in the languages of earth. They have made their appearance on the lonely mountain-top, on the storm-beaten ship at sea, in the streets of the city, on the hills, in the highways and fields and threshing-floors, in the night and in the broad day, in the calm and in the storm, speaking words of peace and smiting with the sword, bringing health and prosperity and wasting with the pestilence, talking with men under the shadow of trees and tents and temple roofs, at city gates, in humble dwellings and in the depths of the dungeon's gloom. In all these places and circumstances men have seen and heard the living inhabitants of other worlds.

And these celestial visitants have come from their far distant homes to take part in the affairs of men. They have shown themselves better acquainted with human history and better able to do our work than we ourselves. They have defeated great armies, they have overthrown populous cities, they have sent forth and arrested the pestilence. They have rested under the shadow of oaks at noon as if weary; they have eaten bread as if hungry; they have received hospitality in human homes at evening as if coming in from a journey; they have guided and protected travelers on their way; they have rolled away the stone from the tomb; they have kindled the fire of the altar and stood unhurt in the midst of the flame; they have clothed themselves in garments that shone like the lightning, and they have appeared in so common a garb as to be taken for wayfaring men needing lodgings for the night.

It adds immensely to the solemn interest of our daily life to know that we may have such unseen witnesses of our conduct and partners of our toil at any moment. It gives us a higher and truer estimate of our own place in the great commonwealth of intelligent beings, to find that we are objects of intense interest to the inhabitants of other worlds. It enlarges the range of our thought, and lifts our desires and aspirations above all earthly and perishable things, to know that our present habitation is only one little province of a universe of worlds, and that this mighty empire is bound together by ties of intelligence, co-operation and sympathy to its utmost extent.

The deliverance of Peter from prison by the angel of the Lord at night shows that these mighty visitants from other worlds have little regard for the pomp and splendors of earthly state. Suppose a prophet had said the day before that on that night a mighty being from the central province in God's great empire would visit Jerusalem on a special mission from the Most High, and only one man in all that city would be honored by receiving that celestial messenger. Could any have guessed that that man would be found in a prison sleeping upon a stone floor, chained right hand and left to soldiers, who must be answerable with their lives for his safe-keeping?

There were many other persons besides Peter for an angel to see, many other places besides a prison for an angel to visit. There was a king in Jerusalem at the time, who had carried the splendors of his reign beyond the utmost reach that Solomon in all his glory ever attained. It was a season of sacred festivity, and devout men from every nation under heaven had come up to the Holy City to worship. There was the temple glittering with gold and precious stones, the most gorgeous sanctuary that had ever been reared for the worship of the true God by human hands on the face of the whole earth. There were the tombs of the kings and prophets—there were the holy places that had been consecrated by human faith and Divine interposition in ancient time.

But the mighty angel who came down to Jerusalem that night did not show himself in the palace of the king. He did not enter the Holy Place of the temple He did not address himself to devout pilgrims who had come with alms and with offerings from the most distant nations. He did not come to visit the monuments and revive the memories of the glorious past. The one man whom that mighty servant of God had come from a distant world to see was shut up in stone walls, asleep on a stone floor, bound with iron chains, only waiting for the morning to be led forth and mocked by the multitude and murdered by the king.

It is a sad thing for us to be obliged to confess that when the holy messengers from distant worlds have come to visit their friends and associates in the service of God on earth, they have so often been obliged to look for them in prisons or in caves of the earth or in exile. And yet it is a blessed thing that human faith has made the vilest dungeon a holy place, and the instruments of torture more sacred than the sceptres of kings. The subterranean galleries of the catacombs, where the Roman Christians hid themselves and worshiped God in the dark days of persecution, are visited with more faith and affection to-day than the ruins of the palace where the Cæsars reigned.

If the very chain with which Peter was bound when the touch of the angel awakened him from sleep were now kept in Jerusalem, and there were no question about its identity, every intelligent traveler visiting that city would wish to see and to handle that chain. And not necessarily from any superstitious regard for a material and senseless piece of iron, but from the feeling that Christian faith and suffering consecrate everything they touch in the estimate of those who themselves believe and are ready to suffer for their faith. If the cell in which Peter slept and the stone floor on which the feet of the angel pressed were preserved to this day unchanged, any intelligent traveler would think it something to remember and to tell of, that he had entered that cell and set his foot upon that floor. If any city in America contained the prison in which John Bunyan wrote the Pilgrim's Progress, or the castle in which Martin Luther translated the Bible into his mother tongue, the most unromantic and unbelieving person in that city would direct a stranger to the prison and the castle as places that every one would like to see.

So much consecration do rude homes and stone walls and vile dungeons derive from the faith and toil and suffering of the servants of God. And the whole earth will become a sanctuary and all human possessions will be made holy when all men have learned to walk with God, and to live in sympathy with the blessed inhabitants of other worlds. Let love to Christ become the law and the life of everything we do, and then the place where we toil and the home where we rest will become as attractive to angels as the dungeons where the martyrs suffered.

Peter slept so soundly upon the stone floor, with both hands chained and a guard upon both sides, that the light which shone from the presence of the celestial

messenger did not wake him.   He must hear the
angel voice and feel the touch of the angel hand.   A
man with a good conscience can sleep on a very hard
bed and in the midst of very great danger.   The
anxieties and perils and worries of life and the dread
of death would not weary and wear us out so much
and so fast if we went to our daily duties with such
high and happy faith in God as martyrs have shown
in the prison and the flames.   If we fully believed
that God has given his angels charge over us to keep
us in all our ways, we could fulfill our day of duty
without fear, and we could gratefully accept such sleep
as God gives to his beloved when the night comes.

I know the doctors say that sound sleep comes of a
good digestion.   And while I do not deny that, I know
another thing quite as well as the doctors—a good
digestion depends greatly upon a good conscience.   To
be in the best health of both body and mind, we must
be at peace with Him who satisfieth our mouth with
good things and reneweth our strength like the eagle's.
And it makes very little difference how humble or
exalted the chamber in which we lie down to rest, if
we have done our duty well and we trust wholly in
Him who giveth his beloved sleep.   The sleep that
renews the life and restores the soul and gives a fore-
taste of heavenly rest is the sleep which God gives to
them that love him.

The time is not far distant when the sleep of death
will steal upon us all.   What strange and bewildering

joy it will be to be waked from that last sleep by the touch of an angel's hand! What new life and liberty for the soul to stand forth released from the suffering body, and to see by its side, clothed in light, an angel-guide ready to start upon the heavenward journey, and saying, "Rise up quickly and follow me!" What surprise it will be to the soul to find itself able to obey that command, and to follow the angel-guide, swift as the light, to the paradise of God!

The care with which Peter was kept was a confession that even Herod was afraid of him. Sixteen armed soldiers, all answerable with their lives for his safe-keeping, and a cell made of massive rock, and two chains and three guarded and bolted gates to secure one unarmed, non-resistant, defenceless man! Surely it was taking great pains to hold one prisoner. And we have much reason to be obliged to the king for making the guard so strong, just as the sealing of the stone and the setting of the watch over the sepulchre of Jesus only helped and confirmed the demonstration of his resurrection; just as we may well thank the proud and passionate Voltaire for saying he was tired of hearing that twelve men established Christianity throughout the world—he would yet live to hear it said that one man had banished Christianity from the face of the earth. Voltaire worked hard and long to fulfill his boast. But he has been dead ninety years, and yet the religion which he hated was never so full of life and power, never so widely diffused among men, never so likely to live for all time, as it is now.

We may count ourselves debtors to the cultivated and remorseless criticism which has exhausted the resources of genius and learning and industry in the endeavor to shake our confidence in the sacred records, for all its efforts have only served to lay bare the ever-lasting foundations on which our faith rests. We may be thankful for the bigotry which determined to crush out the spirit of Christian liberty in the Old World two hundred and fifty years ago, for that oppression drove our fathers into exile, and gave them the sanctuary of the wilderness for a home, and made them the guar-dians of truth and freedom for the world. And so every link in the two chains which bound Peter that night, every stone in the wall of his prison, every bolt in the triple gates, and every one of his sixteen guards prove to us that the power enlisted for the defence of the religion of Jesus is mightier than the armies of kings.

Peter was accustomed to see miracles and manifesta-tions of Divine power in behalf of men; and yet I do not wonder that he was bewildered and thought he had seen a vision that night. Let us try to imagine the circumstances, that we may the better understand his feelings. He is awaked suddenly from deep sleep, and his cell, which had never seen a sunbeam, is all ablaze with light. There stands before him a being radiant with celestial beauty, gentleness and might. He hears a voice which he cannot choose but obey, "Arise." He lifts his hands and they are no longer chained. He stands upon his feet and he is free. Again the voice in quick, commanding tones, "Gird thyself—bind on thy sandals." He tightens the leathern belt about his loins, never once ceasing to gaze with dazzled eyes at the stranger. He ties on his cast-off sandals without knowing where he found them, without looking at his hands to see what they are doing.

And then he stands up bewildered and wondering what next. The armed soldiers are still as if they had been changed to stone on the stony floor. Again the voice, "Cast thy garments about thee." And he does so, knowing as little as before what he is doing. "Follow me," and the angel moves toward the closed and bolted door. And all the while this impulsive man, Peter, who was always talking, even when he had nothing to say, has not said a word. He steps over the prostrate guards, who, asleep or awake, do not seem to know what is going on, and he moves after his strange guide. They approach the door—it is shut; they are outside of it—it is still shut. How they passed it Peter does not know. He has not seen it open or close. It was before them; it is now behind them, and they move on. There are soldiers within and soldiers without. But they give no heed when the apostle and his guide pass between them. They approach the second gate on the other side of the court of the prison. That, too, is shut and guarded within and without. They have already passed it, and everything is behind them as it was before them. There is no creak of hinges, no clank of bolts, no sign of alarm or of attention from the fourfold guard. It is all light as day about the man and the angel, and yet it seems to the man as if he were dreaming. The bolts, the gates, the guards seem to have lost their substance and their reality to him. He passes them all as if they were thin air, but how he does it he cannot tell.

At last it looks more like reality when he comes to the outer iron gate, for that swings open, and he can see the motion, and the two pass out into the public street. But then there is no sound of unbolting, no stir or look of the soldier-guards within or without, as if they knew that anybody were passing. And the gate is shut the moment the angel and the man are in the street. Peter follows his guide bewildered and wondering what will be the end, and in a moment more he finds himself alone.

Now at last he has time to think. The streets are silent. No light shines from the blank walls of the houses. The splendor that flowed from his mysterious guide is gone. But the bewildered man begins to come to himself. He recognizes the place. It was along this very street that the rude soldiers led him a week ago, with the ruder rabble hooting after him, and the occupants of the houses stepping out to join in the mockery. It was just here that he expected to meet the faces of the mob in the morning when the order came to lead him forth to torture and death.

Not quite sure that it is himself or that he is fully awake, he feels in the dark for the crease of the manacle on the swollen wrist. The mark is there, but the chain is gone. Did he bind on his sandals when told in the prison? He stamps upon the ground. Yes, they are on his feet now. And his girdle and cast-off robe that lay beside him on the stone floor in the hot and stifling cell? Yes, he has them all. And it is no dream. God's mighty angel has led him along the street where he expected to be led in mockery by Herod's men of war. He is free, and the fanatical populace of Jerusalem will clamor in vain for their victim on the morrow.

And so God's angel shall come in the appointed time to deliver the disciple of Jesus from the prison of the flesh. And oh how much more glorious than the change which so bewildered the mind of the apostle when he went out from the dungeon in Jerusalem, and could not for a while believe that it was himself abroad in the open streets! The heavenly messenger finds the one for whom he is sent racked with pain. The shadows of death are deepening around him. The voice of wailing and sorrow is in his chamber. The faces that bend over him are bedewed with tears. His mind wanders, his senses are benumbed, everything grows dark and confused around him. He cannot hear the voices of his beloved, he cannot feel the touch of their hand. Everything is going from him—feeling, thought, desire, life—all fading, sinking, gone!

But no! A strange glory is shining around him. Forms of celestial beauty approach. Strains of unearthly music fill the air. The pain, the darkness, the sorrow are all gone. There is no sun, but it is all light. He listens, and in the chorus of voices he hears one that passed away from the earth years ago. And now it is the same voice, only purer, sweeter, more full of love than it ever was on earth. And now he recognizes a face over which he saw the shadow of death pass long ago, and now it is the same and yet so beautiful, so angelical, just what he wished it to be, what it was to his mind and heart even when worn and deeply furrowed with the lines of sickness and pain. And now there are more of the loved and lost ones of other years around him. They come swift as thought. There is a tremor of light in the air, and they are by his side. And they all seem like angels, yet so natural, so human, so like themselves. They all know him, and their presence makes it seem as if this were home, and yet not the home that he left darkened with shadows and saddened with wailing and tears.

Can this be heaven? And is it himself that is here? And is he like the rest, glorious, beautiful, happy? And death, and pain, and sorrow, are they all past? Will not a word or a motion or a moment prove it all a dream, and wake him to hear the voice of weeping and to feel the fire of fever upon his lip, and to see a sad company bending over him in an agony of grief?

But we try in vain to express in words the blessed bewilderment of the happy soul in the first moment of waking from the sleep of death to the life of heaven. If the apostle could not for a while believe the reality of what he had seen and heard when delivered from prison by the angel at night, how much greater shall be the wonder, the surprise of the ransomed soul when taken from this suffering, crumbling prison of the body, and set down free and every faculty all thrilling with immortal life in the golden streets of the New Jerusalem.

It is here that we sleep and dream. The great reality of life is yet to come—a life that never rests from activity, that never tires with toil, that never grows old with time—a life that shall keep pace in duration with the eternal years of God. Here the soul is bound, like Peter in the prison, with two chains—one the burden and sorrow of life, the other the fear of death. Faith in Christ alone delivers us from the double bondage. Faith in Christ alone can prepare us to be waked by the touch of the angel of death, and to see ourselves surrounded with a greater light than shone in the prison of the apostle when his angel deliverer said to him, " Arise, follow me." Immortal man, let not the cares of this world, the deceitfulness of riches, the seductions of pleasure, the dreams of ambition lead you to forget that your true life begins

30

with death, and your real home is not earth, but heaven. Let nothing bind you with such strong attachments here that you would rather stay in the prison of the body and wear your chains than go forth into everlasting light and liberty, when God's angel comes with the message, " Rise up quickly, and follow me."

Midnight in the Prison at Philippi.

And at midnight, Paul and Silas prayed, and sang praises unto God: and the prisoners heard them.—ACTS xvi. 25

MIDNIGHT IN THE PRISON AT PHILIPPI

est dungeon of the prison where the
ned as if of all criminals they were the
kept on singing until all the prisoners
at the angel. Shrieks
there were heard
but the unhappy in
by the sound of

ere the men that drew the attention of
at that solitary hour? And how about
a place? The day before they had
river's bank, in a quiet place
alking with that way that can
and salvation.
to excite the people or to d
They were only minis

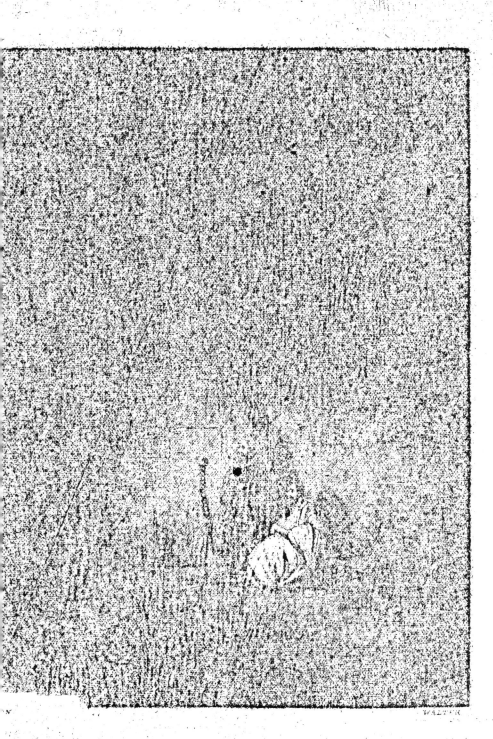

XXIII.

MIDNIGHT IN THE PRISON AT PHILIPPI.

PRAISE and prayer were strange sounds to be heard at midnight in the heathen prison at Philippi. And the two men whose voices broke the silence of the hour were in a sad condition to sing. But their song swelled loud from the deepest and darkest dungeon of the prison where they had been confined as if of all criminals they were the worst, and they kept on singing until all the prisoners waked and wondered at the sound. Shrieks and groans and execrations had many times been heard in that dark abode. Never before had the unhappy inmates been disturbed at midnight by the sound of praise and prayer.

Who were the men that drew the attention of all the prisoners at that solitary hour? And how came they to be in such a place? The day before they had been down by the river's bank, in a quiet place outside of the city walls, talking with the company that came and went about Jesus and the way of salvation. They were doing nothing to excite the people or to disturb the peace of the city. They were only ministering comfort and rest to sorrowing and weary hearts. They were only answering for others the most solemn and important question that can ever engage the human mind: "What must I do to be saved?"

While thus employed they were repeatedly interrupted by the cries of a poor slave girl who was hel in double bondage by her human masters and by the demons of darkness. One of the two men, Paul, by virtue of the Divine power given unto him in the name of Jesus Christ, delivered the unhappy slave from her spiritual tormentors, and so her masters could no longer make gain of her pretended inspiration. They were greatly incensed because their fraud and cruelty were now exposed, and their opportunity to profit by imposture was lost. In their rage and excitement they laid hands upon the two peaceful strangers, hurried them back into the city, gathered a crowd about them in the market-place, and vehemently charged them with causing the tumult which themselves alone had excited.

The rude idlers of the town ran together from every quarter, and cries were lifted up from many voices. No opportunity was given to the two defenceless men to speak or explain what they had done. The attention of the magistrates was drawn to the tumult. The officers of the Roman government were great sticklers for order, and they sometimes restored quiet by the most cruel and hasty process. In this case, seeing that Paul and Silas were set upon and denounced by all the rest, they took it for granted, without delay or inquiry, that they were the guilty cause of the disturbance. They accordingly commanded them to be taken from the hands of the rabble and stripped and scourged by the public executioner in the market-place. Their garments were torn off, they were thrown violently upon their faces to the ground, their hands and feet were held down by strong and cruel men, while others beat with blow after blow upon their naked backs with tough and flexible rods of elm, that tore the flesh and drew blood at every stroke. If they tried to speak or to ask a hearing of the magistrates, they were seized by the hair of the head and their faces ground into the dust. The heartless rabble looked on with eager eyes, and shouted savage applause, while the blows fell thick and fast upon the quivering flesh. The sight of blood and the writhings of the victims only roused the brutal passions of the crowd to a wilder pitch of excitement, and made them encourage the cruel lictors to strike with the greater force and upon the part where the blow would cause the greatest suffering. Such exhibitions were always witnessed with fiendish delight by the rabble in Roman towns, and many times the leading motive of the magistrate in condemning the accused was to please the people with the sight of torture and blood.

When the executioners were weary with giving many blows, and their heavy rods were dripping with blood, the poor men were lifted up from the ground and taken away to prison. The rabble went hooting after them—the magistrates sent the solemn charge to the jailor at the peril of his life to keep his captives safely. Being taken in at the main gate, they were led through the crowd of prisoners in the outer court. They were seen by all, bruised and bleeding and their lacerated bodies covered with dust. A more secure and horrible place was sought for these men than for the common criminals. And they were accordingly taken into the deepest recesses of the prison and let down into a damp, cold, pestilential dungeon. The jailor descended after them, laid them upon their inflamed and tortured backs on the stone floor, stretched out their feet and hands and pinioned them down between strong timbers, so that they could not rise or relieve themselves by changing their position. Thus bound and secured, the jailor left them, neither giving them water to assuage their burning thirst, nor anything to alleviate their painful wounds. He climbed up out of the dungeon, and the iron covering crashed down behind him upon the stone floor over their heads like the fall of a millstone upon the pavement. And there they were for the night, suffering hunger and thirst and cold and torture, in darkness so deep that they could not tell the day from the night.

Such was the reception given to the first missionaries of the cross who passed over to Europe from the Asiatic shore to proclaim the glad tidings of the great salvation. They came to feed the hungry and clothe

the naked and comfort the sorrowing, and they were stripped of their garments and scourged in the market-place. They came to proclaim liberty to enslaved millions, and they were bound and consigned to the deepest dungeon. They come to bring light into the hearts and homes of all men, and they were imprisoned in utter darkness. They brought a message from heaven which has been for ages the source of power and prosperity to the mightiest and most enlightened nations of the earth, and they were treated as if they were robbers and deceivers of mankind.

So the world crowns its worst enemies and crucifies its greatest benefactors. So hard is it even now for men to accept the richest blessing when it is offered as a free gift. So slow of heart are millions to believe that the humbling, self-denying religion of Jesus does most to improve man's condition in this world, while in the world to come it ensures glory and life everlasting.

The excitement of the day was over. The lictors had bound up their bloody rods and laid them aside for the next victim. The magistrates had gone to their homes, flattering themselves that by promptness and energy they had suppressed a popular tumult and vindicated the majesty of Roman law. The jailor had fulfilled too well the charge to put the two prisoners beyond the possibility of rescue or escape. The other inmates of the prison congratulated themselves that they at least had not had their flesh seamed and torn by the cruel rods, nor had they been buried alive in the cold dungeon of the inner prison. The rabble of the town had slunk away to their wretched homes.

Midnight had come down with its deep shadows upon the sleeping city. There was silence in the deserted streets, silence in the outer wards of the prison, silence in the cells where wretched men were shivering on the stone floor, silence in the inner prison. But no, from that dungeon deep and cold, where the two tortured men had been bound with their inflamed flesh to the hard and rough stone, there comes a sound. Is it a cry of pain? Is it the wail of tortured men in their agony? Is it a maddened supplication for death to come and release them from their misery?

No, far from it. It is the voice of singing. It is a strain of joy and triumph. It is a psalm of victory and thanksgiving. We do not know precisely what it was that they sung. But we may be sure that it was in that ancient and inspired Hebrew strain which delights in ascribing glory unto God and in declaring unshaken trust in him under the sorest affliction: "Oh sing praises unto Jehovah. For he heareth the poor when they cry, he despiseth not his prisoners, he bringeth them out that are bound with chains. He breaketh the gates of brass, and smiteth the bars of iron in sunder. Oh sing praises unto Jehovah, for he is good, for his mercy endureth for ever."

And still that glorious song swelled loud and clear from the depths of the dungeon's gloom, until it was heard through all the wards and outer courts of the prison, and all the wretched bondmen within the walls were awake and listening to the strain. When they saw the swollen and bleeding flesh of the two men as they were taken into the inner prison the evening before, they thought their sleep would be disturbed that night by groans and cries of agony. And now they are waked by the strains of joy and exultation.

And while they listen and wonder what all this can mean, suddenly there comes a mysterious and awful sound, as if the solid earth were rent asunder beneath the whole city. The foundations of the prison are shaken. The bolted doors are all thrown open. The chains and fetters of every prisoner are loosed and all are free. The jailor, who had slept through all the singing, is waked by the earthquake. He sees the prison doors open. He supposes the prisoners to have gone. He knows that, by the stern usage of Roman law, his life will have to be paid as the forfeit for their escape. In despair he determines to anticipate the shame of a public execution by plunging his sword into his own bosom. He would be like Brutus and Cassius, who ended their last struggle against Cæsar on the plains near this same city of Philippi, by falling upon their own swords. The jailor's hand is upon his sword, and he is just about to give himself the fatal blow, when a voice comes up from the dungeon of the inner prison, saying, " Do thyself no harm, for we are all here." It is all dark. The jailor himself cannot see the one who speaks. But the voice is so loud, clear and calm, it is so full of earnestness and assurance, that the excited man becomes himself again. He drops his sword, calls for a light, rushes into the inner prison through the open doors, leaps down into the subterranean dungeon, lifts up Paul and Silas from the pit and brings them out into the open court of the prison.

And now there comes over this man a strange fear, a mighty and an irrepressible longing which declares itself in the most momentous inquiry man can ever make: "What must I do to be saved?" Saved, not simply from the terrors of the earthquake; that is already past and has done no harm. Saved, not simply from punishment under Roman law for the escape of the prisoners; for the prisoners are all here. But saved from that awful and infinite peril of which the accusing conscience whispers in the secret place of every human soul. Saved from the wretchedness of living without God and dying without hope. Saved with that everlasting salvation which is preached by these persecuted prisoners in the name of the most high God.

This is the grand question which is to be first asked and first answered for himself by every considerate, conscientious man. It is not to be deferred till the time of trouble and alarm. We are not to wait till the pleasures of earth cease to allure, and the terrors of death take hold of us, before we ask what is to become of us in the endless future beyond the grave, before we seek some rescue from the guilt and woe of sin in our own hearts. This poor jailer at Philippi was indeed driven by terror to acknowledge himself an inquirer for the way of salvation. And no man should be ashamed to confess himself afraid of what he feared— afraid to live a life of sin and die a death of despair, afraid to wrong the strivings and pleadings of infinite love, and to reject the offer of eternal salvation. This is what a brave man should be most afraid of.

The good soldier who is least afraid of the terrors of death is most afraid to disobey the orders of his commander. He is ready to face the storm of battle, but he is not willing to have it said that his country called for him in the hour of her peril and he answered not. And no man should be ashamed to have it said that he is afraid to disobey the infinite God, afraid to refuse when the cause of truth and righteousness for all ages and all worlds demands a service at his hands. It is the first and best evidence of a right mind when one begins to ask with deep earnestness, " What must I do to be saved from making my life a failure, myself a wreck, my whole toil and effort and sacrifice a waste? What must I do to be saved from living in a state of opposition to God and in perpetual conflict with my own conscience? What must I do to cast off the galling chains of evil habits and passions, and rise up free in the Divine and glorious liberty of the children of God?"

Riches and poverty, sickness and health, prosperity and adversity are trifles not worthy to be named in comparison with the soul's eternal salvation. Salvation is the full possession and perfect enjoyment of every possible means of good for ever. And in this world there is no perfect enjoyment of anything, and the happiest hour is the quickest to fly. What is it worth to man's immortal self to enjoy the highest health and success for a few years, and die the owner of millions of property, and then go into the other world to be poor and wretched and in want of all things for ever? And how rich and happy is he who lives a few years in pain and sorrow, suffers disappointment and neglect and has not where to lay his head, and then with all his immortal powers bursts into a new and glorious life, with the certain prospect of perfect and endless blessedness before him, and all the pain and sorrow of earth for ever behind!

It is a wonder how this excited and terrified man at Philippi could have become so suddenly and supremely anxious about the one subject of greatest concern to us all. His question is still the question of the age, of the world, and of every man in it. Not, What shall I do to be rich, to be honored, to be free from toil and pain and want, to live the longest and to be most successful in this world? But, What shall I do to be blessed for ever, to have every want of my soul supplied and every faculty of my being ennobled and glorified for everlasting ages? What shall I do to prepare for the society of angels, for the occupations of heaven, for a home in that city whose builder and maker is God?

This is something worth being inquired about earnestly, constantly, till the great inheritance of salvation is secure and the soul is at rest.

We all have too many fears and anxieties about our safety and success in this world to enjoy life as we go along. It would add immensely to our present peace and contentment if we were supremely interested about our condition in the endless life to come. Paul and Silas sang praises to God at midnight in the dungeon of Philippi, triumphing over the tortures which had been inflicted upon them, because they looked upward through the gloom and saw the crown of life in waiting for them, and they suffered only because they were helping others to attain that crown. They could sing on their way to glory, although the path they had to tread was one of pain and conflict. Despised and persecuted as they were, the journey of life to them was the march of a conqueror who advances with the exultations of triumph in his heart and the palms of victory on his brow.

*   *   *   *   *   *

In the subsequent history of the great apostle who was the chief actor in this memorable night scene at Philippi there is another experience of prison life, which shows still more clearly the sustaining power of faith in a better life to come. A reference to the latter will show that the joyfulness with which Paul endured afflictions for Christ's sake in the earlier part of his ministry was not a transient enthusiasm, but a faith that waxed stronger and stronger to the last.

In the city of modern Rome, at the foot of the Capitoline Hill, adjoining the ruined Forum, is a deep, dark and terrible dungeon called the Mamertine Prison. It consisted originally of two vaulted chambers, one above the other, excavated in the rock of the ancient hill. The upper dungeon was far below the surface of the ground, and the lower deep of the one beneath could be entered only through a small circular opening in the stone floor of the one above, as a man might descend into a well or a cistern by a rope. No window or door or loophole was left for the light of the sun or the fresh air of the open heavens to enter that dread abode. The floor, the walls, the roof are all of stone, damp, dark, cold, the sight of which, as seen by the dim light of the taper, makes the flesh creep and the heart shudder with horror. That terrible dungeon was hollowed out of the rocky hill twenty-five hundred years ago, and in all the intervening time it has not been possible for the most ingenious cruelty to build a better place in which to break a man's heart.

The tradition of the Catholic Church confidently affirms that the Apostle Paul was confined in that lower dungeon when he sent his last message of love and counsel to his young friend and disciple Timothy. This tradition is credited by some writers of repute outside of the Romish Church. If we venture to assume its credibility for the purpose of illustration, we shall not make the apostle's condition worse than it was at the time. And such a definite view of the dread reality of imprisonment under the Romans will help us to appreciate the feelings with which he wrote his last triumphant words: "I have fought a good fight, I have finished my course, I have kept the faith. Henceforth there is laid up for me a crown of righteousness."

Let us try, then, to imagine the condition of this heroic and much-suffering man, sending forth from the dungeon of the Mamertine prison a shout of victory which has nerved martyrs in the midst of the flames, and which shall sound through all time and to the ends of the earth. We see an old man with white hair and a feeble frame lifting himself up slowly and tremblingly from the wet and miry floor. The chilly damp of the prison is upon his brow, and racking pains are shooting through every limb. But the light of heaven flashes in his glorious eye, and he has the calm, earnest look of one who is already conversing with the awful realities of the unseen and eternal world. He has been waked by sharp suffering from short and uneasy sleep on the cold stone, and now he is walking painfully backward and forward the length of his clanking chain to get a little warmth and to relieve his tortured frame by motion.

He has been accustomed to the dry air and the hot sun of Syrian plains and Arabian deserts, and the chill of that cold prison-house pierces like icicles to his very heart. His dungeon is the sink of the larger and

31

crowded one above, and its condition was declared by the heartless and stoical heathen writers of the time to be " terrific" and not to be described.   His fetters per-mit him to walk but half the space between the walls, and his feet make a path in the miry filth of the stone floor.   He has no change of clothing, no bed, nor chair nor table.   When the stone covering is lifted from above to fling down a little black bread for his daily food, it admits no light, no breath of pure air, for the dungeon above him is as dark and close as his own.

He has no means of measuring the time.   He cannot tell the day from the night.   The weeks and months of captivity are to him all one night of uniform and terrible darkness and solitude.   He lies buried so deep beneath the surface of the ground that the roar of the imperial city, with its million inhabitants above and around him, seems like the dying echoes of distant thunder or the breaking of waves upon some far-off coast.   The triumphal procession of a conqueror might pass through the adjoining Forum and climb the nearer hill of the Capitol, with a hundred trumpets sounding and thousands shouting from streets and housetops, and the captive in his dungeon not know that Rome had kept a holiday.

After long intervals of perfect solitude and dark-ness. a faithful friend, who has braved death to see him, is permitted to descend and stay with him for an hour with a taper's light in his terrible den.   For so long a time he sees the horrors around him, which before the darkness had mercifully hidden from his sight. He avails himself of the opportunity to dictate his last letter to his young friend Timothy at Ephesus, whose face he longs to see once more before his martyrdom. And in this letter, dictated under the sufferance of racking pain and surrounded with unutterable horrors, he is communicating with the living world for the last time.

What thoughts, what emotions will crowd upon the apostle's mind as he pours out all his heart to his beloved and sympathizing friend! What will he say of his situation and his sufferings? Of what wrongs will he complain? What afflictions will he deplore? What fears and disappointments will he confess?

He has been a man of lofty aspirations. He has spent the best of his life in laboring for the highest interests of man amid the pomp and marvels of the great. He has traveled upon the track of empire. He has made himself known in the most ancient and renowned cities of the earth. He has stood before governors, kings and emperors, and always for the same purpose and pleading the same cause. He has reasoned the rabble into calmness when in one instance they were impatient to tear him in pieces, and in another they were just as eager to worship him as a god. He has spoken in the assembly of philosophers with a power that put their wisdom to shame. He has made proud kings and profligate princes tremble by the awful solemnity of his appeal to a judgment to come.

He is now within a bowshot of arches and towers, temples and monuments, trophies and palaces, the wonder of the world for splendor, the utmost achievement of genius and wealth and power. He has been led to his dark imprisonment along the Appian Way, through a street of tombs. more gorgeous than the homes of the living. He has walked, chained to a soldier's hand, beneath the shadow of the Cæsars' palace, that covers a whole hill with the dazzling magnificence of imperial state. He passed to his dungeon through a wilderness of architectural wonders in the Forum, in full view of the spot where Cicero harangued and the first Cæsar fell, over the triumphal way where the car of the conqueror climbed the hill of the Capitol.

Looking for the last time upon the light of the sun in heaven amid a scene of such surpassing earthly magnificence, he has been consigned to the deep pit where murderers and conspirators have died of torture, of strangulation and starving. The walls around him are reeking with crime. His feet sink in the mire as he walks the stony floor. Bearing a commission higher than the sceptre of the Cæsars, he has been left to weep and suffer and pray in darkness and solitude. He is the most tried and provoked, the most wronged and unappreciated, man in all the empire.

What, then, will he say when the opportunity is afforded him to speak to the world for the last time?

Will he use the language of complaint, of disappointment or of despair? Will he mourn that the pomp and splendor of the imperial city are hidden from him? After all his toils and trials and sufferings and perils on land and sea, among strangers and among his own people, will he count himself to have lost the work of his life because it must end in a dungeon and he must die as a malefactor?

No, far from it. This last message which comes up from the darkness of the prison and from the heart of the most injured and afflicted man in Rome is full of light and joy. It begins with thanksgiving and it ends with triumph. It is the coronation hymn of a conqueror who has gained the greatest victory and is to receive the most glorious crown. He has not, indeed, forgotten the wrongs which he has suffered. He has not grown insensible to injury. He has not become indifferent to bodily pain. It almost makes one shiver with the chill of the dungeon when he tells Timothy to bring the cloak which he left at Troas and to do his best to reach Rome before winter. It touches our hearts with unspeakable tenderness to read the affectionate remembrances which he sends, forgetful of his own sorrows, to many beloved friends by name.

No, the heart of this aged prisoner has not grown old, his mind has not become suspicious or resentful, he has not lost any of his human sensibilities or attachments under all his wrongs and afflictions. And yet with all his longing for absent friends, and with his tender susceptibility to the terrible injuries heaped upon him, he glories and rejoices. From the depths of the dungeon's gloom he sends forth a light which shall shine to the ends of the earth. He counts himself to have already gained the victory. He sees the crown waiting for him. He has a Defender higher and mightier than the Cæsars. He confidently expects to be delivered from all evil and to obtain an everlasting kingdom. He is satisfied that he has expended the labor of his life upon the best cause, and that it shall not be lost to him or the world. He would not exchange his foul dungeon for Nero's Golden House if, in so doing, he must disown the principles which he has maintained or dishonor the cause for which he has suffered. Paul in prison is greater, nobler, happier than the man whose imperial palace, at the other end of the Forum, covers the whole Palatine Hill, and whose single word can deliver the apostle from his dungeon or doom him to immediate death.

And we all know very well what gave Paul, in prison and condemned to death, such an advantage over the world's great master. It was simple, earnest, persevering devotion to Christ. His greatness was due to the fact that he was a Christian. He might have been rich and learned and honored in his time, and we never should have known anything about him. It is simply because he was a good man that his memory lives in the hearts of millions, and his influence is destined to flow on, diffusing light and blessing, through all generations. It now makes a memorable moment in a man's life to stand for once on the uncovered stones of the Appian Way, over which Paul, the prisoner of the Lord, passed on his way to Rome, or to go down into the dungeon where there is a possibility that he was once imprisoned, or to pass out of the Ostian gate upon the Campagna, and survey the scene where tradition tells us that he suffered martyrdom. The house of the Cæsars has become the habitation of owls and doleful creatures. A few broken columns and crumbling arches are all that remain of the architectural magnificence of the Forum. The Coliseum is great only in ruin. The name of Nero is remembered only to be execrated, but the memory of Paul grows brighter and fresher with the lapse of time. It lives in more loving hearts, and is cherished in more cultivated minds to-day, than ever before. The work of his life is still one of the great powers operating most efficiently for the world's advancement in all that is great and good.

And there is no way in which any man can now make so much of life with all its powers, faculties and opportunities as by giving himself, as Paul did, to the Divine task of making the world better and happier. In any other way he may never do anything for which the world will ever thank him. But let him give time, talent, money, education, personal influence and accomplishments to the work of bringing wanderers back to the right way and showing men where the essential good of life is to be found, and he will make for himself an everlasting name—he will have many to do him honor when time shall be no more.

Paul's Night in the Deep.

When the fourteenth night was come, as we were driven up and down in Adria, about midnight the shipmen deemed that they drew near to some country. . . . And so it came to pass, that they escaped all safe to land.—ACTS xxvii. 27, 44.

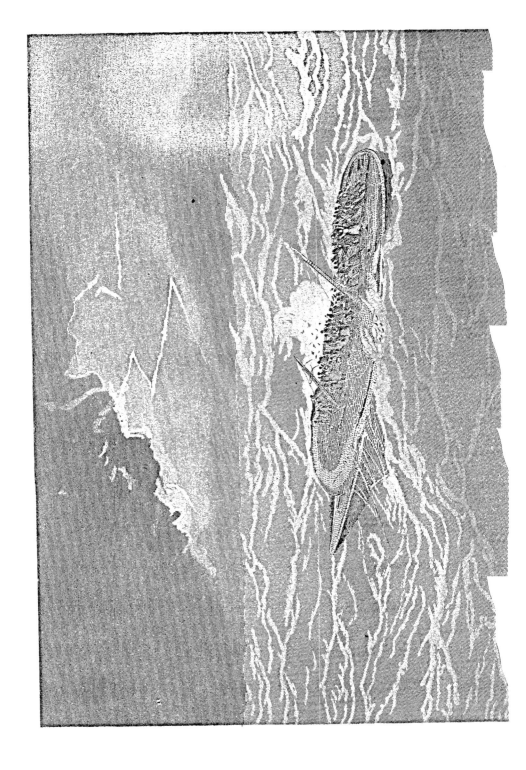

491

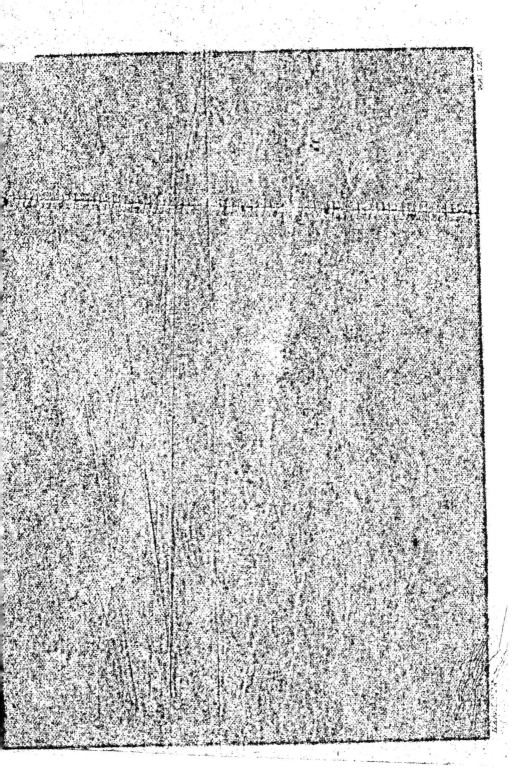

XXIV.

PAUL'S NIGHT IN THE DEEP.

THE tale of suffering on the sea and of shipwreck on the shore is always sadly and fearfully interesting. The long conflict of weary men with the winds and the waves; the signal of distress that is never seen and the cry for help that is never heard; the hunger and thirst that torture the maddened crew with visions of hope and dreams of despair; the wail of the storm that breaks on the shore with the burden of sorrows on the sea; the waiting in anxious homes for the beloved that delay their return, and the mourning for those that come not back, —all have been many times told in solemn prose and sounding rhyme.

But never since men began to sail on the sea has any shipwreck been invested with deeper interest to all minds than the one in which the Apostle Paul bore a part, and by which he was cast with two hundred and seventy-five others safe upon Malta's rocky shore. We all know the story and how it ended with safety to the servant of Christ. And yet so vivid and truthful is the sacred narrative that we cannot read it for

491

the hundredth time without feeling some solicitude for the life of that wonderful man on the last night of his long voyage, walking up and down the heaving deck, among hardened soldiers and reckless seamen, waiting for the day. It was a strange thing for that defenceless Hebrew prisoner to stand forth on that dark and terrible night in the deep, both as the commander and comforter of men who thought it a small matter to take his life lest the feeble and exhausted old man should plunge into the wild breakers, swim ashore and escape their hands. And our wonder at the dignity and the composure of the apostle will be increased if we glance at the leading circumstances of the long voyage.

They had been driven fourteen days and nights before a raging north-east storm, without a sight of the sun or the stars. At that time safe navigation depended far more than now upon a clear sky and a fair wind and a visible shore. They had no chart on which the true course had been delineated for the captain's eye. They had no sextant or quadrant with which, should the sky be clear, to wrest from the far distant orbs of heaven the secret of the ship's place on the sea below. They had no chronometer with which to mark the slow progress of the weary hours while the ship went plunging and rolling through the darkness over the black and bounding deep. They had no compass to point with its trembling finger to the quarter of the heavens where God has stretched out the north over the empty place, and commanded the pole star to keep its everlasting throne.

Their ship was little better than a canal-boat or a scow. It was bluntly rounded at both ends, as if bow and stern had been made after the same model, with no delicate and sharpened lines to cut the water. It had but one mast, and that was set upright in the middle, so that the full pressure of a cross wind upon the sails would pry the planks and timbers apart like a wedge. The whole arrangement of spars and rigging was well fitted to scud before the wind, but it left the ship almost powerless to bear up against a breeze from any other direction than behind. The vessel was large enough to carry three hundred men and a cargo of wheat in the hold, and it had ventured out upon a stretch of sea as long in the passage as it now takes to cross the Atlantic Ocean, and it was in the perilous season of the October gales; and yet it had nothing for a helm or rudder save two long paddles loosely lashed to the sides and running down to the water near the stern.

The first day of the storm they ran under the lee of a small island, and the seamen improved the opportunity to take in sail and haul up the long-boat which had been towing behind. Fearing lest their loosely-joined hulk would go to pieces, they passed ropes beneath the keel, bringing the ends up on either side and tying them across the deck as one would tie a bundle of sticks with twine. The second and third day all joined hands, soldiers and sailors, prisoners and passengers, Paul and his companion Luke with the rest, in throwing overboard everything that could be reached of the furniture and lading of the ship. The wheat was down in the hold and the hatches could not be safely opened to bring it up, while the sea was flooding the deck from stem to stern at every plunge of the vessel.

And now came on the long and fearful struggle with the tempest. The wind blew a gale; the waves ran wild and high; the rain poured down in torrents; the angry elements beat with ceaseless rage upon the torn sail, the shattered mast and the reeling deck; the groaning timbers parted and let in the water as fast as a hundred hands could bail it out; everybody on board was wet through and through; there was no opportunity to take food or rest. And so were they driven fourteen days and nights helplessly before the tempest, until no hope was left that a single life of passengers or crew could be saved.

At last the quick ear of the sailors discovered that a new and more terrible voice had been added to the wild chorus of the storm. It was midnight, and nothing could be seen through the darkness. But there was no mistaking the sound. It was the roar of breakers upon a rocky shore. They cast the lead twice and found that they were rapidly approaching the unseen coast. They dropped four anchors out of the stern to stop their course, and then wished and waited for the coming day. In the mean time taking advice, of Paul, whose word had come to be of more worth with the seamen than the captain's, they refreshed themselves with food and employed the time between midnight and morning in throwing the wheat into the sea.

When the day dawned they cut away the hawsers, leaving the anchors in the deep, and drove the lightened ship toward the shore. It struck at some distance from land, and was soon broken in pieces by the violence of the waves. The whole two hundred and seventy-six persons were cast alive and struggling into the midst of the breakers. Exhausted as they were with cold and hunger and weariness, after so many days and nights of restless plunging and rolling on the sea, they could have had little strength left to battle with the billows of that rocky shore. Wild, haggard and enfeebled as they were by a half month of famine and terror and torture, we should say that most of them must sink without a struggle the moment the broken ship cast them into the waves.

But no, they all escaped safe to land. Some by swimming, some on boards, some on fragments of freight and furniture thrown out of the ship, all found their way through the boiling breakers to the solid land. The angel of the Lord had stood by Paul in the visions of the night on that tempest-tossed ship, and had said to him, " God hath given thee all them that sail with thee," and that word must be fulfilled.

Neither wind nor wave nor hunger nor cold nor weariness nor shipwreck could take the life of one of those two hundred and seventy-five persons sailing with Paul in that ship, because God had given them to his servant in answer to his petition, and for his sake the very men who counseled to kill him should be saved. This persecuted prisoner of the Lord who is going bound to Rome to bear testimony unto Jesus in the palace of the Cæsars and before the world's great master, must be permitted to fulfill his high commission. And the warring elements of the air and the deep fight a continued battle of fourteen days and nights in vain for the destruction of that ship, until the ambassador of Christ and all who sail with him are safely landed on Malta's rocky shore.

So much is it worth to a man to be found at the post of duty when suffering and peril come. Such protection does the bare presence of the servant of Christ afford to many who never know to whom they are indebted for their safety. The great sea had tossed the ships of Solomon and of Xerxes, of Pompey and of Augustus; it had been freighted with the spoils of nations and with the gems and gold of "the gorgeous East." But it never bore a richer treasure than it carried in the life of that one man who was going bound as the prisoner of the Lord to be brought before Nero. The deep might have swallowed up the navies of Salamis and of Actium with less disaster to the world than would have been caused by cutting short the career of him who had received a Divine commission to preach the gospel by his bonds in "all the palace of Cæsar."

And He who makes the winds his ministers and who holds the sea in the hollow of his hand would not permit the raging elements to endanger the life of his servant till his work was done. God will take care of the life of any man who lives only that his duty may be done. So long as God has work for him to do, and it is better for him to live, his life is safe. And when his work is done he shall enter into rest.

God will take care of the influence and reputation of the man who lives only to do his duty. Paul was counted a fanatic and an outcast. His name is not mentioned in the classic histories of his time. The great masters of the world knew him only as the propagator of a hated and pestilent superstition. The author of the Roman Annals and the biographer of the Cæsars would have thought it beneath the dignity of history to say that such a man ever lived. And yet now it would be hard to find one who would not rather have the reputation of Paul than of Nero. In all human history there is not another name which represents so great power over the most active and cultivated mind in this most advanced and progressive age. And it is safe to say that when all the accounts of time are balanced upon the books of eternity, it will be found that Paul has exerted more influence upon men, and has attained a higher place among the masters of the

32

world, than all the Cæsars and Napoleons that ever lived.

Paul's many nights in the deep, and his escape out of all perils while as yet he had anything to do for his Master, should teach us that the way of duty is ever the way of honor, of happiness and of safety. Dangers, trials, sufferings may be met in the discharge of duty, but the servant of God is always safe. None who live for Christ can ever be lost. When all the storms and wrecks of time are past, and the great company of the ransomed is gathered in the glorious light of eternity, it will be found that none who trusted in Jesus have failed to escape safe to the heavenly shore. All who ever enlisted under the Captain of salvation, and whose names were written in his book of life, shall appear when the roll of the ransomed is called and the mansions of rest are thrown open to welcome them in.

Some shall come out of great tribulation, from dungeons and tortures and martyrdom. Some who shine in glory like the stars of the firmament shall come out of great obscurity, having had no record in the proud annals of earthly fame, carrying the seal and promise of coming greatness only in a pure heart and a lowly walk with God. Some will be there whose earthly life was a pilgrimage of pain, whose perishable body was a network of nerves to gather in sufferings and sorrows for the soul. Some shall be there who lived long years under the shadow of thick clouds, wrestling with doubts and fears, like Bunyan and Brainerd and

Cowper and Payson, doing desperate battle with spectre hosts from the pit of darkness, yet ever yearning for the light and waiting for the day. Some shall enter into rest fresh from the fields of toil, and some wearied and worn out with long effort and patient endurance of temptation. Some that shine with angel brightness in the countless throng shall come from humble homes which they have consecrated by Christian faith, and from lowly occupations which they have ennobled and glorified by doing all things for the glory of God. Some shall come from the envied seats of riches and power among men, having laid all their earthly honors and possessions at the feet of Jesus. The war-worn soldier of Christ shall be there, having fought the good fight and wearing still the scars of his earthly campaigns illuminated as badges of honor in the service of his King. And there shall be the little child that fainted beneath the burden of life at the beginning of the journey, and breathed forth its gentle spirit into the bosom of waiting angels, and was borne to the gardens of Paradise in the bloom of its young immortality. All shall be there. All shall escape safe to the heavenly shore. When Christ counts up his chosen and beloved, after all the storms of earth have spent their fury and the wrecks of sin have strewn the shores of time, none who relied on him for rescue shall be lost. No follower of his shall be wanting when the hulk of this frail mortality is broken in pieces, and the rescued souls are gathered upon that blessed shore where the tempests of passion never rage, and the billows of sorrow never swell.

Oh how unlike the gatherings of earth will be that glad meeting when Christ shall call his ransomed home! Here we come together from time to time as the years roll round, but the ranks are not all full. The family circle forms again when the festive days return, but there are more faces in the silent pictures on the wall than greet each other around the social board. To one and another beloved name there are none to answer. And as time passes on and the storms of affliction and sorrow beat around us, we are all getting more names upon the roll of our acquaintances whose places are vacant, who gather with us no more, who answer not when their names are called.

When we visit a former home after long absence and inquire for the friends of other years, we are told of one and of another that he has gone the way whence he will not return. When the regiment comes home from the war with the names of victory upon its banners, and the surviving heroes are hailed with acclamations and crowned with garlands as they bear their torn battle-flags along the streets, the vacancies in the ranks are often more than the places that are filled. Among the thousands that shout for joy over their return there are many who weep for those who come not back. While the multitude rend the air with their loud huzzas of welcome, there is many a heart breaking with silent grief for those who sleep afar in bloody graves;

who fell out of the ranks on the weary march or in the deadly charge, and left no subsequent history but the one word, "*Missing.*" When the storm rages on the deep, and strong ships go down before the gale, and the shore is strewn with wrecks, many families wait with unutterable suspense to know whether their beloved were among the lost.

And so in all the returns and gatherings of earth there are some missing. Many times the lost are more than the found. The farther we go on in the journey of life the fewer of the friends of youth are left to keep us company. But of all those who enlist under the Captain of salvation, none shall be lost—none shall be wanting when the war-worn hosts enter the everlasting gates of heaven and pass in triumph through the golden streets, welcomed by the shout of angels to the throne of their King.

Every act of obedience to Christ is a step in the immortal march to glory and to victory. The sea is calm at his command. The stormy wind fulfills his word. All are safe who sail in the ship with him. Take Christ for your Guide, and he may lead you along a rough and thorny road and up the steep hill-side. He may expose you to the chill of night and the heat of noon and the cutting blast. You may have to press on when weary, and fight on when faint, and hope on when discouraged. But you cannot lose the path of life. You cannot fail to reach the heavenly rest.

Nothing like this is true of any other guide You

may follow pleasure, and be led along a flowery path to the sound of music and the step of dances for a while. But the end will be pain and sorrow. You may follow pride, but you will find it a cruel master, crushing with heavy burdens and scourging with scorpions all the way, and bringing to shame at last. You may follow selfishness, and it may promise every indulgence at first. But it will poison every fountain and blast every flower and wither all the joys of life as you go on. You may follow ambition, and climb for a while the dazzling and dizzy steep of fame only to be hurled down with a more furious and fatal descent at last. You may follow the enticing spirit of procrastination, and put off the most urgent duty to a more convenient season. But you will be left to mourn at last, and say, How have I hated instruction and despised reproof!

But if you follow Christ, he will make all the sorrows and trials and losses of earth your servants and ministers to help you on in the heavenward way. He will not suffer the powers of darkness to hurt a hair of your head. Through all the perils and temptations of earth and time he will bring you at last to the heavenly Zion. with songs and everlasting joy upon your head.

This is the one great cardinal truth in Christian faith worthy of all acceptation : all who trust in Christ are safe—safe now, safe everywhere, safe for ever. Heaven and earth may pass away, but his word, which is the shield and hope of his followers, shall never pass away. It shall never be written in his book of life against the name of any soul that trusted in him, "*lost*," "*missing*." When life's long battle is done and the muster-roll of the sacramental host is read before the throne of Immanuel, the ranks shall be all full. To every name a ransomed soul shall answer: "Here am I, saved by thy blood, victorious by thy might, O King, bringing the spoil of all my victories to increase the splendor of thy many crowns."

And this infinite surety of salvation in Christ is offered with infinite liberality to the needy and the perishing. The ship of salvation which he launches upon the perilous seas of time is large enough to hold all who wish to sail with him; it is strong enough to outride every storm; it is open and free for all to enter. The everlasting riches of heaven can be secured with far more certainty than the perishable riches of earth. Many divers plunge into the deep in search of goodly pearls, and return exhausted and empty-handed. All who seek the one pearl of infinite price are sure to find. The earth has been tunneled and bored a thousand times for mineral treasures without yielding any reward for the labor or the cost. No man ever sought the true riches of faith and hope and peace with God, and then found that he had spent his labor for naught. The opportunity to secure an everlasting inheritance in heaven is far more free and universal than the ability to own an acre of ground or the meanest abode on the face of the earth. No obstacles can close the kingdom

of heaven against him who sincerely desires to enter.
It is wide enough to take in all that come, rich enough to
make the poorest within richer than the richest with-
out ; glorious enough to make the least and lowest of
its subjects more exalted than the mightiest of the
princes of the earth. The kingdom of heaven has a
post of honor and of profit for every applicant, occupa-
tions suited to every capacity, sources of light and joy
for every heart. It is easier to get an introduction to
the society of saints and angels, and to live with them
upon terms of friendship and equality for ever, than to
secure the least and the lowest of the aims of human
ambition on earth. You have only to come and knock,
with nothing but the name of Christ and your own
necessities to recommend you, and the everlasting door
of the heavenly kingdom will be thrown wide open
to receive you, and jubilant voices will sing your
welcome, and angel messengers will fly to the burning
throne to bear the glad tidings of your coming. If
men were only half as anxious to have their names
written with honor in the books of heaven as they are
to stand well in some little circle of fashion and fri-
volity on earth, they could look down with pity from
their serene and lofty elevation upon the petty rivalries
and jealousies of human society in this world.

Thus free and glorious and secure is the redemption
purchased for us by the blood of the cross. The ship
of salvation is girt around by the bands of everlasting
strength. It is borne onward by winds that sweep

toward heaven. It is guided by the star of immortal hope. It has Christ at the helm, and it cannot fail to reach the port of peace. All are safe who sail the treacherous seas of time with Christ on board. All others are destined to wander from the true course, to lose sight of the sun and stars, to founder in darkness without a hand to help or a hope to sustain in the final hour.

I have seen the mountain pine clinging to the edge of a lofty precipice. Its hardy roots had sought for a little earth in the cleft of the rock. It was a spot . where the snows of winter outlasted the spring, and the desolating storm of summer swept by in its wild wrath, and the thundering avalanche came rushing down. And I wondered that anything so full of life could live for years upon a spot so high and hard and cold. But I have seen a greater wonder of life and growth than that. I have seen the blessed fruits of faith and love spring up in the uncongenial soil of an utterly depraved heart. I have seen the proud, the profane and the selfish humbling themselves at the foot of the cross, pouring out their hearts in penitence, gratitude and praise, giving their time, their efforts and their possessions in willing consecration to Christ. I have seen the gay and the thoughtless forsaking their vanity, giving up the frivolities of worldly pleasure and self-indulgence, and beginning life all anew, setting out for heaven with earnest and cheerful step. I have seen the frail and the fearful advancing to meet the king of terrors without an expression of alarm, entering the valley of the shadow of death without fear.

All this is done by that infinite grace of God which throws open heaven's eternal mansions to the wanderers of earth, and which seeks its own highest glory in saving the lost. On this great mission of redemption the Eternal Son came forth from the bosom of the Father. He descended into the lowest depths of our human woe, girt with the awful attributes of infinite might and infinite mercy. He performed his work so perfectly that now in this world, for whose salvation his glory shines, his mercy pleads, there can be no excuse for impenitence, there can be no place for despair. We can go to the lowest and worst of men, to the most troubled and tempted, to the most fearful and despondent, to the most reckless and unthankful and say, "Christ died for you and that is the reason why you should love him. Christ has submitted to the utmost degree of shame and agony for your sake, and that is the reason why you should trust him. Christ is addressing you this very moment with the message of peace, with the offer of pardon, with the gift of eternal life, and that is the reason why, without a moment's delay, you should cast all the burden of your sins at the foot of his cross."

A giant steamer was out in mid-ocean. The wind was fair and strong. The engine was toiling with limbs of iron and heart of fire to hurl the mighty fabric on its way. The sails were all spread to help the groaning wheels. The masts and spars spread forth their strong arms to gather up the force of the wind, and the ship went bounding over the deep like a sea-bird fresh upon the wing. It was a return voyage, and a few more mornings would lift the hills of home and native land from the waste of waters. A hopeful and happy throng of passengers was beguiling the twilight hour with walking the heaving deck. Their talk was of storied scenes that they had visited in other lands, and then again of home and of friends waiting to welcome them back. There were cheerful voices and joyful looks and loud laughter. The difficulty of walking on the unsteady floor only increased the pleasure of the hour. There was a sudden lurch of the ship, a cry of terror, a plunge in the waves, and one of the happy company was struggling for life in the deep. Quick as thought, but none too quick for rescue, a rope was thrown to the drowning man, he caught it before he was swept back on the foaming wake of the ship, and strong arms drew him on board without waiting to lower a boat. And the rescued man had grasped the rope with such desperate energy that he could not unclasp his own hands when safe on deck. And when others came to his help they found the hempen strand imbedded in the living flesh. That is the way man clings to anything that will save him from a watery grave. With such quick decision he grasps, and with such desperate energy he holds on when life is at stake. And shall he not grasp as unhesitatingly the only Hand that can save him from a bottomless deep? Shall he not be still more in earnest when the soul's eternal life is in peril?

When all the storms and wrecks of time are past, and the ransomed of the Lord have all escaped safe to the heavenly shore, may you whose eye falls on this page, and he whose hand traces the line, be counted in that glorious company, ascribing unto the Author of our salvation glory and dominion, world without end. Amen.

The Teachings of Night.

Night unto night showeth knowledge.—PSALM xix. 2.

XXV.

THE TEACHINGS OF NIGHT.

IN the beginning God made the light, and so time began. He separated the light from the darkness and so divided the sovereignty of time between day and night. The bright and the black prince were made equal in command, and each was appointed to relieve the other in the endless task of counting the years of eternity. The two stand forth as co-heralds to proclaim the Divine glory through the whole creation, the one always speaking when the other is silent; and there is no speech nor language where their voice is not heard. The day comes in shining glories from the gates of the morning, and night follows close with its dusky robe and starry crown, and both preach the same sermon, ever old and ever new, upon the glory of God. Though all human voices on earth were silent, and the angels in heaven should cease their song, still would the day and the night proclaim the goodness and the glory of God. The great Creator never leaves himself without witness of his infinite perfections in the grand temple of his works. For the day never fails to lift up the mighty chorus of the sun and the seas, the mountains and the hills, the forests and the streams, the forms and voices of all living things in his praise. And the night is ever faithful in bringing forth the hosts of stars upon the field of light, or in leading up the solemn procession of clouds and darkness, to proclaim the presence and power of Him who holds the stars in his right hand, and whose throne is in the thick darkness. The sun comes forth with dazzling magnificence as the grandest material representative of Him who dwells in light that is unapproachable and full of glory. The starry host, by the vastness of their number and distance, by the unchanging order of their march, and by their silent obedience to everlasting law, show forth ever-increasing knowledge of God from age to age. The inspired apostle says that even the heathen are without excuse for their ignorance and depravity, because they refuse to listen when the day uttereth speech—they refuse to learn when the night showeth knowledge.

We should ever hold ourselves ready to receive instruction both from the day and the night. In the present instance let us take our lesson from the calm and meditative teacher that speaks by silence and brings forth knowledge out of darkness. What salutary impressions can we gain from the night, considered not in its astronomical aspects, but simply as the visible contrast of the day, the season of darkness, of silence and of repose?

Night teaches us the solemn and fearful lesson of

the individuality of our being. Far more than the day it shows us what it is to be alone with ourselves and God. It drives all the faculties and sensibilities of the soul inward upon itself. You spend a wakeful hour in darkness and in silence upon your bed at night. There is no sight to be seen, no sound to be heard. The voices of the day are hushed. The diversions and activities of busy life are all removed. You have nothing to do but lie awake in the night-watches and think. Without light, without sound, without fear, without pain, a solitary thinking mind, with the curtain of complete darkness shutting you in on every side, you still must feel that there is another Being whose dread omniscience is haunting the secret depths of your soul. With no thought of what your fellow-men may do or be or say, you can only think of what you yourself are and ought to be when alone with God. Every fibre and feeling of your whole being tells you that the eye of the Infinite One is upon you, and that there is no escaping his presence. You seem to yourself to be alone in the universe with God, and you feel for the time that it were better for you never to have had any being than not to be at peace with him, who is around you and within you and everywhere, and who seems to you in the darkness and solitude to be the only being in existence outside of yourself.

Thus the night, with its silence and darkness and solitude, may impress you far more deeply than the day with the sense of God's presence, with the bare,

33

solitary conviction of your direct, individual responsibility to him. The night will give you the clearest idea of what it is to be all thought, feeling, conscience, soul, and to have your whole being searched and penetrated by the presence and scrutiny of the infinite God. And if you feel that that great and holy One is your Father, your friend and protector, your hope and portion for ever, then the hour of wakeful meditation in the darkness of the night will be to you one of the sweetest and happiest hours of life.

Pastor Harms of Hermansburg used to preach and pray and instruct his people for nine hours on the Sabbath. And then when his mind was utterly exhausted, and his whole body was thrilling with pain, and he seemed almost dying for the want of rest, he could get no sleep. And he used to say that he loved to lie awake all night in the silence and darkness and think of Jesus. The night put away everything else from his thoughts, and left his heart free to commune with the One whom his soul most devoutly loved, and who visited and comforted his weary disciple in the night-watches. And so God's children have often enjoyed rare seasons of communion with him in the solitude of exile, in the deep gloom of the dungeon, in the perpetual night of blindness, at times when all voices and instructions from the world have been most completely cut off, and the soul is left alone with God.

And the hours of darkness, of solitude and of silence are fearful and sometimes maddening to those who are afraid to be alone with themselves and God. I shall never forget words that I once heard involuntarily from the lips of a man who supposed himself to be alone in the darkness and solitude of his chamber by night. He spoke of a great and dreadful crime which he had committed in some land beyond the seas. He cursed himself in vehement and bitter words for his wickedness, and then as passionately called upon God to have mercy upon his soul. At one time, fearing lest his confessions of crime had been overheard, he sprang up wildly and called for an answer if any one were in the room or within hearing. He listened in the silence, and the bed shook with the beating of his heart. He called again and again, and then lay down to repeat his imprecations and prayers as before, trying to quiet his fears by saying aloud, " Then I am alone and no one has heard me, and all will be safe if I can get away from here in the morning." And yet what distressed and terrified that wretched man most of all was the conviction in his own heart that he was not alone in the deepest solitude—there was One from whose presence he could not escape, though he should take the wings of the morning and dwell in the uttermost parts of the sea. The night compassed him about with its darkness only to make him feel how dreadful a thing it is for the guilty to stand face to face with the omniscient God. When the heart is pure it will be the highest blessedness to see God and to feel ourselves alone with him.

We are indeed made to be social beings. And in all

the great joys and conflicts of life, in the highest and deepest experiences of success and failure, we long for the presence and sympathy of friends. We feel as if we must tell somebody the crushing grief or the exultant joy with which our hearts are full. Knowledge confers little satisfaction unless we can communicate it to others. Riches corrode and canker the soul if kept only for self. The impulse of any strong emotion is to make itself known. The mother whose only child has been taken away by death often feels that no sorrow can be like hers, and for years she will tell the tale of her affliction to all who will hear, to keep her heart from breaking with the pent-up grief. In such cases both the joyful and the afflicted would feel it to be more than human nature can bear not to have some one to whom the heart can pour forth its ecstasy of emotion.

But all this sympathy and publicity of feeling are of the light and of the day. The night has a deeper voice, and it speaks with a more solemn emphasis to the soul when it surrounds us with darkness and makes us feel that we are alone with ourselves and God. Jesus himself retired to desert places, and spent the whole night upon desolate mountains, that he might be alone with his Father. He loved the souls of men. He poured out his heart and his life in longing and in sympathy toward the sorrowing and the afflicted. And yet it was in the darkness of the night and in the loneliness of the desert that he strengthened himself for his great work by prayer and communion with his Father.

And he taught us to shut out the world with all its show and noise and seek our Father in some secret place, when we would pour out all our grief and joys with the greater confidence unto his attentive ear. It is not ordinarily in the great and crowded assembly, not in the hours of social intercourse, not when listening to the voice of others, that we come nearest to God and gain our deepest impressions of personal, individual responsibility to him. I do not wonder that devout men in the dark and disturbed periods of the world's history retired to deserts and mountains, and spent whole nights in prayer to God. If it had been done only occasionally and for brief seasons, as it was done by Jesus himself, it would have been profitable. It proved injurious when it became a profession, and built up a barrier between devout men and the duties of social life.

I have myself spent the hours of night alone upon high mountains, when I thought that the darkness, the silence and the solitude made the presence of God to be the more deeply felt. The sense of loneliness and desolation, the awful impression of the nearness of eternity and the spiritual world, were like the feeling which weighs upon the mind when watching alone at night with the dead. The mingled murmur of a thousand torrents rose faintly from the dark cliffs and the deep gorges below. At intervals the prolonged and swelling roar of the avalanche filled the awful solitudes as with the rushing of invisible hosts, trampling the clouds and sweeping the pathless fields of air. Above rose the shadowy forms of still loftier mountains, bearing the name of angels and giants and storms and darkness. And the cold, snow-shining peaks, piercing the silent sky, seemed like the colossal monuments of a perished world standing alone in the midst of a wilderness of death. Everything conspired to fill the mind with an oppressive sense of loneliness and desolation.

And the utter absence of all sounds and forms of life, and all the activities of the bright and busy day in that lofty solitude at night, made me feel more deeply the presence of Him whose mighty hand had piled the mountains above the clouds and "throned eternity in icy halls of cold sublimity." Under the awful impression of the hour it seemed as if all lesser things had lost their hold' upon my mind. "Entranced in prayer I worshiped the Invisible alone." To my excited imagination the loftiest of the snowy heights took the form of a great white throne set up for the Ancient of Days. The gentle wind that came up from the silvery streams and the sea ot pines murmured as if it had been swept by the harp-strings of angels. I should have been scarcely more moved had I actually seen

"the bright seraphim in burning row,
Their loud uplifted angel trumpets blow."

And I thought I had learned from the experience of the hour a new reason why Jesus took his disciples apart into a solitary and exceeding high mountain by night when he would show them his glory. I thought we might all more frequently hear the voice of our Father and see the face of Jesus in his glory if we would learn to shut out the world more completely from our minds, and receive the solemn lesson which the night teaches in silence and darkness.

In our day human life is full of stir and noise and outward show. We do everything in society and by organization. The individual is lost in the multitude. The man is absorbed in the masses. Thought, intelligence, education are so generally diffused that independent thinking is hardly possible. And our religion takes the general form and characteristic of the time. It is social, public, seen and known of men, diffused through the mass, and rising and falling with the tide of common feeling, practice and opinion. This is all well, taken only as a part of our religious life. And if it must be carried to the extreme, it is a much safer extreme than the opposite of ascetic retirement and morbid seclusion from the world. But it would be a grand consummation if, with all our publicity of feeling and practice, our multiplicity of meetings and societies and organizations, we could learn a little more of retirement, of meditation and of individual communion with God. To feel ourselves alone with him for one hour in the whole week, for so long a time to have no thought but of his presence, and no choice but his will, must give earnestness and consecration and peace to all the other seasons of life.

And God folds down the veil of darkness upon the whole world the half of our life-time on purpose that we may shut out all external things, retire within ourselves and meet him alone in the living sanctuary of our own hearts. He covers us with the mantle of night and lays upon us the necessity of repose that we may not waste all our affections and faculties in frantic devotion to the mere show and form of this changing world. He takes all visible things out of our sight, and shuts us up alone with ourselves and him, that he may make us kings unto himself, reigning over the spiritual and immortal sovereignty of mind, possessing the exhaustless revenues and resources of a redeemed and consecrated soul. He would show us that by keeping our hearts pure we can always have unfailing sources of peace and joy within ourselves. We can withdraw from all the troubles and conflicts of the world into the sanctuary of our own hearts, and there the vision of his face shall change night to day and earth to heaven.

And this retirement of the soul in which God's presence is most deeply felt need not take us away from the crowded paths of life or the presence of our fellowmen. Where we see most of man, there we can see most of God. For man is God's crowned and glorious work, made in his own image, and every human soul is the subject of Divine care and a sharer in the Divine bounty.

A man whose published meditations display an extraordinary spiritual acuteness and cultivation, and whose face seemed to those who knew him to be radiant with the light of heaven, once said that he felt God's presence with him in walking the crowded and noisy streets of New York as really as he did in the sanctuary and in the solemn hour of secret devotion. And in fact I know of nothing that will make the devout heart turn with a deeper longing to God than to feel oneself alone and a stranger in a great multitude or amid scenes of suffering and sorrow.

I have laid down to sleep at night upon the bloody field when the music, the magnificence and the splendors of war had rolled away, and left groans and agonies and death behind. Around me were thousands of the dead sleeping in the shallow graves which their companions had made for them in haste, while the hills still shook with the thunder of the long contest, and the blue battle-smoke darkened the heavens with its sulphurous cloud. All through the shattered forests and the trampled fields lay still more numerous thousands of the wounded and the dying, with the bare earth for a bed and the open sky for a covering. In the darkness and silence an occasional cry would come from the parched lips of a dying soldier, in the delirium of death, calling the name of beloved ones in his far-distant home. Many souls were passing to their last account every hour as the heavy night wore away. It seemed as if the veil of the darkness were the shadow of the unseen world resting upon that field, and that it were but a step from time into eternity. Never in my life before had I been in a situation where everything so conspired to make me lay awake all night and think of God and of the awful destinies of eternity. When the devouring fire, and the desolating tempest, and the earthquake shock of battle were past, it seemed as if a still small voice were whispering to the suffering and dying thousands, and the most hardened soldier was glad to hear anybody speak of God.

I have walked alone at night in the crowded streets of a great foreign city. I was surrounded by the unintelligible murmur of unknown tongues. In all the living tide of human faces flowing along in continued succession I could catch no token of recognition, I could see none ever seen before. I felt all the while that if I should fall and die upon the pavement, there would be none to know my name, and only the care of the public health, rather than friendship or affection, would find me a stranger's grave. And yet that feeling of loneliness and of personal insignificance, in the midst of a countless living multitude, impressed me more deeply with my personal relationship to the infinite and eternal God. The utter separation between myself and my fellow-men made me cling the more closely to that fatherly Hand which is always within reach and which is strong enough to sustain all who seek its support. The thought that I was of so little conse-quence to thousands of my fellow-men made me appre-ciate the more highly the ceaseless care of that one infinite Friend without whose permission not a hair of my head could fall to the ground.

To feel ourselves of sufficient importance to be noticed and cared for every moment by Him who has the universe in his charge, is to have the highest and truest sense of our own greatness. And that lesson can be learned by us all from anything that makes us seem to ourselves but a mote floating upon the great sea of existence, of little consequence save to ourselves and to Him who made us what we are, and who makes nothing in vain.

The night of the natural world is the symbol of the deeper night of sorrow and disappointment that settles down upon the soul. And God surrounds us with both that we may feel for his hand in the darkness and find ourselves safe with his protection. We may learn from the night of affliction and trouble many lessons which we could never master in the light of the broad day. When God spoke to men with an audible voice in ancient time, he was wont to address them in the hours of silence and darkness, when the noise of the day was hushed and deep sleep had fallen upon the multitude. And now still he is wont to bring the most precious lessons of faith and patience and love to those whose home is darkened with the cloud of sorrow.

If we only trust him and seek his presence, we shall find that God is with us most sensibly when we need him most, because everything else has forsaken us.

We must not expect always to see our Father's face, and yet we must reverently and trustingly look for him when the night is deepest around us. The darkness which covers our path may be only the shadow of his presence. He is covering us with his protecting hand, as he covered Moses in the cleft of the rock lest he should be consumed by the burning effulgence of his glory. When God's children pray to him for light, he comes to them in answer to their desire in a thick cloud. The light is in the cloud, although to them it seems dark. When their eyes become accustomed to the brightness, they will see the cloud covered with glory. The day which brings the heaviest burden is the day when God comes nearest with blessings in his hands. The duty which imposes the sorest trial proves him to be nearest with all needed help. The temptations, the conflicts, the afflictions which are hardest to meet and which cannot be avoided, are set in our path to show that infinite mercies are waiting for us, and we have only to go forward and receive the blessing.

If we see the Divine favor only in the success which crowns our efforts, in the health which we enjoy, and in the abundance of our earthly goods, God may come to us many times in the greater mercy of loss and disappointment, and we not know of his coming. When you turn aside from the way of duty for profit or pleasure, and God sends his angel to meet you with the drawn sword of disappointment, do not be grieved or angry at the stroke which saves you from destruction. When any peculiarly sore and unwelcome experience is sent upon you, do not cry out in alarm and bitterness of soul, but calmly and trustingly ask, "What new gift has my Father now come to bestow?" Thus the night of sorrow and affliction shall teach more precious lessons than the day of success and joy.

There is a time coming to us all when our souls will be in darkness and despair if we cannot turn to the great Shepherd of the heavenly fold with cheerful and triumphant faith and say, "I will fear no evil, for thou art with me, thy rod and thy staff they comfort me." Human friends can do much to prepare each other for the journey through the valley of the shadow of death. They may go hand in hand to the very brink of the cold river that rolls between this and the unseen land. They may do much to soothe and sustain each other as the last awful hour draws near. But there is a point beyond which human help cannot go. Every one of us must advance to meet the great and final foe with no human hand on which to lean. We must turn away our face from our earthly friends, and pass in under the deep shadow of eternity without their company. Each individual must stand exposed to the dread arrow of the great destroyer, with none to turn aside the shaft.

And yet in that awful hour we need not find ourselves alone. There is a Friend that sticketh closer than a brother. He has been all the way through the valley of the shadow of death, and returned to tell us that it is safe for the feet of them who follow him. We have only to turn to him now with a true heart and he will not leave us to grope in vain for his hand when the night of death is around us and no human friend can take us by the hand and lead us safely on. We have only to choose Christ for our Guide and companion now amid all the gloom and shadows of this earthly life, and we shall walk with him in Paradise in the glory of that land where there is no night.

No Night in Heaven.

There shall be no night there.—REV. xii. 5.

T. MORAN.

J. F. RICE.

NO NIGHT IN HEAVEN.

We have wandered .... and .... away through the .... of the ....
shutting out the .... and turning .... from the .... paths of .... as we have
.... instruction in .... of .... to the voice of inspiration as .... which
.... was still and .... and deep .... We have found light in the .... and the shadows of doubt .... have .... we watched for the morning.

.... looked upon the startled .... waked from sleep by the .... the sacrifice of his son. We .... Sodom receiving the stranger .... with .... of evening and .... them .... city in the .... We have .... pillowed .... at Bethel up the .... of light and along the shining steps .... to the .... of heaven. We .... long travels of the patriarch with .... by the .... mountain stream ....

XXVI.

NO NIGHT IN HEAVEN.

E have wandered with solemn thought and sacred awe through the NIGHT-SCENES of the Bible. Shutting out the glare of day and turning aside from the cheerful paths of busy life, we have sought instruction in the silent shade. We have listened to the voice of inspiration as it spoke when the world was still and dim, and deep sleep had fallen upon men. We have found light in the secret places of darkness, and the shadows of doubt and fear have faded while we watched for the morning.

We have looked upon the startled and sorrowing face of Abraham waked from sleep by the voice which commanded the sacrifice of his son. We have seen Lot at the gate of Sodom receiving the stranger angels with courteous hospitality at evening, and rescued by them from the burning city in the morning. We have gazed from the stony pillow of Jacob at Bethel up the terraced mountain of light and along the shining steps of ministering angels to the throne of heaven. We have witnessed the long wrestle of the patriarch with the mysterious stranger by the lonely mountain stream on his return from Padan-aram. Our faith has been strengthened by the supplications of the weeping Jacob and the success of the prevailing Israel. We have traversed the smitten realm of impious Pharaoh in the calm light of the Passover moon, and heard the wild wail of Egyptian mothers when the destroying angel smote the first-born by night. We have stood on the Red Sea shore and joined in the triumph-song of the ransomed tribes:

"When the Lord looked forth from his pillar of glory,
    And chariots and horsemen were whelmed in the tide."

We have seen unhappy Saul forsaken of God for his transgression, hurrying like a fugitive from justice on his lonely night journey from Gilboa to Endor, that he might seek light in his despair from the demons of darkness. We have heard the song of praise and of trust lifted up by the dethroned and fugitive king David in his dark and perilous night encampment by the Jordan. We have seen Elijah facing the false prophets at Carmel and putting them to death with his own hand, bringing the clouds and the rain with his prayer, running like a wild roe in triumph before the flying chariot of Ahab, and then flinging himself down in despair and wishing to die in darkness and alone in the desert. We have seen Jonah conquering the great and mighty city of Nineveh with a single day of prophecy, and then watching all night to see the bolts of wrath descend, and wishing himself to die because the threatened destruction delayed its coming. We have seen the bodiless hand come forth and write upon the wall of the banquet-room when Belshazzar feasted his thousand lords, and great Babylon fell on the night of mirth and revelry.

We have gone to Jesus with Nicodemus by night, and heard him speak in words to be remembered for ever of the wondrous love of God in giving his only Son for the ransom of a lost world. We have looked out upon the stormy night when the winds were loud and the sea lifted up its waves on high, and we have seen a bright form in darkness walking upon the billows as if the solid earth were beneath his feet. We have seen the fire of coals glaring upon the bronzed faces of soldiers in the court of the high-priest's palace, and heard the impetuous and tempted Peter declare with oaths and cursing that he knew not the Nazarene. We have listened to the agonizing prayer of Jesus thrice repeated beneath the olive trees in Gethsemane. We have walked with the saddened disciples to Emmaus at evening, and come back in the darkness of night with haste and joy to Jerusalem to tell and to hear the tidings that the Lord is risen indeed. We have seen the Divine Saviour after his resurrection walking again upon the shore of the Sea of Galilee in the dim light of the early morning, making the high commission of his foremost apostle to consist in feeding the lambs of the Lord's flock. We have seen the imprisoned Peter waked from sleep by an angel at night, led forth through barred and bolted doors into the open streets of Jerusalem so quickly and quietly that for a time he did not know what had been done by the angel, but supposed he had seen a vision. We have heard Paul and Silas sing praises to God at midnight in the dungeon at Philippi. And we have seen the aged apostle to the Gentiles struggling in the stormy waves, and saved alive from shipwreck on the rocky shore of Malta.

All these have been scenes of earth and of night. Mingled with the brightest manifestations of Divine power, there have been human weakness and pain and sorrow. The lessons that we have learned in our long study of the darker scenes of sacred history have been in some measure dim and uncertain, like the lights and shadows between night and morning. And this very obscurity attendant upon all our present studies is wisely appointed to awaken within us a more intense longing for the blessed morn and the full day of that land where there shall be no night. The deficiencies and imperfections of this present state are our teachers to lift our hopes higher, and to set before us the shadowy outlines of a glory which eye hath not seen, ear hath not heard, nor heart conceived.

Every day of toil along the weary path of life, every sore conflict with the trials and temptations of the world, every feeling of faintness and exhaustion under the burden of earthly care and responsibility, is appointed to teach us what the Bible means when it speaks of heaven as a state of rest. While your heart is all intent and your hands are all engaged in securing the most permanent and desirable residence in this world, you will give little heed to the word when told that earth has no home for the weary soul. But let poverty come upon you like an armed man, let calamity sweep away your possessions as the whirlwind sweeps the withered leaves of autumn, let misfortune make you a wanderer without a house or a home in the wide world, and then you will listen with tearful eyes and throbbing heart to the words of Jesus, " In my Father's house are many mansions; I go to prepare a place for you." If you put forth all your efforts and pour out all your hopes and desires upon the endeavor to stay as long as possible in this world, and to enjoy its pleasures to the utmost degree, you will take little interest in anything that may be said about an endless and blessed life beyond the grave. But let all your experiments in the pursuit of earthly happiness fail; let your desires and expectations come to naught until hope dies in your heart; let affliction follow affliction until the wide earth seems to you but one great charnel-house, where death reigns with undisputed sway over all things beautiful and lovely, and then you will be prepared to see a new meaning and glory in the Divine promise that all who believe in Jesus shall inherit eternal life.

So much does the meaning of the most familiar words and expressions in the sacred Scriptures depend upon the state of mind in which they are read and the course of life and thought which we ourselves are pursuing. So are all the shadows and sorrows of earth and time wisely appointed to lift up our hearts and hopes to the light and joy of heaven.

With all our studies and all our deepest experience we shall never fathom the full meaning of the one word—heaven. We are warranted in ascribing to that blessed state all that is most genial and ennobling in occupation; all that is most enduring and satisfying in possession; all that is most pure and excellent in character. The occupations of heaven are endless praise, triumph, joy. The possessions of heaven are infinite glory, riches, knowledge. The character of heaven is perfect love, holiness, peace. These things we can at present know only in part, and the word of Divine revelation itself must of necessity tell us much of what heaven is by telling us what it is not.

We need little perception to see and little sensibility to feel that this world is smitten all over with a direful curse. It speaks in wrathful thunders from the sky. It flames up in baleful fires and infectious plagues from the earth. It defiles the fairest fields with footsteps of blood. It casts the grim shadow of fear and danger and perplexity upon every path. It wrings from every heart the cry of woe. And the word of Divine revelation tells us much of the future and the better life when it says that in heaven there shall be no more curse.

This world is the subdued and vested domain of death. The history of the past is a record of the triumphs of the king of terrors. In all lands the generations of the departed outnumber the living, and all that now live will soon go with bitter pangs and terrible agony to increase the already countless population of the tomb. There is no pathway of life where the destroyer may not be met at any moment. There is no home from which the grim shadow of death can be shut out. The bloom of youth, the strength of manhood, the glory of age are withered in his icy breath as the late flowers wither in the frosts of autumn. And this awful history of the ravages of the destroyer in all lands and in all time helps us most to understand the meaning of the Divine promise that in heaven there shall be no more death.

This earthly life has been fitly characterized as a pilgrimage through a vale of tears. In the language of poetry, man himself has been called a pendulum betwixt a smile and a tear. Philosophy, with affected indifference to all the changes and sorrows of the human lot on earth and with the formality of precise definition, says man is the creature that weeps. And the entranced apostle tells us much of what he saw in heaven when he says that there God's own hand shall wipe away all tears.

In every earthly dwelling there is somebody to suffer pain. In every human family there is some face over which the pale shadow of sickness has passed.

In every company of human beings there are brows furrowed with care and looks changed with sorrow, and frames bending under heavy burdens, and signs of approaching decay that must destroy at last. And who will not call upon every pain-stricken nerve in his body, and every enfeebled and suffering faculty of his mind, to bless God for the assurance that in heaven there shall be no more pain?

Everything in this world is characterized by imperfection. The best people have many faults. The clearest mind only sees through a glass darkly. The purest heart is not without spot. All the intercourse of society, all the transactions of business, all our estimates of human conduct and motive must be based upon the sad assumption that we cannot wholly trust either ourselves or our fellow-men. Every heart has its grief, every house has its skeleton, every character is marred with weakness and imperfection. And all this helps us to understand how much the Bible means when it speaks of a life without sin, of a home without sorrow, of a society where the defiled are made pure and the just are made perfect.

Among all the brief negative descriptions which the Scriptures give of the heavenly state, no one is more full of meaning than this: "There shall be no night there." The night is the emblem and the reality of darkness, of mystery, of gloom. It is always associated with ignorance and error, with wandering from the true path and weary search for the safe way. And the inspired apostle of the Apocalypse tells us much of the heavenly state when he says that there is a time coming when there shall be no more night. The thick veil of mystery which now covers the works and the ways of God, even to the most cultivated and spiritual mind, shall be rent in twain. The misleading mist of baffled inquiry and blind conjecture, and the deeper clouds of utter ignorance, shall never cast their shadows upon the hills of the heavenly country.

The revelations of truth to us here are like the artful intimations of a riddle, clear enough to excite curiosity, yet reserved enough to baffle inquiry. All that we can know only serves to impress us more profoundly with the unfathomed and infinite mystery beyond. We cannot remember the half of what our life was yesterday. We do not know what it will be to-morrow. We do not think to any purpose a tenth of our waking hours, and we spend a third of our lives in that state which has been aptly called the image and twin-brother of death. After all the discoveries and demonstrations of our boasted modern science, we have as much reason as had the friends of Job three thousand years ago, to exclaim, "What can we know?"

The most cultivated mind is the one which, by much meditation and painful study, has attained the deepest knowledge of its own ignorance. It is still the discipline which an all-wise Providence imposes on us all that we shall walk by faith, not by sight. When we claim to have cleared up all the mystery overhanging the present state by the feeble taper of human wisdom, and pride prompts us to walk in the light of our own kindling, then we need the merciful interposition of an invisible and an almighty Arm to save us from wandering without end and falling to rise no more.

And who can possess a human heart and not long to have this great mystery in the kingdom of a wise and beneficent God cleared up? Who ever studied the dark and awful problem of our human destiny, with a quickened and cultivated sensibility, without feeling his heart breaking within him with longing for light to shine forth from the cloud and the clear day to dawn upon the encompassing night? The blind battle of opinions goes on from generation to generation. The greatest and the best of the human race are ranged upon opposite sides, striking wildly at random and wounding they know not whom in the dark. Both parties arm themselves with mighty arguments and many proofs, and neither gains the victory. And who can thoughtfully consider this blind and aimless conflict without wishing that some great arbiter would appear upon the field, and reconcile all differences and silence all debate by the revelation of his own superior knowledge?

The good and evil of life are distributed with strange inequality. Success crowns the wicked cause and disaster befalls the good. Error flies faster than truth; the guilty are acquitted with applause and the innocent suffer wrong. It is only at immense cost and sacrifice that the world is kept from entire subjection to the powers of darkness. And who can see all this without longing to know why the holy and the beneficent One does not show himself more clearly and justify his own ways without waiting for the feeble arguments and the faltering efforts of man?

We may try ever so hard to keep the great reality of the future life constantly in view, and yet it will often hide itself from our vision in dim eclipse. We all know that God is to us the infinite Sun of Truth, and that in his light alone can we see light. And yet the clouds of earth will often drift their darkness between us and him so thickly that we can see his face only as the light of a nebulous star shining faintly through its misty veil from the untraveled depths of immensity. The hours of clear vision, in which a good man can see God upon his throne of coeternal justice and mercy, with no cloud between, are fewer than the fair nights in which the astronomer can explore the paths and trace out the eternal harmonies of distant worlds.

We know very well that all arguments, reasons and evidences are on the side of truth and right in any case, and that it is utterly impossible for any form of temptation to supply us with a justifying reason for doubt, unbelief or neglect of duty. And yet so dim is our poor human vision, so feeble our capacity to comprehend evidences and to draw conclusions, that the infinite Sun of Truth sometimes seems to us but as a feeble taper shining in a very dark place, lighting up only the small portion of our path where we are walking, and leaving the impenetrable darkness of ignorance to shut us in with its blank wall on every side.

I sometimes seem to myself like a traveler in a strange country, making my way by night through the narrow defile of high and precipitous mountains. A mass of earth and rock comes thundering down from the overhanging cliffs and crushes me to the ground. I cry in the solitude and the darkness for help, and suddenly a friendly hand is placed beneath me to lift me up. I lean upon it for support. It is a human hand, warm with the life-blood that flows from a human heart, and yet it is strong enough to overturn the mountains. A human voice speaks to me in tones sweeter than the harps of heaven. It says, " Be not afraid ; I will uphold thee with my hand ; I will lead thee in the right way. I will heal all thy wounds and strengthen thy heart." And I go forward with faltering steps, still too weak to walk or stand without help—too blind to find the way without a guide. In the alarm and embarrassment of sudden surprise, I sometimes let go the hand of my Helper to save myself from falling, and yet fall the more certainly for relying upon my own strength. My Deliverer gently rebukes my distrust of him and lifts me up. I ask his name, and why he helps me, and where he will lead me. But he only tells me to trust in him and cling to his hand, and soon I shall know all. And is it strange that my heart burns within me as I walk in close company with One who saves me from destruction and keeps by my side that I may not fall again, and only tells me that it is not for me to direct my steps, and that hereafter I shall see him as he is?

Any one who has known by experience the conflicts of Christian faith and doubt, hope and fear, will not regard this as an exaggerated representation of the darkness and uncertainty with which we feel ourselves to be surrounded when we have the most intense longing for the perfect knowledge and the endless day of heaven. And all these aimless conflicts of our minds and unanswered longings of our hearts should lead us to rejoice the more in the Divine assurance that a time is coming when there shall be no more night. The dim, obscuring glass, the changing and tantalizing enigma through which we now see the providences of God and our own duty, shall all pass away. The night shall melt into morn and the mystery shall be clothed with glory.

The redeemed soul, irradiated through its whole being by the light of heaven, and studying the book of God's providence, in the splendors of the eternal throne, shall find no leaves sealed up, no pages written in too dark a character to be read. The veil of the flesh shall be removed, and the spiritual vision shall be purged from the dross and defilement of sin. And to souls thus purified knowledge shall no longer be a dangerous gift. They shall not be forbidden to look within the ark of God's covenant and learn the reason for the allotments of his justice and mercy, which it is now impossible for us to comprehend. The ways of God, that now seem to our feeble and perverted vision most dark, shall then be irradiated with a glory above the brightness of the sun.

And have you not thought enough of these things to long for a state where this great mystery, this thick cloud of darkness shall pass away and there shall be no more night? Have you not learned by deep searching into the depths of your own spirit by long and baffling conflict with ignorance and error, something more of the meaning of the Divine promise that the life of heaven shall be one eternal day, and the blessed shall dwell in everlasting light? And is not the possibility, the reasonable and strong hope of reaching that beautiful land at no distant day, enough to give us patience and watchfulness and energy through all the weary journey? Should not the very gloom through which we must now pass keep alive in our hearts a more intense longing for the home where there shall be no night of ignorance or uncertainty—

"No dreadful hour
Of mental darkness or the tempter's power;
Across whose skies no envious cloud shall roll
To dim the sunlight of the raptured soul"?

In this world we associate weariness and danger and all forms of trouble and wickedness and suffering with the night. Those who can sleep do, indeed, welcome the night as the season of rest. But there are many tossing upon feverish beds to whom "tired Nature's sweet restorer" will not come. And to them the slow hours of the night creep on their sluggish way as if leaden weights were hung on all the wheels of time. To them, the veil of darkness which shuts out the diversions and silences the voices of the day is like the pitiless door of the prison-house and the stone walls of the dungeon. And besides the very necessity of night as a season of repose is a sad confession of the frailty and imperfection of our mortal state. We must permit the powers of life to sink down into utter weariness and inactivity for a third or fourth of the time given us in this world, or we cannot live at all.

It will be the perfection of our immortal being to be made capable of living in a land where there shall be no night—no night of rest, because none are weary—no night of watching, because none are sick—no night of terror, because there are none to molest or to make afraid.

"No night shall be in heaven: no gathering gloom
Shall o'er that glorious landscape ever come;
No tears shall fall in sadness o'er those flowers
That breathe their fragrance through celestial bowers.

"No night shall be in heaven: forbid to sleep,
These eyes no more their mournful vigils keep;
Their fountains dried, their tears all wiped away,
They gaze undazzled on eternal day.

" No night shall be in heaven: no sorrow reign,
 No secret anguish, no corporeal pain,
 No shivering limbs, no burning fever there,
 No soul's eclipse, no winter of despair.

" No night shall be in heaven, but endless noon;
 No fast declining sun, no waning moon;
 But there the Lamb shall yield perpetual light
 'Mid pastures green and waters ever bright.

" No night shall be in heaven: no darkened room,
 No bed of death, nor silence of the tomb,
 But breezes ever fresh with love and truth
 Shall brace the frame with an immortal youth.

" No night shall be in heaven. But night is here
 The night of sorrow and the night of fear:
 I mourn the ills that now my steps attend,
 And shrink from others that may yet impend.

" No night shall be in heaven. Oh had I faith
 To rest in what the faithful Witness saith,
 That faith should make these hideous phantoms flee
 And leave no night henceforth on earth to me."

THE END.